NEW POLITICAL ECONOMY

Edited by
Richard McIntyre
University of Rhode Island

A ROUTLEDGE SERIES

New Political Economy

Richard McIntyre, *General Editor*

Political Economy from Below
*Economic Thought in Communitarian
Anarchism, 1840–1914*
Rob Knowles

Structuralism and Individualism in
Economic Analysis
*The "Contractionary Devaluation
Debate" in Development Economics*
S. Charusheela

Encoding Capital
*The Political Economy of the Human
Genome Project*
Rodney Loeppky

Miracle for Whom?
Chilean Workers under Free Trade
Janine Berg

Market Sense
*Toward a New Economics of Markets
and Society*
Philip Kozel

The African-Asian Divide
*Analyzing Institutions and
Accumulation in Kenya*
Paul Vandenberg

Everyday Economic Practices
*The "Hidden Transcripts" of Egyptian
Voices*
Savvina A. Chowdhury

Prison Labor in the United States
An Economic Analysis
Asatar P. Bair

PRISON LABOR IN THE UNITED STATES

An Economic Analysis

Asatar P. Bair

Routledge
New York & London

Routledge
Taylor & Francis Group
711 Third Avenue,
New York, NY 10017

Routledge
Taylor & Francis Group
2 Park Square
Milton Park, Abingdon
Oxon OX14 4RN

Routledge is an imprint of Taylor & Francis Group, an Informa business

First issued in paperback 2012

Library of Congress Cataloging-in-Publication Data

Bair, Asatar P.
    Prison labor in the United States : an economic analysis / by Asatar P. Bair.
    p. cm. -- (New political economy)
  Includes bibliographical references and index.
  ISBN 0-415-96154-8
  1. Convict labor--United States. 2. Slave labor--United States. I. Title.

HV8925.B35 2007
331.11'73--dc22   2007015164

Visit the Taylor & Francis Web site at
http://www.taylorandfrancis.com

and the Routledge Web site at
http://www.routledge.com

ISBN-13: 978-0-415-96154-7 (hbk)
ISBN-13: 978-0-415-54199-2 (pbk)

To my Felicity;
and to the freedom in captivity and the captivity in freedom

Contents

List of Figures   ix

List of Tables   xi

Acknowledgments   xiii

Introduction: Prisons and American Society   1

Chapter One
Slavery   9

Chapter Two
Conditions of Existence for Slavery in U.S. Prisons   21

Chapter Three
State Welfare and the Production of the Prison Household   49

Chapter Four
The Production of Commodities in Prison   87

Chapter Five
The History of Prison Slavery in the U.S.   109

Chapter Six
Consequences of Prison Slavery   127

Notes   155

Glossary   175

Bibliography   187

Index   197

List of Figures

Figure 1.1   Slavery and ownership.   19

Figure 2.1   Percentage of inmates enslaved, 2001.   46

Figure 5.1   Percentage of inmates enslaved, 1885–2001.   116

Figure 5.2   Incarcerated population in the United States.   120

Figure 5.3   Rate of incarceration, 1945–2005.   121

List of Tables

Table 3.1   Potential and Actual Income of Inmates by Class   58

Table 3.2   Provision of Commodities and Use-Values to Inmates   60

Table 3.3   Actual Income of Inmates by Class   62

Table 3.4   Prison Household Production, Total   66

Table 3.5   Prison Household Production, Each Inmate's Share   67

Table 4.1   Total PIE Payments to Inmates, Less Deductions   90

Table 4.2   Actual Income of Inmates by Class, Including All Deductions and Charges   92

Table 4.3   Florida Department of Corrections Annual Budget Report, Cost of Incarceration, 1999–2000   99

Table 4.4   PRIDE Revenues, 2000   100

Table 4.5   PRIDE Expenditures, 2000   101

Table 5.1   Value Produced by Inmates, 1885–2001   117

Table 6.1   Beetham's Criteria for Legitimate Power   147

Acknowledgments

This work has come out of my dissertation on the same topic; I'd like to thank my dissertation advisors, Stephen Resnick, Richard Wolff, Lucas Wilson, and Bernard Morzuch, for their patient and careful guidance at every stage of the dissertation process.

My thanks go to Ric McIntyre, the editor of the New Political Economy series, for his close reading of my work and his insightful comments. I'd also like to thank all my teachers at the University of Massachusetts Amherst, in particular Sam Bowles, my undergraduate mentor, who inspired me to become an economist; my gratitude also goes to Nancy Folbre, David Kotz, Herb Gintis, Leonce Ndikumana, Mohan Rao, Gerald Friedman, Carol Heim, Dan Lass, Joe Moffitt, Bob Pollin, Lee Badgett—I know I was often a difficult student; I appreciate your efforts to educate me.

Thank you to my colleagues in the Association for Economic and Social Analysis, especially Blair Sandler, who helped my at many stages along the way, introducing me to the grand art of T'ai Chi Ch'uan, and lending support and sympathy throughout the process. Thank you to my fellow graduate students, particularly Tony Guglielmi, who developed a course on the economics of U.S. prisons that served as my inspiration for this topic. Thank you to my students in the economics of prisons course that I ended up teaching; your interest in the topic and unexpected questions inspired me to learn more and to question my assumptions.

Robert Burns read many drafts of my work; during our conversations I gained from his command of the intricacies of Marxian value theory, as well as his encyclopedic knowledge of the Simpsons and the Daily Show. Maliha Safri always provided both sharp insights and a sense of humor; Kenan Ercel, Yahya Madra, Ceren Ozselcuk, Phil Kozel, Vamsicharan Vakulabaranam, Jeff Carpenter, Erik Olsen, Ellen Russell, Joe Schneider, Steph Eckman, Lawrance Evans, Bob Reinauer, Noah Gordon—you made being in grad school seem like the coolest thing on the block; thanks for your friendship.

I'm grateful to my colleagues at Riverside Community College, Dariusch Haghighat and Ward Schinke, for their strong encouragement during the completion of my dissertation, and also to my colleagues at the City College of San Francisco, particularly John Whitehead and Marc Kitchel, for their unwavering support.

I'm grateful to have received the kind support of my family; it meant a great deal to me that you were present at my dissertation defense. My apologies to those I may have forgotten; my friends, colleagues, family, and teachers have done the best they could; any flaws in my work owe purely to my own limitations.

Asatar P. Bair
San Francisco

Introduction:
Prisons and American Society

The United States has recently achieved the rather dubious honor of being the world leader in both the number of people incarcerated and the rate of incarceration in proportion to the total population. As of 2005, there are over 2.1 million people incarcerated, an incarceration rate of 491 per 100,000 people.[1] Even more stunning, over the course of a year, between 12 and 14 million people will have some contact with the prison system.[2]

We have embarked on a bold social experiment: we built the largest, most comprehensive, and by far the most expensive prison system of any society in history.[3] Perhaps the historians of the future will remember this as the hallmark accomplishment of the United States of America during the late 20th century.

The staggering costs of the prison system are beginning to cause a variety of social tensions. While budgets for education and social spending are slashed, while local and national roads and communications infrastructure crumbles, the budgets for departments of corrections have quietly skyrocketed, growing by 11% per year from 1990–1996, faster than any other category of state spending.[4] This has led many to call for some way of reducing the costs of incarceration.[5] Proposals to reduce the number of people incarcerated have been rejected in favor of making the prisoners themselves work to produce commodities for sale on the market. In 2001, inmates in United States prisons and jails produced $1.8 billion worth of commodities.[6]

It is generally agreed that prison should serve several purposes: to punish those who violate the law, to rehabilitate offenders, and to reduce crime both by incapacitating those believed to be criminals and to deter others from undertaking criminal activity. Thus, prisons have a unique and important role to play in society. There has been much debate and discussion in the short history of large-scale prisons over exactly how these aims can and should be met.[7] Prison labor is often believed to be both a punishment and a method of rehabilitation. Some have argued that these aims may at times conflict.

Prisons are unique sites in American society. Violence is rampant—there are over 36,000 reported assaults each year in prison, and countless unreported ones. Sexual assaults occur with a regularity and brutality that is, to say the least, rare in other areas of American life.[8] Prisons have a unique code of conduct, and violations of the unwritten rules of prison life—whether they are committed knowingly or not—are punished harshly. In addition, prisons have so many written rules that nearly every human task, from eating, to sleeping, to moving around, requires a ritual of permission and obedience to correctional authorities. It also seems to be the case that some correctional officers wield their power for their own personal gratification, enforcing rules on a capricious and arbitrary basis rather than to ensure the safety of inmates and staff.[9]

Both the level of violence in prison and its unique rules—written and unwritten—have effects on the inmates. One example of this that psychologists have noted is that prisons tend to dull one's responses to mid-range stimuli. The more time inmates spend in prison, the more they tend to react to other people by either ignoring them, or in violence. In prison, such ordinary human acts as making eye contact, interrupting a conversation, or laughing can all be invitations to serious violent conflicts. This is said to be an important survival mechanism in prison, where small actions can take a larger significance in the creation of a prison hierarchy, with the strong on top and the weak on the bottom.

It would be quite difficult to understand prison life without referring to the role of race. There is perhaps no site in American society where racism appears quite as clearly than within the criminal justice system, where people of color, and especially African Americans, are treated far more harshly than whites. People of color are the targets of racial profiling and police brutality, of racial inequality in the court system that assigns them higher bails, worse plea bargains, higher conviction rates, and longer sentences when compared to similar crimes committed by whites.[10] As a result of this, the rate of incarceration for African Americans stands at eight times that of whites.[11] While African American men account for 8.3% of the population, they comprise 64.4% of the population behind bars. An African-American man has an astonishing 28.4% chance of being incarcerated for a significant period in his lifetime, compared with a 5.1% chance for a white male.[12]

Racism leads to severe tensions within prisons, where the overwhelming majority of the correctional officers and staff are white. Though prisons are not officially segregated, there is a kind of social segregation that is nearly absolute and is enforced by the inmates themselves—each race or ethnic group tends to stay with its own kind.

Prison life is shaped by the society's general view of inmates. Inmates are well aware that in going to prison they have been placed in America's lowest caste. Some consider their outsider status to be a badge of honor, which leads to an internal commitment to the criminal lifestyle, as it has become no longer merely a way of making a living, but a matter of self-identity.

Politicians and correctional officials seem prefer not to dwell on the violence, arbitrary use of power, and racism of prisons, focusing instead on the role of institutional programs, such as drug rehabilitation, therapy groups such as anger management, vocational training, religious services, and education. All of these programs are intended to change inmate's habits and proclivities as well as the economic opportunities available to them in the hopes that they will choose not to return to a life of crime when they are released from prison. Studies suggest that these programs do play an important role, even though they are rapidly vanishing from prisons across the country, cut from state correctional budgets.

The reason for these cuts is that in the last 25 years, more emphasis has been placed on punishment, retribution, and incapacitation rather than rehabilitation or looking at the root causes of crime such as poverty and unemployment. Indeed, just as the number of people in poverty grew dramatically during the Reagan and Bush years, so did the number of people incarcerated. As the focus shifted to punishment many institutional programs were cut, such as higher education for inmates, even though higher education is believed to reduce recidivism by many correctional professionals, inmates, and their advocates.

The only institutional program that has become more available to inmates over time is prison labor. Some have suggested that prison labor is slavery.[13] This is a provocative claim, one that bears further examination; oddly enough, there are almost no scholarly works which make a systematic argument that prison labor is or is not slavery.[14] This book aims at just such an examination.

Chapter One builds the analytical framework needed to understand slavery, discussing what slavery is and what it is not in general terms. The problem with many arguments concerning slavery is that they tend to focus only on one element of slavery, a kind of reductionism that does not reflect the diversity of forms of slavery throughout history. For example, slavery is often seen as the ownership of human chattel; by this definition, slavery *does not exist* in U.S. prisons. Inmates are clearly not property. For example, inmates cannot be sold or used as collateral. Nor is it a tenable argument to claim that prison labor is slavery because it is forced. In many prisons, there is in fact a waiting list for employment in prison industries (one possible kind of labor inmates may perform).[15] It's equally unsatisfactory to argue that because inmates receive low wages they are enslaved. Enterprising capitalists have often sought to pay low wages, and are sometimes successful at exploiting the desperation of those who will accept wages below the going rate. This does not make these wage 'rip-offs' into slavery. Furthermore, most economists view the payment of wages to be indicative of capitalism rather than slavery.[16]

In Chapters One and Two, I draw upon classical and contemporary works within the tradition of Marxian economics to show: a) there are many forms of slavery, b) slavery as the ownership of human chattel only one form of slavery among many, and c) slavery—defined as the 'slave fundamental class process' (*SFCP*)—does exist in prisons. Inmates are enslaved because a combination of political, economic, and cultural forces compel them to perform both necessary labor (that amount of labor needed for their own consumption) and surplus labor (labor above and beyond the necessary labor) in prison, and the product of this labor is appropriated by another party—termed here the *slavemaster*, or simply *master* for short. What makes this specifically *slave* exploitation is that the labor-power of the inmates qua slaves is owned and reproduced by their masters.[17] In most cases, the slavemaster is the warden of the prison or the head of a state agency in charge of prison industries, but the appropriator may also be a private enterprise, given permission to appropriate inmate slave surplus labor by the head of the department of corrections in a given jurisdiction.[18]

This book makes two claims; first, a portion of the inmates in U.S. prisons are enslaved persons—not figuratively or metaphorically, not merely reminiscent of the era of slavery, but *actual slaves*.[19] Second, prison slavery has effects on American society that have never before been understood, for the simple reason that no one has attempted to analyze the class structure of prisons. I show that these inmates are enslaved even though they are not property, they are not compelled to work by simple threats of force, and they sometimes receive money payments.

Prison slavery is shaped by the flow of value that inmates receive from the state, which consists of food, clothing, shelter, medical care, and other goods and services. Because inmates receive this value flow whether or not they are actually enslaved, I consider it a form of welfare from the state. This state welfare affects the reproduction of labor-power in prisons, for inmates receive a set of goods and services which they consume without payment. A portion of these goods and services is produced by some of the inmates in the form of cooked meals, clean laundry, maintenance of facilities, and so on. I call this 'prison household production.' Like the cooking, cleaning, and other tasks typically done in the average household outside prison, prison household production is a non-market activity; although the goods and services produced in households have value, they are not commodities. Prison household production is different from the production of commodities in prison; for example, different facilities are involved, there is often a different pay scale in each, with commodity production being higher, and there is generally a higher regard given to commodity production both by inmates and correctional officials. I analyze these two productive sites as different instances of slavery; the tensions and conflicts between inmates in the different sites, with non-laboring inmates, and with correctional officials are illuminated by this class analysis, presented in Chapter Three.

As part of my research for this study, I visited 27 different prisons in 10 states, observing production facilities, interviewing correctional officials and inmates, and seeing for myself what prison labor looks like in a sampling of U.S. prisons. As a result of this research, I was able to obtain financial data and concrete observations which I apply to the class theory developed in Chapters One and Two. Using data from the state of Florida, I systematically analyze all of the value flows in prison commodity production. This is the first study which provides a rigorous, class-based empirical analysis of prison labor. One finding from these data is that inmate-slaves are actually exploited at a quantitative level (Marx's 'rate of surplus value' or 'rate of exploitation') which is actually far *lower* than the exploitation occurring in the capitalist firms in the U.S. outside prisons. Of course, the experience of enslavement makes the exploitation qualitatively different from capitalist exploitation, but it seems an important statement about society that inmate-slaves are actually less exploited than 'free' wage workers. The results of this quantitative part of the study can be found in Chapter Four.

In Chapter Five, I consider the modern history of prison slavery, showing how changes in incarceration trends, the social construction of race, the labor movement, and penological reforms have impacted prison slavery. Chapter Five looks at the Holy Grail of penology: the economically self-sufficient prison, or the prison which covers all its expenditures by the use of inmate-slave labor, requiring no state expenditure.

Chapter Six considers some of the effects of prison slavery on inmates and society. One effect of the *SFCP* in prison on society concerns crime and violence. The ways in which different forms of exploitation (e.g. capitalist, slave, feudal) affect the level of crime and violence in society is a complex topic that has never been rigorously examined. Though an examination of this sort would require a comprehensive focus on the various class processes taking place at a variety of sites in the U.S., it seems likely that the level of violence in society is shaped by the unique form of slave exploitation occurring in prisons, which exposes inmates to entirely different political, economic, and social processes than those experienced by other Americans. Enslaved inmates may become angry as a result of their slave exploitation, and violently displace that anger onto others in society. In addition, inmates who are released into society after serving their sentences may find that the exploitation they experienced as slaves in prison makes them unfit for participation in the largely capitalist class structure of American society. Perhaps this is simply due to the stigma of being incarcerated, or perhaps it is due to the inmate being trained to unquestionably obey orders, to avoid initiative, to blend in and avoid being noticed—perhaps the very traits that allow inmates to successfully participate in the *SFCP* in prisons make it unlikely that they will succeed in the vastly different capitalist class processes occurring outside prisons. This would be in direct contradiction to the finding expressed by many writers that working a job in prison helps these inmates succeed economically upon their release. Because these writers did not see the *SFCP* in prisons, they missed the exploitation that also occurs in prisons, and hence cannot explain the effects of that exploitation on inmates during their incarceration and after their release.

If former inmates cannot participate in the capitalist class structure, they may turn to illegal economic activities for sources of income. These illegal economic activities may contain all sorts of class processes, including ancient, slave, feudal, capitalist, or even communist. The experience of slavery in prisons may lead to inmates being enslaved in a form of the *SFCP* occurring outside prisons, perhaps in prostitution.[20] Of course, these ex-convicts may take the place of the slavemaster in this example, appropriating the surplus labor of their slaves. It may be the case that for some inmates, the experience of being a slave in prison makes them determined to avoid being exploited outside prison, and this may mean that the inmate becomes an exploiter.

Criminal activity may also be conducted in other class structures. For example, an individual thief may well be taking part in an ancient class process of individual production and appropriation of surplus labor. In the drug trade, production may be organized as a feudal class process, with the 'drug lord' appropriating the surplus labor of his or her 'serfs'. Other criminal activity may be conducted as a capitalist class process, with some criminal operating as entrepreneurs, and hiring workers on a wage basis.

Since illegal economic activities include contracts that cannot be legally enforced, enforcement must be undertaken by the individual parties, leading to the constant threat and use of violence as a matter of business. This is one way that crime and violence may be increased by the *SFCP* in prisons.[21]

These criminal class structures may be a temptation to others in society as well. Workers may see criminal activity as a way to escape exploitative class structures, or to provide opportunities for the rapid accumulation of wealth they may not believe are possible in the largely capitalist economy. Unemployed persons may turn to criminal class structures out of desperation or frustration with their inability to obtain a decent job. To prevent workers from fleeing the capitalist class process, the state creates a system of laws and punishments for violations of these laws, with the final consequence being the prison system.

Crime can reduce the amount of surplus value extracted by capitalist firms. The instability caused by violence may disrupt the production process, interfering with the production or realization of surplus value. On the other hand, if the state looks to taxes on firms to pay for the rising costs of more prisons and law enforcement, this represents a claim on the surplus value of the firm. Firms must take a portion of their surplus and distribute it to the state. Thus firms may have an economic interest in lowering the costs of the prison system, or displacing the cost of it onto other taxpayers.

The tax payments which the state demands from workers and capitalist enterprises to pay for the prison system may become onerous as the number of incarcerated persons rises. The demand for lower tax payments while maintaining the threat of incarceration as a method of preventing criminal activity may lead to greater demands for inmates themselves to pay for their own incarceration through their labor.

Even if the *SFCP* in prisons is not successful at offsetting the costs of incarceration, the fact that inmates are performing labor may be seen as a just punishment for their crimes. In other words, capitalist workers, themselves caught in exploitative labor processes, may feel that inmates deserve to be punished by labor, even slave labor, for their attempt to escape from the rules of the game to which all workers are bound.

The *SFCP* in prisons may function to force poor urban dispossessed groups to reduce their expectations. American culture continually produces and reproduces a vision of happiness, success, and fulfillment that is outside the grasp of most people. What happens when these dreams are shattered by the reality that very few will ever get rich, and that working the same dead-end job one's entire life will not lead to this dream? Some may respond to this inevitable disappointment by turning to crime. The presence of the *SFCP* in prisons may send a message that there is no viable escape from the exploitation of their lives, and thus, the best thing to do is accept it. As the famous exhortation of Margaret Thatcher goes, "there is no alternative"—no other option besides the exploitation of the capitalist labor market.

Prison slavery may also undermine the legitimacy of the legal system. Slavery is incompatible with modern social norms. This is why those who support the growth and development of prison slavery in the U.S. do not call it slavery, but rather argue that it is wage labor much like the capitalist workplace outside prisons. Those who label prison labor as slavery generally do so to attack it on moral and ethical grounds. As this work will show, the argument that prison labor is the same as capitalist wage labor is untenable; prison labor is in fact a form of slavery. To the extent that people are aware that the judicial system punishes people in a manner that is a direct contrast with the values most people hold may lead to people losing respect for the law, and consequently refusing to follow it the way they might if the system of corrections did not rest upon hypocrisy.

The preceding paragraphs sketch some of the relationships between violence, crime, and class processes in American society and the class processes occurring in prisons. This specific class analysis clarifies the consequences of slavery in prisons—consequences which would inevitably be understood differently or not at all without the class focus. Thus we hope to provide a new perspective on crime and punishment that can provide new approaches and solutions to the problems of crime and exploitation.

Chapter One
Slavery

WHAT IS SLAVERY?

Before we can discuss whether or not prison labor is slavery, we have to define slavery. This is difficult, for slavery is an institution with a long history and many, varied forms. Any theory employed to understand economics or society must by necessity be limited in its consideration of only a select number of social processes occurring at a given time and place. Societies are complex—each may contain a nearly limitless number of people, objects, ideas, and relationships. This makes it impossible for any theory to hope to be truly comprehensive—it would require an infinite amount of knowledge and time to evaluate all social processes and the relationships between them—if we had such knowledge, presumably we would not need to create theories at all. [1]

Because of the complexity of social relationships, it is necessary for each theoretician to select a few aspects of a society on which to focus, while excluding the rest. In terms of theorizing the causes of whatever social relationship is the object of the theory, different theoreticians may well select different causes. Even when theorists agree to consider a certain aspect of society—say, the ways in which production of goods and services is organized—they often differ on what are the important features of production. After all, each production process is different from every other production process. The task of theory is to show the common elements in each kind of production. Marxists have traditionally called such common elements a 'mode of production,' but there is a great deal of disagreement and difference over what constitutes a mode of production, and how one mode of production may change into another.

A classic example is the debate between two prominent Marxist theorists, Paul Sweezy and Maurice Dobb (1976), on the transition between one mode of production, feudalism, and another, capitalism. Each of these theorists had different ideas about what made a mode of production capitalist or feudal, and hence while they agreed that a transition had occurred from feudalism to capitalism, they naturally disagreed about when and for what reasons it took place.

The features that mark one mode of production as different from another are always relative to the theorist. An example is the agreement among many social scientists that free markets, private property, and personal freedom are the core features that distinguish capitalism from other kinds of production. However, it can be shown that even when these conditions are met, the result is clearly not capitalist. In the antebellum South there was widespread exchange of commodities in markets, there was private property—in fact, property relations extended to people, and personal freedom existed—for whites—but the resulting society was not capitalist.[2]

In discussing slavery, I'll use the term "slave fundamental class process" or "slave class structure" rather than "slave mode of production."[3] Slavery may be defined in many ways, reflecting the problems discussed above with selecting a few characteristics of a social system as definitional. Slavery at a given time and place may be strikingly different from slavery occurring at another time and place. It may be difficult to distinguish slavery from feudalism or capitalism. Davis (1984), for example, writes, "the more we learn about slavery, the more difficulty we have defining it."[4] Fierce (1994) argues that in seeking to determine whether a site is slavery, one's own theoretical position is critical. Fierce refers to a form of prison labor occurring in the late 19th and early 20th century called convict leasing.

> A persistent underlying theme is the comparison with slavery, with which convict leasing shares important, if imperfect, likenesses. In several instances the reference to slavery is explicitly. That is so because the evidence of convict treatment under leasing as presented here—that is, length and conditions of the work regimen, medical and health care, diet, clothing, worker-supervisor relationships, general labor exploitation, and perhaps, most of all, punishment—conjure up an image that is a vivid reminder of slavery. In the final analysis readers must decide whether or not the treatment that Black convicts faced in the system of southern convict leasing is mindful of their definition of slavery.[5]

The definition of slavery, then, is always dependent on the theory of slavery being employed. In this sense, there is no such thing as 'slavery' in the abstract—there are only particular forms of slavery that exist at given times and places. This means that a different theory of what slavery is may perceive slavery where other theories may have seen capitalism, feudalism, or some other system of production. Furthermore, as the preceding argument implies, it is important to clearly specify what characteristics are seen as definitive of slavery for that particular theorist.

THE STRUCTURE OF THE SLAVE FUNDAMENTAL CLASS PROCESS

The theory of slavery employed here is one possible way of understanding and defining what slavery is, and hence what separates slavery from other social systems. This particular definition does not represent what Anderson calls an "easy supra-historical mélange" in other words, an ahistorical, absolute theory of slavery.[6] Rather, the elements selected here to define slavery are only a few of the infinity of possible specific social processes that exist along with different forms of slavery. Slavery is seen here as having two distinct parts. First, slavery has a *class structure*, defined as the form of production and appropriation of surplus labor that takes place at a given point of production.[7] This particular class structure is called the slave fundamental class process. As noted earlier, within the slave class structure, the producers of surplus labor are called "slaves," while the appropriators of surplus are called "slavemasters," or simply "masters." Exploitation occurs in the *SFCP* because the masters appropriate a surplus that they did not produce themselves. The class structure of the *SFCP* has the following features.

The slave performs necessary and surplus labor and is required to deliver his or her total output to the slave master. This clearly separates the *SFCP* from feudalism, in which the serf producers do not deliver the entire product of their labor to their lord qua appropriator. However, in capitalist production, like the *SFCP*, the total product of the worker's labor is appropriated by the capitalist, so this criterion by itself is insufficient to define the *SFCP*. A further defining characteristic of the *SFCP* is that the reproduction of a slave's labor-power is intertwined in the relationship between master and slave. In other words, the master must provide to the slave a portion of the slave's labor, if the master wishes the slave to be able to continue to labor. This quantum of labor is the necessary labor, while all else is surplus labor. These features of the class structure of the *SFCP* separate it from other fundamental class process.

The processes necessary to "reproduce' workers" labor-power, i.e. to make it possible for workers to continue to labor, may include cooking and eating meals, rest, cleaning, child-rearing, entertainment, and so forth takes place outside of the productive process, and is not a direct concern of the capitalist appropriator. Capitalists may be concerned with the general features of the market for labor-power, but are not directly involved with the reproduction of labor-power, which generally takes place in the private households of workers.[8] In slavery, the reproduction of labor-power is bound up in the relationship between master and slave due to the master's ownership of the slave's labor-power. Since the master owns the slave's labor-power, if the master wants the labor-power to be reproduced, so that slaves can continue to provide labor, the master is obligated to maintain the slave, just as a horse must be fed, or a machine must be serviced and maintained if it is to operate properly.

In feudalism, serfs typically worked their own land part of the time, and their lord's land part of the time. Serfs have traditional rights to the land (tenure) which separate them from slaves, which have no right to land or other property.[9] Serfs are not required to deliver the total product of their labor to their lords; the products of the labor serfs perform on their own land is kept by the serfs themselves. Again, in feudalism the reproduction of labor-power takes place outside of the relationship of appropriation between lord and serf.

Communism also differs from slavery in that there is no master—those who perform surplus labor are the same as those who appropriate surplus labor. Furthermore, this appropriation is done collectively.[10] Thus, in communism there is no exploitation, while in the slave, capitalist and feudal class processes there is exploitation. This is one reason Marxists have long regarded communism to be superior to these other class processes, making a communist society their goal.

The above is a 'thin' definition of slavery. The class features of the *SFCP* are few; nothing has been said about culture, politics, the law, etc., not because the social processes occurring in these areas are less important, but in order to keep class conceptually distinct from all else.[11] In addition to the class structure, slavery also has a "non-class structure" composed of a potentially infinite number of social, political, physical, religious, political and other sorts of processes; as the name implies, these forces are not directly related to the production and appropriation of surplus labor, but rather they form the conditions of existence for the slave class structure. Neither the class structure nor its conditions of existence is seen as the "essence" of slavery, rather the two sides exist in a complex, overdetermined, dialectic.

It is these conditions of existence, in short, that answer the question: what is it that creates the situation where person or group of people must deliver the entire product of their labor to another person or group, where the entire sustenance of the producers is in the hands of the appropriators?

Not all definitions of slavery, even those which use a notion of class as an entry point, include or make explicit any reference to the production and appropriation of surplus labor. Eugene Genovese uses the concept of the ownership of people to define class in his work on slavery in the U.S. South.[12] This is a different concept of class, which does not explicitly refer to the labor process; I will discuss this approach in more detail shortly.

Each specific occurrence of the *SFCP* will have different political, cultural, and economic conditions of existence, which means that different forms of the *SFCP* may vary widely. For example, the particular form of the *SFCP* existing in Jamaica in 1798 was strikingly different from the *SFCP* existing at the same time in West African households.[13] Despite these differences, I believe there is one element of the non-class structure which is common enough and important enough to merit further discussion, a political condition of existence for the *SFCP* which, from my perspective, is important to consider in any discussion of slavery as a class process.

This element is the ownership of a slave's labor-power by a person other than the slave. Every person has a certain capacity to perform work, to take given raw materials—products of nature and labor—and transform them into new products. The capacity of a person to undertake work in a given amount of time is labor-power, which exists regardless of whether or not a market happens to exist for labor-power. Due to a combination of political, economic and cultural processes, the labor-power of the slaves is owned by the slavemaster.

The idea that slavery involves the slave's loss of the right to sell his or her own labor-power is given a central role in the work of Kevin Bales, who writes:

> [T]he labor power of the enslaved person becomes the property of the slaveholder. It is a commodity over which the slaveholder has complete control. A free laborer can enter or withdraw from the labor market at any time, but a slave cannot. He or she cannot sell his or her own labor power and thereby commodify it. This is true whether the period of enslavement is fixed, temporary, or indefinite.[14]

In an earlier work, Bales writes: "My own definition of a slave would be *a person held by violence or the threat of violence for economic exploitation*. I appreciate that this is general in the extreme, but I believe that any useful definition must be kept general so as to encompass the wide variations of form that slavery takes."[15] Bales later refines the definition of slavery to "a state marked by the loss of free will, in which a person is forced through violence or threat of violence to give up the ability to sell his or her own labor-power."[16]

Bales deserves acclaim for focusing the world's attention on modern forms of slavery that persist today. His work is richly detailed and shows the energy of an activist as well as the close observation of a scholar. His work also illustrates the point that even similar-sounding definitions of slavery can often arrive at quite different conclusions, for by abstracting from the question of who appropriates the surplus that is produced (and under what circumstances this production and appropriation takes place) in favor of concentrating on the labor power, Bales ends up concluding that prison labor is only slavery if the prisoner is unpaid or was imprisoned unjustly.

> Prison labor is a particularly thorny question, because the accusation that it constitutes enslavement depends primarily on the legitimacy of the government in control and the fairness of the criminal justice system. When people are held against their will without due process, threatened or coerced with violence, and robbed of their labor-power— all features of the current situation in Burma, according to the International Labor Organization—then it is reasonable to assess this as a form of state-sponsored slavery. When an inmate of a British prison is voluntarily enrolled in a work project for which he is remunerated, this can hardly be described as slavery.[17]

It seems superfluous to argue that prison labor is only slavery if the criminal justice system is totally compromised. What if a country has a relatively good criminal justice system, but once a person is incarcerated, their labor-power is forcibly taken from them?[18] Bales seems to suggest that a legitimate government (by which I presume he means a democracy) cannot enslave people through its prison system. This conclusion is somewhat odd, for prison labor seems to fall squarely within Bales' own definition of slavery. Bales argues slavery has three characteristics: "loss of free will, the appropriation of labor power, and the use or threat of violence."[19] Bales does not really offer a full argument on prison labor, for the above quote is nearly the extent of Bales writing about prisons in his two books.[20] However, Bales asserts that in prison labor, the loss of free will is "not a necessary condition of the practice," while the appropriation of labor power is 'sometimes present, sometimes not,' and violence or the threat of violence is "present in the practice." It's difficult to argue that prison labor involves the exercise of free will, for inmates are incarcerated against their will by violence. Whatever choices they make within the prison are shaped by the total control exercised upon them by correctional authorities. Bales is correct that not all inmates' face an appropriation of their labor power, a point which I'll address in some detail in Chapters Two and Three. However, this is largely due to structural forces, such as the competition with enterprises outside prison.[21] I discuss the development of this situation in Chapter Five.[22]

Fogel and Engerman also argue that the ownership of one person's labor-power by another person is a key element of slavery; while they prefer to use the neoclassical term 'human capital' rather than the Marxian term "labor-power," it is clear from the following that what they mean by 'human capital' is a person's capacity to perform labor in a given amount of time.

> [T]he crucial difference between slave and free society rests not *on the existence* of property rights in man, in human capital, but on who may hold title to such property rights. Under freedom, each person holds title, more or less, to his own human capital. He is prevented by law from selling the title to this capital except for quite limited periods of time and then only under a very restricted set of conditions . . . In slave societies, however, a large number of individuals were permanently deprived of the title to their own human capital.[23]

It certainly clarifies the ownership relation when the slavemaster sells the slave's labor-power to another party. This creates a market price of slave labor-power, which is conceptually different from the price of labor-power which arises from individuals selling their own labor-power, although the magnitude may be the same. Despite the importance of the ownership of labor-power, it is not sufficient to define the *SFCP*. In feudalism for example, it could be argued that the lord owned the labor-power of the serfs. In feudal Europe, for example, laws and customs existed such that lords could exercise exclusive command over the serf's labor for a certain portion of the time. Thus it was illegal for the serf to sell his or her labor-power, the original meaning of the term *felony*. As argued above, the *SFCP* has a unique class structure which is clearly differentiated from feudalism and other class processes.

Unlike slavery, workers can sell their labor-power to whomever they choose. In other words, workers own their labor-power, and the wages they receive are paid to obtain access to their labor-power for a given length of time. This is not the case in the slave class process, where slaves cannot choose to sell (or not sell) their labor-power to whomever they choose in exchange for a wage. If masters choose to motivate their slaves with monetary rewards for certain actions, this is not to be considered a wage, as a wage indicates a relatively free exchange has been made, while a financial reward to a slave merely indicates that the master has decided it enhances the productivity of the slave when money is an incentive.[24]

The following argument discusses the role of this non-class process—ownership of human labor-power—within U.S. prisons. The above discussion merely indicates that I consider such ownership of labor-power to be important and interesting, and does not indicate a privileging of the concept of ownership over the concept of class. Based on the epistemological position employed here, such privileging would be untenable.

As mentioned above, production and appropriation of inmate slave surplus labor is divided into two spheres of production: commodity production, where inmate slaves produce goods and services for sale, and prison household production, where inmate slaves produce goods and services for use within the prison rather than for sale. The different institutional arrangements that exist in different states and jurisdictions under the laws that apply to prisons and to production and sale of commodities within prisons leads to several different kinds of appropriation.

Appropriation of Surplus Labor in Commodity Production

1. **State Appropriation.** Here the appropriator is the head of a state agency (usually a part of the department of corrections within a state, though sometimes a private or quasi-private enterprise) which is given responsibility for industrial production in all the state prisons. This responsibility extends to the production, appropriation, distribution, and realization of surplus value; though the appropriation is done by the head of this state agency, the head of the department of corrections is the ultimate owner of the inmate slave labor-power.

2. **Private Appropriation in State Prisons.** A private enterprise may be given permission to appropriate inmate slave surplus labor. In this model, the private enterprise directly reproduces the labor-power of the inmate slaves by paying them, and the department of corrections takes a portion of the payment. There are 5 different sub-forms of production and appropriation in this category.

3. **Private Appropriation in Privatized Prisons.** Another kind of private enterprise may appropriate inmate slave surplus-labor, namely an enterprise engaged in running private prisons. Such enterprises are paid by the state to incarcerate inmates, a controversial and recent change in corrections in the U.S. Here the private enterprise is given permission by the head of the department of corrections to house the inmates, and also to appropriate their surplus-labor as slaves.

Appropriation of Surplus Labor in Prison Household Production

1. **State Appropriation.** In prison household production taking place in state-run prisons, the appropriator of inmate slave surplus labor is the warden. The warden is supported in his position as slavemaster by the state, which provides the warden with a budget to cover certain expenses, such as the cost of means of production, raw materials, and payments to slaves. However, the state also demands that the warden provide all inmates with welfare.[25]
2. **Private Appropriation.** In the case of a private prison, the appropriator of the prison household use values produced within the private prison is the private enterprise charged with running that prison. At the present time, there are far more inmates in state prisons than in private.

SLAVERY, OWNERSHIP AND THE SLAVE FUNDAMENTAL CLASS PROCESS

Slavery is most commonly understood in ways that abstract from the production and appropriation of surplus labor. The ownership of another human being as chattel or property is overwhelmingly used to define slavery.[26] One of the most famous instances of this theoretical understanding appears in the definition given by the League of Nations committee on slavery: "the status or condition of a person over whom any or all the powers attaching to the right of ownership are exercised."[27]

As argued above, the slave fundamental class process exists when the total product of the slave's labor is appropriated by the master, and the reproduction of the slave takes place within the relationship of master and slave. It may be that a part of conditions of existence for the *SFCP* is the political process of ownership of human beings. It may also be that a person's labor-power is owned rather than the person. Thus for example, the owner of the person's labor-power does not own the person, but owns the person's capacity to perform labor. A historical example of this would be medieval feudalism in Europe, where serfs were unable to sell their labor-power, since it was owned by their lord. However, the lord did not own the person of the serf.[28]

This is an important distinction for our purposes, for in the case of prisons, the labor-power of the slaves is owned by the head of the department of corrections, but not their person. The head of the department of corrections has complete command over the labor-power of the slaves. He or she can enslave inmates in the *SFCP* in commodity or in prison household production, or even command that the inmates do not participate in the *SFCP* or in any other form of labor.

Although ownership may be a condition of existence for the *SFCP*, this does not make the two identical. Ownership is not a class process; a particular form of slavery may involve ownership but may *not* involve an *SFCP*. Imagine a situation where a man owns another man, has owned him since birth, and enjoys the right to buy and sell this person as he sees fit. Say the person is understood by all to be a slave. This slave could be involved in, for example, the ancient, or individual class process. The slave could be engaged in production of goods, performing necessary and surplus labor, and appropriating his own surplus labor.[29] Thus this man, although he is a slave due to his status as owned property, is not involved in the *SFCP*, but rather the ancient fundamental class process. We could imagine alternate scenarios in which the slave is involved in communist, feudal, or capitalist class processes, or no class process at all. If no surplus labor is performed, there is no class process. This may mean that the slave performs no labor, simply that no surplus is produced. The slave may perform unproductive labor, for example, labor that does not directly produce surplus. In addition to these possibilities, it is also possible that this slave is involved in multiple class processes, which means that he occupies multiple class positions.

The above shows that the presence of slavery as an ownership relationship reveals nothing whatsoever about the class processes in which the slaves (or the owners, for that matter) are involved. Furthermore, the existence of the *SFCP* does not imply that ownership exists. For example, it is possible to imagine a situation in which private property does not exist. Imagine that a society consists of two groups of people: free persons and slaves. Free persons share the goods, land, and other resources with each other. Within this society is a group of slaves. These slaves are not owned by anyone, since property does not exist as a concept. What makes this second group slaves is that they perform necessary and surplus and the product of their labor is appropriated by the free persons, their labor-power is possessed by the free persons, and their labor-power is reproduced by the free persons. In this situation, the *SFCP* takes place without ownership of people.

Ownership is not an essential feature of the *SFCP*. Some forms of slavery have involved both ownership and the *SFCP*, such as antebellum slavery, while other forms of slavery have involved ownership without the *SFCP*, while other forms of slavery have involved the *SFCP* without ownership. A useful way to illustrate this conception of slavery is depicted in Figure 1.1.

The area labeled "Ownership of human beings" represents one subcategory of slavery, while the area labeled "Slave Fundamental Class Process" designates another subcategory of slavery. As noted above, ownership

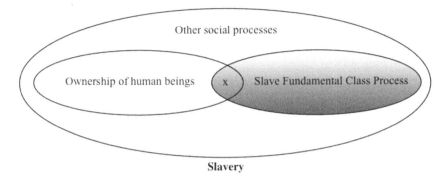

Slavery

Figure 1.1 Slavery and ownership.

can exist without the *SFCP*, or with the *SFCP*, which is represented by the area labeled "x" above.

Feiner (1981) and Weiner (1999) both argue that property ownership is different from the *SFCP*. Feiner (1981) writes:

> the concepts of ownership and possession, while they may serve as a very general definition of what human chattel property is, do not impart to the concept of slavery any *class* content.[30]

Feiner argues further that when slavery is seen solely as the presence of human chattel property, rather than as one condition of existence for the *SFCP*, human chattel becomes theoretically indistinguishable from other kinds of property.

> When this occurs, human chattel and the class process of slavery are reduced to these essential property relations which express the underlying class relations. When these concepts (conditions of existence, subsumed classes, etc.) are present, however, it is not only possible, it is imperative to recognize that when human chattel property is used in the production of surplus labor, this "property" becomes a unique and historically specific form of labor.[31]

Feiner argues that the ownership of human chattel was a condition of existence of the *SFCP* which took place in the antebellum south, but this condition of existence is not seen as the essence of slavery.

The above argument shows that the *SFCP*—a class process—is distinct from the ownership of human beings—a non-class process. This distinction is important in the case of prisons, as we shall see.

Chapter Two
Conditions of Existence for Slavery in U.S. Prisons

Inmates enslaved in correctional facilities[1] in the U.S. perform many different kinds of concrete labor at many different sites inside and outside the prison walls. Although this study analyzes two of these sites, commodity production and prison household production, it is not a comprehensive analysis of the class dynamics within prison.[2] For example, only the slave labor is analyzed, not the labor of the guards or other correctional staff, which make up the group termed *prison authorities*. This refers to the group of people who work within the Department of Corrections in a given federal or state jurisdiction, including the warden and the warden's staff, the correctional officers and other personnel who work at a given prison, as well as various different administrators and staff who work in the Department of Corrections but may not be in direct contact with inmates. As noted earlier, the individual with the most official power here is the head of the department of corrections in the given state or other jurisdiction.

It will be shown that the class process in both areas of production—commodity and prison household production—is the *SFCP*. To show this we will proceed to analyze a few of the non-class processes that participate in overdetermining the *SFCP*. It will be shown that when inmates are enslaved in the *SFCP*, they are required by the combination of these non-class processes to deliver their total product to their masters, they are not free to sell their labor-power, and that their labor-power is reproduced within the relationship between master and slave.

As noted above, not all inmates are enslaved. Many aspects of the non-class structure described below apply to all inmates, creating a situation where an inmate may be enslaved, even if he or she is not enslaved at the moment. The boundary between slaves and non-slave inmates is porous, and does not fall neatly along the lines of "working" and "non-working" inmates in the way these lines are drawn in most discussions of prison labor.

For convenience, I've divided the conditions of existence for prison slavery into the categories political, cultural, and economic. These conditions of existence link those inmates in the *SFCP* to the appropriators of slave surplus labor. These forces make it possible for the entire product of inmates' labor to be taken from them, while the reproduction of their labor power is controlled by their masters (our class criterion for the *SFCP*).

These processes are not intended to define the *SFCP* as a transcendent category that exists outside of time and place. In this sense, there is no such thing as slavery, only particular forms of slavery that exist within particular societies at particular times. Similarly, there is no single 'ideal form' of the *SFCP* to which all other forms can be compared. The *SFCP* has existed in so many different forms that there can be no single set of non-class processes that all of these forms have in common.

These processes also provide dimensionality to the otherwise spare class definition of slavery, giving the prison *SFCP* depth and revealing both its similarities to, and differences from, other forms of slavery. Thus we need not merely look backward at other historical forms of slavery in determining whether a social site is or is not slavery, which would inevitably privilege some historical period or geographical location as the 'essence of slavery.'

POLITICAL CONDITIONS OF EXISTENCE

The conditions of existence that have to do with the exercise of power are considered political, in the broad sense of the term. These include laws, rules, and customs that convey authority on one party and require obedience of another party.

In prisons the labor-power of inmates is owned by the correctional authorities charged by the state with maintaining the incarceration system. Since the warden of the prison has the most immediate control over the inmates, he or she may have de facto ownership of the inmates' labor-power, but the true ownership lies with the head of the department of corrections in the state, usually a political appointee of the governor of the state. Regardless of who ends up appropriating the slave surplus labor, the head of the department of corrections has the final say over the use of the labor-power, since it is he or she who must approve all slave labor programs in prison.

Marx notes that in capitalism, the capitalist owns a worker's labor-power for a given amount of time (however much time was purchased) whereas in the slave class process, the master owns the labor-power of the slave forever. The ability of the head of the department of corrections to compel inmates to perform slave surplus labor combined with their position of appropriation may be understood as a sort of permanent ownership of labor-power in the sense that, as long as an inmate is in prison, the prison authorities own his or her labor-power, whether or not the inmate is enslaved.[3] The department of corrections can gain a rental income by granting outside enterprises access to the use of slave labor-power—a fact that provides further evidence of the ownership of inmate slave labor-power that the head of the department of corrections. This rental income would not be possible without the ownership of slave labor-power. Slaves, however, may not sell their labor-power to anyone who is not authorized by the head of the department of corrections. Thus the legal ability of prison authorities to compel inmates to perform slave surplus labor clearly separates the way labor-power is used in prison in comparison to capitalism outside prison, in which wage laborers possess the freedom to sell their labor-power to whichever exploiter they choose.

One issue that arises in considering the ownership of inmate slave labor-power is the large proportion of inmates in many U.S. prisons who do no labor. If there is a substantial proportion of the inmates who do not labor, it may seem to indicate that inmates do own their labor-power. One reason for the high level of non-working inmates is the lack of development of prison production, both in commodity and in prison household production. Historically, nearly all inmates were enslaved, until the mid-twentieth century, when a series of laws were created to reduce the scale of prison commodity production. Currently, commodity production is undergoing rapid growth. More industrial capacity is being created in prisons, and along with that industrial capacity it becomes possible to expand the *SFCP*. However, admissions to U.S. prisons have also seen rapid growth; if the number of positions in the *SFCP* is growing, but the number of inmates is growing as well, then the proportion of inmates in the *SFCP* may not be growing, and may even fall.

The general reason for the relative lack of development of prison industries is related to the protests of unions and private capitalist firms over competition from prison industries which had far lower costs than did the private capitalist firms. Hence, the federal government passed laws which restricted the ability of prisons to sell the commodities they produced. State prisons could still produce commodities, but could only sell the commodities within the state where they were produced. However, as the membership of unions declined, their political influence waned, and federal law was changed to remove some of these restrictions. This has allowed for the expansion of the *SFCP* in U.S. prisons. Before 1979, the ability of prison authorities to use the labor-power of the inmate slaves was limited. Also, the culture of corrections has shifted to emphasize to a greater extent the role of work in prisons. This has influenced more departments of corrections to utilize inmate slave labor-power more vigorously than they had in the past, which would tend to lower the proportion of non-working inmates.

As shown above, the proportion of non-working inmates has more to do with structural and institutional factors than with individual choice. However, given the limited development of prison industries, and hence the limited number of jobs there, prison authorities may be able to present participation in the *SFCP*, including the income granted to inmate slaves for such participation, as a reward for good behavior. Thus prison authorities could be assured of the participation of the inmates most likely to work hard and be productive, the inmates who would respond to such a financial incentive. We would expect that if the *SFCP* were expanded, such incentives would be less effective.

At the same time as the ownership of inmate slaves' labor-power by the prison authorities pushes the inmate slaves to performs surplus labor in the slave class process, it may at the same time undermine the slave class process. Inmate slaves may resist their exploitation just for the sake of spiting the power of the prison authorities, even if they must pay a high price for their disobedience.

Prison authorities have been granted the legal basis to compel labor and appropriate the entire product of slave labor.[4] Later we will examine which groups within this general category of prison authorities perform the functions of appropriation, supervision, and the receipt of distributed surplus labor. For now we will be content merely to show that the legal basis for the compulsion and appropriation of surplus labor is in place. The compulsion of labor is a political process; it involves the wielding of power, and the laws, traditions, and customs that support such authority. The fact that prison authorities can legally compel the labor of inmates has been well-covered in the literature on prison labor. Many authors have pointed out that the 13th Amendment to the Constitution outlawed "slavery" and "involuntary servitude" outside prisons, but not within them.[5]

> *Amendment XIII. Section 1.* Neither slavery nor involuntary servitude, except as a punishment for crime whereof the party shall have been duly convicted, shall exist within the United States or any place subject to their jurisdiction.

For many authors, particularly on the left, this political process is enough to show that slavery exists in prison industries in the U.S. However, this represents an essentializing of one non-class process—the wielding of power—as the determinant of an entire social system. Such essentializing is at odds with the approach used in this work. Instead, the power relationship between prison authorities and inmates is seen as one non-class process among an infinite number that together overdetermine the slave class process in prison industries. In fact, just as the exercise of power over inmates pushes them into slavery, it also pushes them in the opposite direction, towards refusing to participate in the *SFCP*. For an example of the latter, consider the ever-present risk of riots in prison. It is well-recognized among prison administrators that prisons can only be run with the inmates' tacit consent. If even half the inmates withdraw their consent, the prison is no longer controlled by the warden or the guards. The risk of provoking inmates may well prevent prison authorities from using the full range of coercion available to them.

Because of the rapid growth of prison populations in recent years and the resulting overcrowding of prisons, prison industries have not been able to enslave all the inmates in the *SFCP* in commodity production—in fact, only a small proportion of inmates are enslaved in this area. Many prisons have long waiting lists for enslavement in commodity production.[6] As we shall see, economic factors play a significant role here.

Just as the mere existence of extremely unequal power relationships is not enough to label prison labor as either slavery or the *SFCP*, it is also the case that this legal loophole in the Constitution is not evidence enough to support the claim that inmates are owned property. Property ownership in human beings must be supported by an entire network of laws which specify what can and cannot be done with one's property, whether that property takes the form of land, machinery, horses, or human beings. This set of legislation simply does not exist in United States law after the end of the Civil War. Thus, inmates cannot be considered owned property. They cannot be bought and sold, they cannot be willed to one's descendants; they cannot be used as collateral to borrow against. As discussed earlier, if ownership of human chattel is seen as the essence of slavery then slavery clearly does not exist in prison industries, because inmates are not owned property. However, a different form of slavery, based on a different understanding of slavery, slavery as the *SFCP*, can exist and does exist in U.S. prisons.[7] This highlights the difference between a class approach, which considers the surplus value produced by slaves, and approaches which look to ownership, a non-class political or legal process.

Although inmates are not owned property, the Constitution allows prisons to force inmates to work with or without any sort of compensation in return. Legislation in many states has added to this Constitutional basis by mandating that able-bodied prisoners be made to work to pay for the costs of their imprisonment. In the federal prison system, for example, all prisoners must work by law. Oregon recently passed legislation mandating a 40-hour workweek for inmates.[8] Many other states have passed similar measures. It may be the case that because of the circumstances of production, inmates need not be forced to work at all. Inmates may well be eager to work. The critical point is that the legal and political infrastructure exists to compel inmates to perform surplus labor.

Prison authorities have the power to control nearly every aspect of the slaves' lives. Again, this power is vested in the hands of the warden, as the decision-maker regarding most aspects of life within a given prison. This power over the day-to-day lives of all inmates allows the warden to inflict both severe punishments on slaves and non-slave inmates alike, as well as to offer them substantial non-monetary rewards, giving the warden a substantial degree of control over inmates' behavior. Because this power exists, even if it is not exercised over each individual, it is incorrect to say that prison labor is voluntary. Although slaves may choose to be enslaved in prison, it is a choice made under the shadow of extreme punishment, and hence is quite different from the choices regarding labor made by individuals outside prison.[9]

Some of this power is legal in nature, and some is illegal. One legal form of power is the ability to place inmates in solitary confinement with little to no provocation. Inmates have little or no legal recourse for being given a higher security classification, which includes being placed in solitary confinement, or "administrative segregation," the more current term for the isolation of a prisoner. Prison authorities have designed an elaborate system of rewards and punishments to control inmate behavior. This includes taking away such things as television, visitation rights, pillows and bedding, taking away the regular food and replacing it with worse fare, and so on. The result of these punishments is generally reduction in the amount of state welfare which flows to an inmate.[10]

An illegal form of power is the ability of the prison authorities to use force to punish inmates for various actions, including, for example, not working, producing inferior products, or being disobedient. The use of force is illegal in every prison in the U.S. except in the case of self-defense or keeping order within the prison, yet violent abuses of inmates are so commonplace, and accountability so slight, that this form of power exists on a de facto basis.[11] The power of the prison authorities pushes inmates to perform surplus labor, even when no explicit threat is made. The presence of such unequal power between prison authorities and inmates is a constant pressure on inmates to behave, to work, to be silent rather than speaking up, since those who question enslavement or refuse it are disciplined. This clearly supports the *SFCP* in prisons. At the same time, the presence of this power also pushes inmates in the opposite direction, to *not* produce surplus, as the exercise of power may cause resentment to build among the inmates, resentments which are sometimes expressed by the refusal to perform surplus labor, despite (but also because of) the likely possibility of punishment. Thus the very mechanisms designed to produce obedience (including obedient labor and surplus labor) may also produce disobedience. An example is the state of Oregon's measure mandating a 40-hour workweek for all state inmates, for no pay. Inmates immediately protested this measure and they were placed on lockdown, halting the production of slave surplus labor.[12]

The political processes secure the appropriation of surplus labor by the prison authorities or those they have designated to appropriate. If the prison authorities did not own the inmate slave labor-power, could not compel their labor, and did not have the power to punish (and reward) inmates in all sorts of ways, the *SFCP* may well cease to exist in prisons; yet at the same time these processes also generate resistance.

CULTURAL CONDITIONS OF EXISTENCE

Cultural conditions of existence are those processes that create certain meanings in a social site, influencing how an individual thinks about his role in society, and more generally, how he gives meaning to his life. These processes shape the production and appropriation of surplus labor in many ways. This study follows the work of Patterson (1982) in considering a defining mark of slavery to be the presence of several specific cultural and ritualistic processes within a given social formation. The ways in which slavery is understood shape a slave's identity and situate him or her within the society, producing an understanding of what it means to be enslaved, and hence shaping the production and appropriation of slave surplus labor.[13] These non-class cultural processes take place in prisons. The following account will show how these processes take place in U.S. prisons, and how this secures the existence of slavery.

An important cultural process is the discourse that claims inmates are inferior to other U.S. citizens, even that they are less than human, and hence they deserve all manner of punishment. The primary way in which the inferiority of prisoners is constructed is through the creation of a category into

which all prisoners fall: *the criminal*. There is a powerful tendency within
American culture to understand criminals as something other than human,
hence the use of the words "animal," "beast," "brute," or "inhuman" in
describing those convicted of a crime.[14] This cultural discourse distances
'the criminal' from the rest of us, a distance which allows us to believe
that the criminal deserves punishment of the worst kind, producing a tension between social norms limiting torture and the social thirst for punishment.[15]

Part of this discourse that defines "criminals" as inferior also associates being convicted of a crime with shame and dishonor. Slaves are seen
as individuals who lack honor; for example, their word means nothing—
you cannot trust a slave. This is seen in the Roman law excluding as evidence in a court of law any testimony that a slave delivered other than that
given under torture. Even if an individual slave displays honor, or performs
actions seen as honorable, he is still a slave. A slave may be admired by others in a given society, but that slave still lacks honor as a slave. Criminals
are seen as inherently dangerous, untrustworthy, violent, disloyal, selfish,
greedy individuals who will lie, cheat, steal, kill, and rape with impunity.
Being incarcerated, or having once been incarcerated, cements a person into
the category of criminal, forever branding the person with dishonor, a condition of existence for the *SFCP* in prisons.

Patterson gives this notion of honor and dishonor a great deal of
emphasis, arguing that the stereotype of "Sambo" in the U.S. South as a
"degraded man-child" was a powerful ideological and cultural apparatus
which took away the honor of the slaves by describing them as naturally
childlike, irresponsible, lazy, docile, and infantile, incapable of honesty, giving to exaggeration and theft.

> The stereotype is, in fact, an ideological imperative of all systems of
> slavery, from the most primitive to the most advanced. It is simply
> an elaboration of the notion that the slave is quintessentially a per-
> son without honor. The key to Sambo, Elkins rightly notes, is the total
> absence of any hint of "manhood," which in turn is a perfect descrip-
> tion of the dishonored condition.[16]

This thesis departs from Patterson's position in that the cultural process of slave inferiority and the dishonor that is part and parcel of it is not
seen as the essence or "quintessence" of slavery in an absolute sense, but
rather as an important process among many others which together form
a complex relationship with the slave class process. The notion of slave
inferiority suggests that enslaved inmates, as despised criminals, lacking in

honor or decency, deserve their punishment of forced labor, which is not generally seen as slavery. The language used asserts that the relevant distinction is between "working" and "non-working" inmates, as if these are the only choices. As Chapter Six shows, this is a false dichotomy that is oppressive either way, though for different reasons.

The cultural process described above supports the *SFCP* by propagating the idea that the inmates should be in their class position, and should not attempt to change it. It undercuts support from individuals and institutions outside prisons who may seek to aid inmates in altering their class position. More insidiously, the notion of slave inferiority may persuade the inmates themselves that their nature is to obey their masters and produce surplus labor. They may agree that they deserve whatever punishment they receive, that they do not deserve the right to appropriate their own surplus labor or even to receive the necessary labor which reproduces them as slaves. Thus possible sources of class conflict are eliminated, supporting the *SFCP*.

This cultural process of understanding slaves as inferior may interact with the political processes described above in complex ways. When slaves are seen as inferior beings, as less than human, all sorts of actions against them become justified. Hence, in prisons, violence against inmates is always due to their own provocation, just for being criminals who have broken the law. This gives prison authorities more power, and legitimizes whatever brutal excesses they may commit. It allows us all to ignore what is done in prisons, since it is only done to "despicable criminals."

At the same time the idea of inferiority may undermine the production of surplus. Inmates may agree that they are inferior, worthless beings, possibly leading to depression, acts of violence, or self-destructive behavior, or all of these. If inmates become mired in aggression, depression, and self-destructive behavior (which are all very common in prisons) the production of surplus labor may be curtailed. Perhaps inmates will not pay attention during the production process, making costly mistakes. Inmates may seek to mutilate or even kill themselves in their depression, or may involve themselves in dangerous conflicts with other inmates or correctional officers, thereby either making themselves medically or for security reasons otherwise unfit for labor, lessening the available pool of slaves.

Another cultural process which occurs in prison is the creation of a new identity for the incarcerated. This is secured by a set of rituals which strip an inmate of his old identity and create a new identity as a convicted criminal, an inmate, whose role is now to obey the prison authorities. This process undermines resistance from the inmates, who may now see themselves as different individuals than they were outside the prison walls. As free citizens, they may vigorously resist a situation in which someone else owns their labor-power. As inmate slaves, they may not make the same demands, because of the creation of an slave identity that is obedient to the correctional authorities. Even if an inmate is not enslaved, this process takes place, perhaps to a different degree in each individual. Some may resist it in various ways, others may not. The point is not that slaves are a homogeneous mass, but merely that this slave identity creation is an aspect of prison life that takes place and acts to co-create the slave class process.

Patterson (1982) argues that there are two different elements to the process of creating a slave identity. First, there is naming the slave. Second, there are a number of different physical markers that have at various times been given the meaning as the marks of enslavement. Third, there is a severing of the relationships a slave had with their family and community before being enslaved. Since one's name, physical appearance, and relationships all affect a person's identity, when they are drastically and permanently altered by enslavement, the person's understanding of him or herself as an individual is also affected. Many cultures regarded the changing of a person's name to be definitive of that person's identity. Patterson notes the similarity with prisons:

> The changing of name is almost universally a symbolic act of stripping a person of his former identity (note for example the tendency among modern peoples to assign a new formal identification, usually a number, to both prisoners of war and domestic convicts).[17]

Patterson argues that the names that slaves have been given historically have a variety of meanings. In ancient Rome, Greek names often were used to convey slave status. On one large plantation in Jamaica, slaves were given names like "Beauty," "Carefree," "Monkey," "Villain," and "Strumpet."[18] These names participate in objectifying the slave, summarizing the slave's personality or central characteristic in one word. An important function of names in American slavery was also an attempt to remove African customs, traditions, and religious practices and substitute the Christian values, morals, and customs of the European masters. Masters found that the slaves who put effort into remembering and preserving their African heritage were the slaves most likely to resist the masters, to attempt escape, and to foment rebellion among the other slaves.

In prisons, the replacement of a person's name with a number, which an inmate must then memorize, is a symbolic stripping of his or her old identity, and creation of a new identity, which has unique characteristics in the prison setting and based on the name that is used. Nearly every word has some sort of meaning or connotation. If used as a name, the word takes on additional significance. However, the unique feature of a number is that it generally has no particular meaning.[19] Symbolically, this means that the numerical name given to an inmate is one which gives that inmate no particular new identity, except as an inferior, degraded person, a criminal. Even an insulting name like "Monkey" at least gives a slave a kind of identity. A monkey, after all, also has good qualities. A number, on the other hand, has neither good nor bad features. It has no connotations. In this sense, perhaps it serves to cut off the inmate from their personhood even more effectively. This reinforces the cultural process discussed above, namely, the creation of a discourse of slave inferiority. A person is no longer recognized for their own uniqueness, but reduced to an category, the universally despised category of "criminal."

In addition to the use of names to create a slave identity, masters also gave meaning to aspects of a slave's appearance, through certain physical characteristics, through dress or ornamentation, and by other means. One marker of slave status was race, as discussed earlier. Patterson notes that other markers were also used, such as tattoos, branding, cropping of ears, and many others. Slaves have sometimes been identified by ritual scarification, or the absence of ritual scars.

None of these visible markers of slave status is an essential feature of slavery. It is noted due to its prevalence in various forms of slavery, and because there is a clear relation to prisons, where inmates are marked by their clothing. Clothing is a powerful visual marker, which often says something about a person's identity. In many societies, including American society, the choice of clothing is a form of self-expression or identification within a group or profession, and thus carries a powerful set of meanings about a person's character, social status, economic status and so on.

Both inmates and prison authorities have at times recognized the symbolic power of requiring inmates to wear certain uniforms. Until relatively recently, inmates wore clothing with wide black and white stripes. Inmates have repeatedly demanded that the stripes be changed, recognizing that striped clothing has connotations of 19th century prisons and, for example, the practices of convict leasing and chain gangs which have now become emblems of brutality. Even more recently there have been proposals by some politicians to bring back the stripes—a political move designed to show that the politician is tough on crime. Bringing back stripes means, in the most simplistic symbolic and political level, an increase in punishment, a change in our understanding of what it means to be incarcerated, harking back to an earlier era of incarceration that ended because of popular outrage over the treatment of inmates. One popular Arizona sheriff has decreed that the inmates in his jail (who have been convicted of no crime, but are awaiting trial) will wear pink underwear. This is explicitly designed as an assault on the masculinity of the overwhelmingly male population of that jail, a way of publicly mocking the lack of power that these inmates have over their own appearance.[20]

The process of trading in one's own clothes in exchange for the uniform of a prisoner is a ritual of enslavement, where a person is stripped of their own autonomous identity, as expressed in their choice of clothing, and given a new cultural symbol, which marks the person as an inmate. The person is then universally recognized as an inmate, as a prisoner, as a criminal.

The last element of the creation of a slave identity concerns the change in the enslaved person's relationships. When a person is enslaved, that person is often taken away from their family and friends either physically or ritualistically (and often both). In other words, a slave is cut off from the web of human relationships which give shape and meaning to a person's life. Patterson describes this process as *social death*. The slave is considered socially dead, as he or she is cut off from the family and community relationships that are understood to be the basis of a person's life in relation to society. Without these relationships, a person no longer exists as a person, or at the least, their status has been permanently altered. Patterson notes that many cultures view the enslavement of a member of the family as the permanent removal of that person from the family and community. Even if the slave were to escape, he or she would have no place to go.

In U.S. prisons inmates are separated from their family and friends through their incarceration. Visitation rights may also be rescinded by prison authorities. Inmates can also be reassigned to other prisons, which may be considerable distances from their family and community. However, the main way that prison severs kinship and community connections is simply through time. Prisons prevent the contact and socialization that forms the basis of most relationships, substituting only a brief visiting period, generally accompanied by harsh experiences for visitors, such as extensive searches. Many visitors reflect that their feeling is that the prison authorities would prefer it if they did not visit.

Inmate accounts reflect the difficulty of being slowly separated from family and friends. In the documentary film entitled *The Farm: Life at Angola Prison*, one inmate advises new inmates to accept that most of your friends and family will "cut you loose." According to this inmate, the exception is usually your mother or a close sibling.[21] Even your closest family may reject you. Families may show their rejection of an incarcerated family member by never referring to that person in conversation within the family or with others, or by not having any pictures in their house of that person, for example. Inmates tend to understand this element of prison as a kind of death.[22]

This non-class process of creating a slave identity pushes inmates to perform surplus labor. For example, inmates may seek to escape from the pain of this separation from loved ones through work. Civilian supervisors in charge of various production processes in prisons have often remarked to me that enslaved inmates often work harder than workers outside prisons. One reason for this may be that enslavement, carrying with it all the activities and preoccupations of labor, has the virtue of preventing inmates from painful reflection upon their shattered relationships and new slave identity. Thus, we arrive a seemingly paradoxical result—that inmates may prefer enslavement to the alternative. We will consider this paradox in more detail shortly. It is also possible that this process of separation from family and kinship relationships pushes inmates in entirely different directions. Inmates may grow angry or depressed due to their separation, and this may result in them not performing surplus labor. Perhaps inmates want to think about their loved ones, and view slave labor as a dangerous distraction from the hard work involved in keeping their relationships alive.

The creation of a slave identity as separate and different from the inmate's former identity has effects on the *SFCP*. If people see themselves as slaves, they will accept the treatment of a slave. If a person is torn from their old identity, and a new one is forcibly created that emphasizes first and foremost the person's new status as a slave, and the differences between this status and whatever may have existed 'on the outside.' If the person accepts it, then by definition he must identify himself as a slave. If the form of the slavery in question contains the *SFCP*, the slave accepts his performance of surplus labor as an existential part of his being as a slave, like a person would accept his own lungs or heart. Thus the slave will not question whether or not surplus labor is to be performed, and if so, how much—the slave will simply perform slave surplus labor. The slave may not need to be forced or threatened to perform surplus labor, he may simply accept it as his station in life. If so, this is a benefit to the warden or the designated appropriator, as the inmate will not resist his or her enslavement.

The cultural processes described above also allow for an idea which may seem to be contradictory, namely that slavery may not be a punishment, but a form of rehabilitation for inmates, who, due to their inferior status, have not absorbed the benefits of work outside prison, and therefore must be forced to work under the *SFCP* within prisons. Thus, slavery in prisons can be seen as a kind of benefit to inmates, by teaching them "discipline" and "the value of a hard day's work.' Most prison authorities, however, do not consider prison labor to be anything remotely related to slavery. For example, consider the following statement of mission from the Prison Industry Authority of California:

> [To] Create and maintain working conditions within enterprises, as much like those which prevail in private industry as possible, to assure inmates assigned therein the opportunity to work productively, to earn funds, and to acquire or improve effective work habits or occupational skills. [To] Operate work programs for inmates that are self-supporting through the generation of sufficient funds from the sale of products and services to pay all its expenses, thereby avoiding the cost of alternative inmate programming by California Department of Corrections.

As the above quote attests, prison labor in California is designed to closely resemble industries outside prisons. In other words, prison officials would like to overlook the ways in which prisons are different from industries outside prisons.

Wright argues that prison labor is not rehabilitative because it generally does not develop skills that will be useful in finding inmates productive employment upon their release.[23] Since many of the jobs available in prison have disappeared from the American economy outside prison, the skills needed to work these jobs are not that useful for finding work after leaving prison. We will consider this issue in Chapter Three.

A common argument concerns the relationship between "idleness" and prison labor. If inmates are idle, they will be more likely to take part in conflicts amongst themselves or with the staff of the prison. Thus, it is to the benefit of the prison to engage the inmates in the *SFCP*.

Inmates themselves also play a role in reproducing this cultural process, through peer counseling and religious services, when they affirm the importance of work (participating in the *SFCP*), following the rules, and generally "fitting in" to the established order in prison, rather than getting in trouble, which includes resisting the *SFCP*.

ECONOMIC CONDITIONS OF EXISTENCE

Inmates often require a source of money income while in prison, to use for things like buying items from the prison commissary, buying books or periodicals, buying drugs or other contraband, or sending to their families. Entering into slavery often provides enslaved inmates with a money income, since most states and jurisdictions provide an income to inmates who are enslaved.[24] Thus inmates face a dilemma between enslavement and a necessary money income.[25]

This economic motivation acts in concert with the political processes that secure the existence of slavery in prisons. We tend to view force and economic incentives as competing motivations, but in this case, they seem to work well together. From my own observations, the power of the inmates' need for income often allows prisons to use less outright coercion than they might in the absence of the inmates extreme need and desire for an income, even the meager income that participating in the *SFCP* provides. This does not mean that the shadow of force does not fall across the inmates. Force is ever-present in the prison setting, but most wardens and correctional officers know prisons are more effectively governed if force is used sparingly. If some proportion of the inmates are willing to engage in slave labor, why not let them, reward them with an income and let those who are unwilling to work go without an income or obtain one by illegitimate means?[26]

The apparent willingness of inmates to work as slaves has much to do with the income that the *SFCP* provides. It is a paradox for those that consider force to be the essence of slavery: if a slave performs surplus labor willingly for his master, is he then no longer a slave? Slave accounts from the Antebellum south show that many slaves carried out their tasks willingly and were never beaten by their masters.[27] Surely this does not mean that they were not enslaved, nor should it be construed to mean that slavery was pleasant or something other than horribly exploitative. Similarly, if the need for income drives inmates to perform slave surplus labor, we should not make the mistake of thinking that it is anything but slave labor.

A second economic condition of existence for prison slavery concerns the reproduction of slave labor-power. The master qua appropriator of slave surplus labor must give to the slave a portion of the total output he has produced in order to reproduce the slave's labor-power. This is termed the *master's provision*.[28] Slaves are considered to be maintained by this master's provision in the same way a machine or other piece of productive equipment is maintained; the slave does not *earn* his or her living, but rather it is provided to the slave, just as a horse is provided with grain and straw so that it may pull a plough. The responsibility for the maintenance of the slaves is ultimately in the hands of the head of the department of corrections, and is delegated to the warden of the prison in which the inmates are imprisoned. The warden may use his control over the reproduction of slave labor-power to ensure the appropriation of surplus labor in a variety of ways. For example, if an slave is refusing to work or doing inferior work the warden may reduce the quality of his standard of living, perhaps by removing the slaves' bedding, or confiscating "contraband" (e.g. posters, cooking equipment, tattooing equipment, etc.) that had been tolerated before.

Because the reproduction of the slaves' labor-power is intertwined in the relationship between master and slave, the master may use this to seek to secure or accelerate his or her appropriation of surplus labor from the slaves. Perhaps productive slaves can be rewarded with better clothing, shelter or food, encouraging productivity among all the slaves. Perhaps the master may threaten to take away certain elements of the slaves' consumption, a favorite food, for instance. As mentioned earlier, prison slavemasters use these very tactics to cement their ownership and control over inmates' labor-power. At the same time, this can undermine the master's appropriation of slave surplus. Enslaved inmates may resist the master's attempts to reproduce their slave labor power by refusing to eat, bathe, wear clothing, and so forth. This is an extreme protest, but one that has been repeated at various times throughout the modern history of prisons.[29]

The master's provision is affected by a unique feature of modern prisons: prisons involve vast payments of state welfare. Welfare is understood a transfer of value from the state to another party (usually an individual) which takes place regardless of the recipient providing anything in return.[30] All inmates receive welfare from the state in the form of basic consumption goods, including food, clothing, shelter, medical care, etc.

This leads us back to an important distinction, that of the inmate as a person, versus the inmate as a slave. While the state welfare reproduces the inmate as a person, providing him with the sum of social labor needed to maintain him, the master's provision reproduces the enslaved inmate *as a slave*; in other words, the master's provision reproduces his slave labor-power. The receipt of state welfare does not obligate an inmate to perform labor—this is what makes it welfare.

The presence of state welfare allows the master to lower the master's provision significantly below the level of the necessary labor. Hence the master's provision is altered by the state welfare; it may even fall to zero. A detailed analysis of this process is undertaken in Chapter Three, which examines state welfare and the production of prison household use-values which is a part of that welfare.

If the warden or his designated appropriator takes advantage of the state welfare to lower the master's provision, he may realize a significant gain due to the fact that he is taking advantage of an input to production that costs far less than it would if it were obtained elsewhere, namely the labor-power of the inmate slaves. Using the inmate slaves in this fashion is only possible because of all the conditions of existence of the *SFCP* described above, including the fact that the labor-power of the enslaved inmates does not belong to them.

As mentioned earlier, a private enterprise may be the appropriator of slave surplus labor. An enterprise can sometimes earn significantly higher profit rates by exploiting inmate-slaves than they would by exploiting civilian workers outside prison. It is also possible that enterprises may produce in prisons and realize the same profit rate as outside prisons, but produce a commodity which they would ordinarily not produce, because the costs would be too high if they had to pay the going outside rate for labor-power.

We noted above that inmates need for a money income may drive them to the *SFCP*. This drive would be somewhat mitigated by the presence of state welfare. However, most inmates see the state welfare as inadequate, since it only provides them with certain goods (and no money); in addition, they may be repulsed by the idea of receiving state welfare, and hence may enter the *SFCP* as a way of proving to themselves and others that they are not like the lazy, ignorant welfare recipients demonized in the media. Thus the state welfare may push inmates to perform surplus labor. At the same time, state welfare gives inmates the opportunity to not work, perhaps for the first time in their lives. Some may take advantage of this opportunity.[31]

Enslaved inmates sometimes produce commodities, or items produced for sale rather than for use by the direct producers. This is labeled $SFCP_1$ and is covered in more detail in Chapter Four. The state agencies responsible for appropriating a part of the inmate-produced surplus labor face significant political pressure to be self-supporting—in other words, to meet their budgets without requiring funds from the state. Without the state welfare, these agencies would be forced to pay a much higher maintenance fee to continue the $SFCP_1$, which would make them unable to be self-supporting. This may well cause a crisis in the $SFCP_1$.

When commodities are produced, they must be realized—in other words, the commodities must be sold. Thus the activities involved in the selling of prison-produced commodities are an economic condition of existence for the $SFCP_1$. If commodities are produced but not sold, the $SFCP_1$ is endangered and may reach a crisis. The realization of commodities can be hampered if the commodities are poorly manufactured and of low quality, for example. Most prison labor programs producing commodities were created in part to offset the costs of incarceration. If "prison labor" becomes an additional expense, it may be in danger of criticism and possible closure.[32] The need to realize commodities may also exert pressure over the pace of production. If customers place large orders, the production process may be sped up, increasing the intensity of labor or the length of the work-ing day.

The last point above brings us to the final economic condition of existence, which is that the *SFCP* is an economic process which involves the production of goods and services (either as commodities, or as prison household use-values). Marx argues that the survival of a class process depends in part on the development of what he called the "forces of produc-tion." If the slaves only perform enough labor to cover the reproduction of their labor-power, then provided there is no one else reproducing the slaves' labor-power, the slaves will not produce any surplus labor, and hence there will be nothing to for the master to appropriate, no surplus labor for the master to use to secure the conditions of existence of the slave class process. Unless there is some external aid, the class process will cease to exist. It is vital to the continuation of the slave class process that the slaves not only perform surplus labor, but that the surplus labor be large enough to secure all the various conditions of the slave class process.

Since the costs confronting an enterprise of any sort are uncertain, if the master wishes to remain the appropriator of slave surplus labor, he must obtain the maximum amount of surplus labor possible. If he does not, he takes an additional risk. If additional costs appear, if disaster strikes, if any one of a thousand unforeseen events takes place, the class process may be endangered. If that extra surplus labor had been available, it could have been used to avert the crisis.

Marx outlined the basic methods of obtaining more surplus in Capital, Volume I. The classic methods are what Marx called absolute and relative surplus value.[33] Increasing absolute surplus value involves a lengthening in the workday, while the intensity of labor is held constant, so that a greater proportion of the day is spent in surplus labor rather than in necessary labor. Increasing relative surplus labor is raising the intensity and pace of labor, while keeping the length of the workday constant, so that the neces-sary labor is completed in a shorter time, and more of the day is devoted to surplus labor.

The institutional structure of modern prisons limits the ability of the appropriators to increase absolute surplus value. Since prisons are generally not arranged around the labor process, the development of the forces of production is sometimes forced to abide by the rules and customs of the prison, frustrating the appropriators of inmate slave surplus. For example, because of the schedule of many prisons, including the shifts of the correctional officers, mealtimes, etc. it is difficult for appropriators to increase the workday beyond 8 hours, and in many cases the workday is shorter, 6 or 7 hours. If the structure of prisons were changed to accommodate the production of commodities, then prisons may have a unique ability to obtain a longer workday from inmates than what would be accepted by workers outside prisons, due to the incredible degree of power that prison authorities wield over the inmates. In fact, this was the situation in most 19th century prisons. However, an increase in absolute surplus value may undermine other conditions of existence. For example, enslaved inmates may be willing to work a certain number of hours in order to secure an income, but may be unwilling to work beyond this, as increased work time may interfere with other activities, or perhaps inmate slaves may come to feel that the income they receive is not worth the intense exploitation they must endure. If fewer inmates are willing to enter the *SFCP*, it may be threatened with a crisis.

To increase relative surplus value, prison slavemasters can select the most productive and capable inmates from the pool of inmates willing to be enslaved. If an inmate slave is not productive enough, he or she can easily be replaced. Hence, slaves may have to increase the intensity of their labor to avoid losing their income.

Prison slavemasters often offer higher payments to some inmate slaves, as part of a hierarchy of income levels. Those receiving the highest payments are those regarded as most valuable by the prison slavemasters, i.e. the most productive "workers" qua slaves. This is one way of increasing the intensity of labor, through competition for higher payments.[34]

Marx also discusses the importance of the turnover time of capital in forming the absolute mass of profits available to the appropriator. If the turnover time of capital can be shortened, then the capitalist (or slavemaster) can repeat the circuit of commodities for industrial capital—the production and realization of surplus value—a greater number of times in a given time period.[35]

Here again prison slavemasters face a barrier in the form of the institutional structure of prisons. Prisons always stop and search every vehicle that enters and exits the prison grounds to prevent escapes and the smuggling of contraband. This adds a delay to the circulation of capital, as it takes longer to receive needed inputs to production from outside the prison, and to deliver goods to be sold.

Prison slavemasters can use the unique features of prison to realize a potential gain by lowering the value per unit of their commodities. If prison commodities sell on the same markets as commodities produced outside prison, which they sometimes do, then prison industries are in competition with outside industries to lower the value per unit of the commodity. If the prison industries are able to lower the value per unit below the market value of the commodity—the value formed by the socially necessary abstract labor embodied in the commodity, a kind of weighted average of all the individual values of commodities produced by different enterprises—then the prison industries are able to siphon off surplus value from their competition through the marketplace. Marx argues that capitalist firms generally do this by investing in more productive machinery, which lowers the value of the constant capital per unit. Generally more productive machinery is more expensive, which would tend to raise the value of the constant capital, but since the new machinery is more productive, it produces a greater number of commodities, so the value per unit falls.[36]

As noted earlier, prison slavemasters may take advantage of the state welfare to lower the master's provision far below the level of the necessary labor, and perhaps to zero. Thus from the perspective of the slavemaster, the labor-power of the inmate slaves appears to be nearly free. The slavemaster might then seek to substitute labor for capital as much as is possible, reducing the level of the relatively more expensive constant capital while increasing their consumption of the relatively cheap inmate slave labor-power. Perhaps one method of doing this is to actually use older machinery then is generally used in a given production process, and use more inmate labor to maintain the aging machinery. Slavemasters would thus take advantage of what Marx calls "moral depreciation"—the fact that the value of machinery that is less productive than the average level of productivity seen as socially necessary dramatically decreases in value. Since the machinery used in the production process is lower in value, the value per unit falls, allowing the slavemaster to realize a gain in profit relative to other producers outside prisons.[37]

The above are a few of the methods of developing the forces of production in the slave class process in prisons, as well as some of the barriers to this development that exist. Given the complexities of prison production, it is only possible to sketch the development of the forces of production. Many other examples of this development no doubt exist, and the above remarks should not be seen as comprehensive. However, the general point is that the development of the forces of production in prisons is a condition of existence which, in conjunction with the infinite number of other conditions of existence, a few of which have been described above, enables prison slavemasters to appropriate the surplus labor of inmate slaves.

THE PARADOX OF THE PRISON SLAVE FUNDAMENTAL CLASS PROCESS

Several noted Marxian theorists have suggested that exploitation of a worker is linked to the worker's choices, arguing that if a worker freely chooses to engage in a given labor process, then that labor process must not involve exploitation.[38] In other words, exploitation inevitably involves some kind of coercion. If the coercion was not present, workers would not participate in their own exploitation. This argument seems strongly linked to the neoclassical definition of exploitation, and may represent the influence of neoclassical economic theory on some Marxists.

Within neoclassical economic theory, the notion of exploitation is understood to occur in the economic sphere of distribution. Neoclassical economics focuses primarily on one form of distribution, which is markets. Markets can be used to decide, in a decentralized fashion, who gets what and how much. When all markets are competitive, the value of the marginal product of labor is equal to the real wage rate, and hence exploitation for neoclassicals does not exist, as the wage is said to be 'fair.' Exploitation can only exist when the marginal product of labor is greater than the wage, which can only happen when markets are not perfectly competitive. Specifically, workers are exploited by employers only when there is a monopsony in the demand for labor. The classic example is the company town, where there is only one employer. Since workers are not free to choose the employer, they can be forced to accept a wage which is lower than the marginal product of labor. The solution to the problem of exploitation in neoclassical theory is perfectly competitive markets, in which the utility maximizing choices of individual workers and consumers are brought into balance with the profit maximization of firms.

Since slavery represents the ultimate case of exploitation, it would then stand to reason that slaves would not choose to be enslaved, they must be forced into slavery. This conclusion is the result of essentialism. Neoclassical economics makes human choice into the essence of all social and economic relationships.[39] Thus, freedom equals choice, and slavery, being the antithesis of freedom, involves the lack of choice. Marxian theory, in contrast, focuses on class, the relationship to the surplus labor performed at a given site of production. The reasons why a person may produce surplus labor which someone else appropriates—the Marxian definition of exploitation—may be nearly limitless, depending on the political, cultural, and economic forces which influence (and are in turn influenced by) that person, including his or her choices.

Thus for Marxism it is not at all illogical to say that a person may "choose" to be exploited, may even choose to be a slave. This would be a purely academic point but for the fact that hundreds of thousands of inmates in U.S. prisons repeatedly choose to be slaves. Judging by the length of some of the waiting lists in prisons of inmates seeking to be enslaved, there is a strong desire for enslavement. In fact, prison officials have stated that the desire for enslavement is so strong that the *SFCP* can actually be used as a tool for correctional management, as a reward for good behavior.[40]

The choice to be enslaved makes sense when considered in the context of prison life. Being enslaved generally provides inmates with an income, which can be used to raise an inmate's own consumption level, or to help support a family on the outside. Enslavement can shorten an inmate's sentence—in California, for each day an inmate spends in the *SFCP* an additional day is removed from his or her sentence, potentially cutting a sentence in half. In other states where such arrangements do not exist, enslavement is positive evidence that an inmate is making an effort at rehabilitation and deserves parole. Enslavement may provide an inmate with access to job training in areas such as welding and metal fabrication, automotive technology, computers, furniture manufacturing, sewing, cooking, truck driving, and other potentially valuable job skills.[41] On a psychological level, being enslaved may be a way of occupying one's mind, a way of forgetting about all the tension, boredom, loneliness and brutality of prison, of making the time go by quicker, by losing oneself in a task. Resisting enslavement, on the other hand, carries the threat of punishment, loss of additional freedoms (perversely called 'privileges' in prisons), a longer sentence, and so forth.

For all of these reasons, being enslaved makes sense, especially given the lack of acceptable alternatives. Thus it is not necessary or particularly believable to argue that inmates have a kind of "false consciousness"—that they do not realize they are being exploited or fail to see their 'true' class interests. Some may not think of their "employment" in prisons as slavery, but many do.[42] They may simply choose enslavement because this is the best choice they can make given their circumstances. This class-based account may also explain why there are relatively few revolts against the *SFCP* in prisons, which makes it different from many other forms of the *SFCP* throughout history.

We should ask ourselves to following question: if those who are arguably the lowest caste in American society, hated and despised by all, who are overwhelmingly poor people of color, who face callous brutality and countless rules, whose labor-power is a mere possession of the state department of corrections, who are cut off from any means of subsistence and have no choice but to rely on state welfare, if these inmates choose, out of desperation and without other alternatives, to be enslaved, should we accept that 'choice'? Should we overlook that they are slaves? Should we celebrate their enslavement as progress toward a safer and more free society? Should we believe that slavery is freedom?

INMATE CLASSES

The following discussion briefly delineates the inmate population in terms of class. Inmates have very different connections to the surplus labor in prison, ranging from direct producer of surplus labor, to an indirect connection (providing conditions of existence for the performance of surplus labor), to no connection whatsoever. Thus inmates are placed in the following classes:

1. Inmates performing surplus labor as slaves (slave producers)
2. Inmates performing labor that does not directly produce surplus, but provides the conditions of existence for surplus labor (subsumed slaves)
3   Inmates who perform no labor, (and hence no surplus labor) and are therefore not enslaved. (non-slave inmates)

The first category contains inmates enslaved in the direct production of goods and services in two separate areas of production, commodity and prison household production. A commodity is defined as a good or service produced for the purpose of exchange. Slaves in commodity production (often called "prison industries" in the literature) perform necessary and surplus labor which is embodied in goods and services which are then appropriated by non-inmates. The details of this production and appropriation are covered in the Chapter Three. The slaves in this sphere of production are labeled $SFCP_1$.

Non-commodity production includes inmates enslaved in the production of use-values which are consumed within the prison. This labor includes food preparation, laundry, maintenance and other tasks. The slaves laboring in this sphere of production are labeled $SFCP_2$. In both the $SFCP_1$ and the $SFCP_2$ slaves perform necessary and surplus labor; in the latter, the products of slave labor are appropriated by the warden of the prison. Thus, the inmates in the first category are all direct producers of surplus labor, albeit at different sites of production, and hence may be considered a class of slave producers.

In the second category are inmates whose labor produces no surplus directly, but rather provides conditions of existence for either $SFCP_1$ or $SFCP_2$. These inmates have an indirect relationship to the production of surplus labor, and are therefore not considered to be part of the slave fundamental class process. Since Marxian theory is focused on class, defined by one's relationship to the surplus, workers are categorized according to whether or not they directly and materially produced surplus. These inmates do not directly produce surplus, but since their labor provides necessary conditions that allow the *SFCP* to exist, these inmates are said to be participating in a subsumed class process. Because these inmates do not produce surplus, they are not exploited. However, since they perform labor under similar conditions as slaves in the first category, it is appropriate to label these inmates as a class of subsumed slaves. In the former, the slaves labor to provide the conditions of existence for the slave class process occurring in the production of commodities, while in the latter, the slaves labor to provide the conditions of existence for the slave class process occurring in prison household production.

It is important to note that this slave subsumed class is not the only group which may provide conditions of existence for the $SFCP_1$ or $SFCP_2$, however, the slave subsumed class is the only group which provides conditions of existence and receives distributions of surplus. The distributions of surplus labor which go to this slave subsumed class are explored in Chapter Two.

In addition, it should be noted that other forms of the *SFCP* contain slaves who are not directly performing surplus labor, but rather who are laboring to provide conditions of existence for the class process. For example, slaves in the U.S. South who worked to maintain the tools and equipment used in the production of cash crops were not producing surplus labor, but were providing conditions of existence for the production and appropriation of surplus labor, and hence they are also subsumed slaves. Even though these slaves are not part of the *SFCP*, they still are not free to sell their labor-power, because it is owned by the master. In addition, the labor-power of these slaves was reproduced by the master, and the slaves were subject to the laws and customs of the American south, the network of non-class economic, cultural and political processes that formed the conditions of existence for slavery in that society at that time.

Finally, the third category contains the inmates who perform no labor. Since these inmates do not perform any labor, they perform neither necessary nor surplus labor, nor do they participate in a slave subsumed class process. Hence these inmates should not be considered slaves, as they have no direct or indirect connection to the slave surplus labor. These inmates are labeled non-slave inmates. Thus the inmates may be divided into these three categories:

1. Slave producers
    a. $SFCP_1$
    b. $SFCP_2$

2. Subsumed slaves

       a. Subsumed to the $SFCP_1$
       b. Subsumed to the $SFCP_2$
  3.   Non-slave inmates

In sum, of the total population of inmates, only the first two of these are considered inmate-slaves. That is, only the inmates engaged in the $SFCP$ or those engaged in directly providing the conditions for existence for the $SFCP$ are considered inmate-slaves. The non-laboring inmates are not considered inmate-slaves, though they may be brought into the labor process—and hence enslaved—at virtually any time.

It is tempting to conclude that life is better for the non-slave inmates than the inmate-slaves in 1 and 2. No such claim is made here. Marxian theory says nothing about whether an individual person considers him or herself better or worse off by being subjected to exploitation. This may seem like a surprising result. It stems from Marx's focus on class rather than on some type of measurement of individual well-being.[43]

The proportion of inmates in these groups is as follows. According to the Correctional Industries Association, 6% of inmates nationwide were engaged in commodity production in 2001. Some states and jurisdictions employ more inmates in prison industries, and some less. The jurisdiction which employs the highest proportion of inmates in prison industries is the federal prison system, in which nearly 20% of the inmates produce commodities.[44] Since no comprehensive numbers have been gathered, it is difficult to say with precision how many of these workers are performing surplus labor, and hence are in the $SFCP_1$, and how many are subsumed to the $SFCP_1$. Observations of several dozen prisons across the country lead me to a sense is that the proportion of subsumed slaves is relatively low; I'll assume it is 10% of the slave workers in each productive site. Specific research is needed here to determine more precisely the proportion of inmates in slave fundamental and slave subsumed class processes.

About 30% of the inmates are performing prison household production. This varies depending on the prison and jurisdiction. In some prisons inmates perform the prison household labor necessary for the functioning of their prison, then they perform prison household production at another prison. For example, in maximum security prisons that follow the "control unit' model—which consists of isolation and lockdown in individual cells for up to 23 1/2 hours a day—the prison household production is done by inmates from a nearby minimum-security prison.[45] Inmates not enslaved in either the $SFCP_1$ or the $SFCP_2$ perform no labor.[46]
As Figure 2.1 illustrates, an estimated 36% of inmates are enslaved in either the $SFCP_1$, the $SFCP_2$, or are subsumed slaves, who work to provide the conditions of existence for prison slavery, but do not directly produce

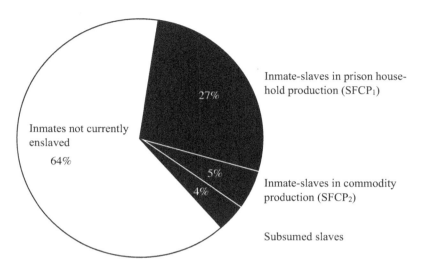

Figure 2.1 Percentage of inmates enslaved, 2001.

value.[47] The remaining 64% of inmates are not enslaved, though they could be at any time, though the productive infrastructure in prisons does not currently permit all the inmates to be enslaved. The proportion of inmates who perform no labor is the single largest class of inmates—with the exception of some states and the federal prison system. The unique class tensions and struggles this situation produces are explored in Chapters Three and Five.

CONCLUSION

This chapter has shown that prisons are important sites in contemporary American society, and uses class to analyze the production which takes place in prisons. We have shown that prison labor is best understood as a unique form of slavery, one which does not include the ownership of human chattel, but does contain the slave fundamental class process. The power wielded by the prison authorities to compel the labor of the inmates, to even own their very labor-power, combines with the cultural processes of objectification, shame and dishonor of the inmates, and the economic processes of income incentives, state welfare and so on to form a particular relationship between the inmate and the warden—that of slave and master. The role of the inmate is to unquestioningly obey, while the role of the prison authorities is to confine the inmates, but also to "manage" the inmates, to discipline them, to extract their surplus labor, to reform them, performing the various functions of the prison system, including punishment, rehabilitation, incapacitation, deterring crime, or some combination of these. Enslaved inmates are in a position of unquestioning obedience and exploitation that dehumanizes them; in the eyes of society they are reduced to little more than the numbers they are assigned.

Supporting slave exploitation—or even tolerating its existence—is a dangerous path for society to tread. If it is deemed acceptable to enslave inmates, who might be next? To allow any member of society to be enslaved degrades us all, dragging us back to a time when concerns of fairness and justice were less relevant than the simple power of brute force to steal the fruits of human labor.

Chapter Three
State Welfare and the Production of the Prison Household

This chapter analyzes a unique feature of prisons, which is the granting of inmates a sum of goods and services free of charge or any expectation or obligation on the part of the inmates to provide any value equivalent. This provision of goods and services to inmates is understood as a payment of state welfare, since it flows to them regardless of whether or not they perform labor.[1] This welfare is given in two forms:

1. the direct provision of commodities to inmates, and
2. the provision of goods and services (use-values) which are produced by other inmates enslaved in prison household production.

This state welfare affects every dimension of production in prisons; hence, it is analyzed separately in this chapter, along with prison household production. As this chapter will show, the specific dynamics related to the production, appropriation and distribution of surplus labor by inmates in prison household production is closely related to the provision of state welfare of the second form above.

Since surplus labor is defined as that quantum of labor performed which is above and beyond the individual's own consumption (necessary labor), before we can analyze the surplus labor performed by inmates, we must theorize the elements of inmates' necessary labor. Since the inmates' necessary labor is interwoven with the state welfare, we must analyze the state welfare, considered in terms of the quantity of abstract labor that flows to inmates. For clarity, this analysis is done with equations; a glossary is provided to help the reader keep track of terms.

WELFARE AND INMATE INCOME LEVELS

The following discussion analyzes two income flows to inmates: welfare from the state, and income from enslavement. Inmates may well have access to other income flows, such as gifts from friends and family outside prison, sources of revenue from activities such as writing, and revenue from illegal activities within the prison. In the interests of concision, this discussion focuses only on welfare and the *SFCP*. The following should be understood as a kind of minimum measure of inmate income, which is often supplemented by other sources.

Because all prisoners receive this state welfare, their income (Y_{inmate}) is always equal to at least this flow of revenue, which is labeled a non-class revenue (NCR_{state}), due to the fact that it is not directly or indirectly related to the production or appropriation of surplus. Thus, inmates occupy a non-class position in that they are recipients of state welfare, regardless of whether or not they perform labor:

$$(1) \qquad\qquad Y_{inmate} = NCR_{state}$$

If N stands for the total inmate population of a prison, then ($N{\cdot}NCR_{state}$) would be the total welfare payment. For simplicity, the term NCR_{state} will stand for the total welfare to all inmates.

The slave class process in the Antebellum south also involved a kind of welfare paid to certain slaves, usually children, pregnant mothers, and the aged. Although nearly every slave worked at various tasks from a very young age to a very old age, slaves were provided with their necessary consumption level even when their own labor produced no surplus.[2] In other words, the value of the labor these slaves performed in a given day was less than or equal to the value of the goods considered at that time and place to be socially necessary for the reproduction of their labor power.

There is one exception to the inmates' right to receive state welfare. This relates to certain infractions of prison rules by an inmate. If an inmate breaks rules, he or she may be placed in administrative segregation, which is a separation of an inmate from the rest of the inmate population. Nearly every prison has some mechanism of separating some of the inmates. Some of the time this involves additional punitive measures, such as the taking away of an inmates' sheets and bedding, or replacing the inmates' food with food of lesser quality, restricting the inmates' access to other prison activities and services, such as participation in the various prison groups that may exist, or taking away access to visitation and television. Since the inmate in this specific situation receives either fewer goods and services from the state, or the goods and services are of lesser quality, this is considered a different category of state welfare, where the inmate receives a punitively lower amount of state welfare:

(2) $$Y_{seg} = NCR_{seg}$$

This lower amount of state welfare is less than what the general inmate population receives; thus

(3) $$Y_{seg} < Y_{inmate}$$

To complicate matters, not every inmate who is in administrative segregation receives a lowered amount of state welfare, as receiving NCR_{seg} rather than NCR_{state} represents an additional punishment that may be applied to an inmate who is already in administrative segregation. Some inmates are segregated for their own protection, due to a gang-related or personal conflict, or due to the threat of sexual assault. These inmates would not be given NCR_{seg} unless there was some additional infraction. However, for simplicity, in this study, the term administrative segregation, or segregation, means that the inmate is receiving a punitively lower amount of state welfare.[3] The warden of the prison is in charge of placing an inmate in administrative segregation. If N_{seg} is defined as the total population of inmates in segregation who are receiving NCR_{seg}, then the total amount of welfare paid would be:

(4) $$\left(N - N_{seg}\right)NCR_{state} + NCR_{seg} \cdot N_{seg}$$

THE LEVEL OF STATE WELFARE AND THE VALUE OF SLAVE LABOR-POWER

Inmates are captives; their fate is necessarily in the hands of the state which apprehends and cages them. Theoretically, criminal justice in a democratic society represents the will of the electorate. The level of welfare inmates receive is a reflection of the laws and cultural climate that shape the prison; if the welfare changes, it will be because of changes in the idea of what level of consumption is considered necessary for inmates. In other words, the laws and customs surrounding prisons participate in overdetermining what inmates receive in state welfare.

The level of state welfare reflects society's notion of what quantity of food, clothing, shelter, and other goods and services are needed to sustain a human being at a level that is considered acceptable. Of course the notion of what is minimally acceptable for a person in society is both complex and contested, a measure which is continually shaped by various cultural, social, religious, political, and economic forces. One could argue that in the U.S. there are two main indicators, the poverty line and the minimum wage. These measures are distinct, yet each aims at the same goal, a measurement of a kind of minimum consumption which is seen as socially necessary [4] These indicators are limited because they say nothing about the expenses an individual may face, such as cost of housing, food, clothing, transportation, utilities, and so forth.

In contrast, prison inmates are actually given a bundle of commodities, as stipulated by the laws which govern each prison jurisdiction. This means it is more straightforward to determine the level of welfare inmates receive, and by extension, the prevalent social view which shapes the level of state welfare. More detail is provided on the specific commodities inmates receive later in this chapter; for now, it suffices to say that inmates have traditionally received a sum of value that is far lower than what would be considered necessary outside prisons. Inmates have often received worse food, clothing, and shelter than non-inmates. Inmates in the 19th and early 20th century received spoiled or inadequate food, slept on flea-ridden hay or crude beds, wore one set of clothes all the time, and had little or no access to medical care.[5]

As ideas about incarceration have changed over the 20th century, incarceration was increasingly recast as a humane cure for social deviance rather than a punishment and deterrent to crime. If prisons were to be humane environments, inmates must be provided with more and better welfare. This is an increase in the level of state welfare. By the same token, the level of state welfare may fall, if people begin to believe that inmates have it easy, that they do not deserve the level of welfare they currently receive, etc. The level of welfare may even fall to zero. In this case, all inmates would either be enslaved or die—a situation that seems accurate in the case of many 19th century prisons.

In short, the level of welfare in prisons is overdetermined by the culture surrounding incarceration, the meanings that are given to imprisonment, the habits and expectations of the inmates themselves, the physical needs of the inmates relative to the particular climate and geography, and the historical context of what is considered appropriate treatment for inmates, along with a host of other factors.

The one exception to the rule outlined above is the level of welfare granted to inmates in segregation, which is lower than the level generally viewed as acceptable within the prison. This represents the understanding in society that prison is punitive, and that correctional officials must be granted the ability to punish inmates for breaking prison rules. Some of these punishments are expected to involve the inmates' standard of living, for example, whether an inmate is allowed contact with other inmates or is confined to a cell all the time and so forth. The prison itself is a form of welfare—it was built by the state to house and confine the inmates. The prison is emblematic of all the contradictions of the welfare that inmates receive, which is both a gift and a punishment. The inmate in administrative segregation is confined to a much smaller part of the prison, he cannot use the spaces he formerly occupied.

This placement of an inmate in administrative segregation, where he receives NCR_{seg} as a method of punishment may serve as a frightening reminder to inmates that their subsistence is in the hands of the authorities they defy. This may be a powerful psychological force which may be brought to bear on inmates who disobey the rules of the prison, including refusal to work.

As discussed in Chapter One, many prison inmates are slaves, owing to their participation in the *SFCP* in either commodity or prison household production. These slaves have slave labor-power, the capacity to work (as a slave) which is in fact owned by the head of the department of corrections.[6] The value of slave labor-power is the value sum needed to reproduce the labor-power of the slave, that is, to allow the slave to continue to labor tomorrow at the same pace and duration as she did today. Marx argues that the value of labor-power is a complex overdetermination of the biological needs of a person combined with social factors.[7]

The value of slave labor-power is termed the *master's provision*, and is labeled V_{slave}. This is the amount deemed socially necessary to reproduce the labor-power of a slave. The master's provision reproduces the ability of a slave to labor as a slave, whereas the state welfare provides an inmate with the food, clothing, shelter, and other items needed for survival at whatever level is deemed adequate by society. This master's provision has taken various forms throughout the history of the American prison system. For most of American history, it has not been in money form, but rather in the form of goods and services. In recent times, enslaved inmates have been given money payments as their master's provision.

Though V_{slave} has sometimes been granted in money form, the term master's provision indicates that it is not a wage, as a wage represents a free exchange of labor-power on the part of the worker, and money on the part of the employer. This free exchange does not take place in prisons. The term master's provision further reflects the idea that the slave is granted his subsistence by his master as a gift rather than by right.

The social, cultural, political, and economic forces which overdetermine the level of state welfare play a similar role in overdetermining the value of slave labor-power in prisons. However, while the level of state welfare reproduces an inmate as a person, a human being who will continue to live due to the state welfare, the value of slave labor-power refers to a much more narrow concept, which is the ability of an slave to perform labor in a given time period. Thus, the value of slave labor-power refers specifically to the *SFCP* and a slaves' ability to continue his condition as a worker qua slave who performs necessary and surplus labor.

The level of welfare and the value of slave labor-power are conceptually distinct categories; they also differ in magnitude in most cases. The reason is that there is a different social understanding of "working" (enslaved) inmates than that of "non-working" inmates. There is a general notion that the former deserve a higher standard of living than the latter. Although there are a few exceptions, they seem to be marginal. This difference is discussed in greater detail below.

INMATE INCOME LEVELS BY CLASS

Marxian theory suggests that any worker producing surplus must receive a sum of abstract labor equal to the value of his or her labor-power, V. Thus, in theory, when an inmate is enslaved, he receives a different income flow from what they received before being enslaved. We will label this new income Y_{slave}. The total income the slave receives would stem from two sources: as a recipient of state welfare and as a slave. Slaves receive a income flow of:

$$(5) \qquad\qquad Y_{slave} = NCR_{state} + V_{slave}$$

Theoretically, the slave receives now far more than is necessary to reproduce his slave labor-power. We will see shortly that this creates a unique opportunity for prison appropriators (the warden, state agency, or other body, as discussed in Chapter One) to *reduce* their payment to the inmate-slave, a clear benefit to the appropriator.

When slaves perform labor above the necessary labor which makes up the value of slave labor-power they are performing slave surplus labor. Since inmates may be enslaved in one of two possible spheres of production in prison, there is a value of slave labor-power for each sphere of production; this means that Y_{slave} includes two potentially different income flows, one for commodity production, labeled Y_1, and one for prison household production, labeled Y_2.[8]

The reason for this difference is that the value of slave labor-power is considered relative to each production process. Hence V_{slave} includes

V_1, commodity production ($SFCP_1$), and V_2, prison household production ($SFCP_2$). Each value sum represents the necessary labor needed to reproduce the slave's labor power in each of these distinct production forms,

$$(6) \qquad\qquad SFCP_1 : Y_1 = V_1 + NCR_{state} \text{ , and}$$

$$(7) \qquad\qquad SFCP_2 : Y_2 = V_2 + NCR_{state}$$

Note that the separation of V_{slave} into V_1 and V_2 is for theoretical clarity, not due to a difference in magnitude. The fact that there is no mention of the difference between commodity and prison household production in the laws governing prisons, or the general discourse on prisons within the culture, suggests that the amount of social labor needed to reproduce a slave's labor-power is the same across both sites of production—hence, $V_1 = V_2$. The term V_{slave} will be used to indicate the value of slave labor-power in general. In addition, the terms $\dot{V}_1$ and $\dot{V}_2$ will be used to refer to the total value of slave labor-power of all the inmates enslaved in the $SFCP_1$ and $SFCP_2$ respectively.

As noted in Chapter One, in addition to being slave producers, inmate-slaves may also be subsumed slaves. In this case they provide the conditions of existence for the $SFCP$, and receive a share of the surplus to reproduce their labor-power. This distribution of surplus received by subsumed slaves is labeled $SSCR$ to indicate that these slaves receive a subsumed class revenue. Recall that slaves may be subsumed to either commodity or prison household production, the income flows are labeled Y_{SS1} and Y_{SS2} respectively. Thus subsumed slaves in commodity production have a total income of

$$(8) \qquad\qquad Y_{SS1} = NCR_{state} + SSCR_1$$

while subsumed slaves in prison household production have an income of

$$(9) \qquad\qquad Y_{SS2} = NCR_{state} + SSCR_2 .$$

As noted earlier, the state welfare does create an opportunity for the slave master to provide the slave with a value sum less than that needed to sustain that slave's labor-power precisely because the inmates' labor power is reproduced by the state welfare, which is provided regardless of whether or not the inmate labors. We will define P_{slave} as the *actual value* provided by the master to the slave, encompassing both P_1 in commodity production and P_2 in prison household production. We will also define $\dot{P}_1$ and $\dot{P}_1$ to be the total master's provision flowing to slaves in the $SFCP_1$ and the $SFCP_2$ respectively. Thus the actual value of the master's provision, P_{slave}, may be far less than the master's provision which is socially required to reproduce the inmate slave labor-power, V_{slave}. This actual master's provision is typically given in money form, generally by means of a transfer of funds to an inmate's account.

In other words, because of the presence of the state's welfare to all inmates, a master has the opportunity to lower the master's provision to a value P_{slave} which is lower than the sum of abstract labor necessary to reproduce the inmate-slaves' labor-power, V_{slave}. This causes the actual income received by the inmate-slave (Y^A_{slave}) to fall below Y_{slave}:

$$(10) \qquad \left(Y^A_{slave} = NCR_{state} + P_{slave}\right) < \left(Y_{slave} = NCR_{state} + V_{slave}\right) \ .$$

The slavemaster in effect takes advantage of the fact that the labor-power of inmates is reproduced by state welfare. Even though the master reduces the master's provision, the reproduction of the slave's labor-power continues, since the reduced value flow from the master is compensated by welfare from the state. The slave master clearly gains from this arrangement. Note, however, that the actual rate of slave exploitation, $\frac{s}{v}$, equal to the slave surplus labor (S_{slave}) divided by the value of slave labor-power, has not changed. The slave master receives the same amount of surplus as before, but the state welfare provides an additional value flow to go to the master equal to the difference between P_{slave} and V_{slave}. This flow of value is not the same as an increase in the surplus because the necessary labor has remained the same; the actual master's provision is simply below that which is necessary to reproduce the slave's labor-power: $P_{slave} < V_{slave}$. Provided P_{slave} is positive, then the income of an inmate-slave is greater than the income of a non-slave inmate:

$$(11) \qquad \left(NCR_{state} + P_{slave}\right) > NCR_{state}.$$

Theoretically, P_{slave} can fall to zero, without jeopardizing the slave fundamental class process. This occurs when the state welfare offsets completely the lack of any provision from the master. As before, there is no change in the rate of exploitation, even though P_{slave} is zero. The state simply supports the slaves to the financial benefit of the master. This is the case in prisons in Texas, Arkansas, and Georgia, and in certain areas of prison production (usually in prison household production) in other states, for example, Florida.

Although P_{slave} may fall to zero, it does not necessarily tend to do so. A positive P_{slave} may persist due to a set of processes which create a recognized difference in "working" versus "non-working" inmates, where "working inmates" qua slaves are seen as deserving of a higher living standard than non-working inmates. This difference may be conceptualized as a reward to the slaves for their labor. Such rewards were sometimes given to slaves in the Antebellum South for doing certain hard jobs, or meeting production quotas.[9] This difference in inmate income versus slave income as the result of P_{slave} often leads to conflicts within the prison. In class terms, we can conceptualize this difference as being between what is needed to reproduce the labor-power of an inmate slave, versus what is needed to reproduce the inmate as a person. If P_{slave} is positive, it reflects the social consensus that a 'working' (enslaved) inmate deserves a higher standard of living than does a non-working inmate:

$$(12) \qquad V_{slave} = (NCR_{state} + P_{slave}), \text{ and } V_{slave} > NCR_{state}.$$

In U.S. prisons the actual master's provision, P_{slave}, in fact falls far below V_{slave}. In addition, the slavemaster can take advantage of state welfare to lower subsumed class payments to subsumed inmate-slaves in commodity and prison household production below the level that would have been necessary in the absence of the state welfare.

It is also possible (and indeed is often the case) that $P_2 < P_1$. For example, in the federal prison system, P_2 ranges from \$0.40 to \$0.60 per hour, while P_1 ranges from \$0.80 to \$1.60 per hour. While such small absolute differences may not be significant in the outside world, they are quite significant in prison, and hence are best viewed in terms of their relative difference. An inmate in the federal system can make 2 to 4 times more income by being enslaved in the $SFCP_1$ as he could by being enslaved in the $SFCP_2$. Since the federal system enslaves all able-bodied inmates who are not in segregation, it becomes clear why long waiting lists exist for enslavement in the $SFCP_1$. In other jurisdictions, especially where the $SFCP_1$ takes place in conjunction with private enterprises, where special laws apply,[10] the relative difference is even greater, where P_1 may be as much as 10 times P_2, although not every jurisdiction is willing or able to enslave all able-bodied inmates like the federal system does.

In either case, it may make sense to use income differentials as a method for obtaining motivated, productive slaves. Masters in commodity production may well benefit by creating a desire in the inmates for jobs in commodity production. This allows these prison slavemasters in commodity production to obtain higher levels of effort and quality from the slaves in $SFCP_1$. If masters care more about the revenue generated from commodity production than they do about the number or quality of the use-values produced in prison household production, they may prefer to have the more motivated, more productive slaves working in commodity production, given that the slaves are not equally productive. This seems to be the driving force in many prisons.[11]

The difference between P_{slave} and V_{slave} is maintained—that is, the V_{slave} does not fall to the lower level of P_{slave}. As argued above, there are reasons why V_{slave} would fall, but this fall in V_{slave} is due to larger social, legal, economic and other processes occurring in society, not the result of a difference between P_{slave} and V_{slave} per se.

In summary, the prison population can be conceived in class analytical terms as follows. All prisoners receive an income of NCR_{state}, whether or not they work as prison slaves (the only exception is the inmates in segregation, who receive a lower amount of state welfare, NCR_{seg}). For those prisoners who work as slave producers, the value flow received in prison household production is $(P_1 + NCR_{state})$ and in commodity production it is $(P_2 + NCR_{state})$. The inmates who work as subsumed slaves in commodity production receive $(SSCR_1 + NCR_{state})$, while the inmates who work as subsumed slaves in prison household production receive $(SSCR_2 + NCR_{state})$. Note that there is a difference between potential and actual income only for the slave producers. The other classes of inmates receive an actual income identical to their potential income. Table 3.1 provides a summary:

The above shows that the inmate population can be understood in terms of class, in addition to other categorizations that may be made, such as race, age, prison terms, and so forth. We will see that these class differences produce tensions and contradictions that lead to conflict in the prison, yet are invisible without the use of the concept of class.

Table 3.1 Potential and Actual Income of Inmates by Class

Inmate Category	Potential Income	Actual Income
1. *Slave Producers*		
a. Commodity production (*SFCP₁*)	$Y_1 = [V_1 + NCR_{state}]$	$Y_1^A = [P_1 + NCR_{state}]$
b. Non-commodity production (*SFCP₂*)	$Y_2 = [V_2 + NCR_{state}]$	$Y_2^A = [P_2 + NCR_{state}]$
2. *Subsumed Slaves*		
a. Commodity production (*SSCP₁*)	$Y_{SS1} = [SSCR_1 + NCR_{state}]$	$Y_{SS1} = [SSCR_1 + NCR_{state}]$
b. Non-commodity production (*SSCP₂*)	$Y_{SS2} = [SSCR_2 + NCR_{state}]$	$Y_{SS2} = [SSCR_2 + NCR_{state}]$
3. *Non-slave inmates, general population*	$Y_{inmate} = [NCR_{state}]$	$Y_{inmate} = [NCR_{state}]$
4. *Non-slave inmates, segregation*	$Y_{seg} = [NCR_{seg}]$	$Y_{seg} = [NCR_{seg}]$

3. WELFARE IN PRISONS

As indicated above, the state welfare is two-fold, the direct provision of commodities, and the provision of prison household use-values produced by inmate slave labor. The former is discussed briefly below. The latter is analyzed in the next section.

The elements of state welfare to inmates are sometimes clearly indicated in official documents within each state. Much of the welfare is compulsory. For example, the state of California provides an extremely detailed listing of all sorts of items inmates are given, as well as the rules they must follow. It describes the various items of clothing issued to inmates—3 pairs of jeans, 3 shirts, 4 undershirts, 6 pairs of socks, etc.—noting that all of it is state property, although it is not labeled a form of welfare.[12] Inmates must wear clothes, and cannot wear their own, so they have no choice but to receive state welfare. The same document describes inmates' rights to clean laundry: "Each inmate shall maintain issued clothing and linen as neat and clean as conditions permit. Weekly laundry exchange shall be provided on a one-for-one basis"[13] Inmates are also provided with products "to keep themselves and their living quarters clean and to practice good health habits."[14] Inmates rights to food are also detailed: "Each inmate shall be provided a wholesome, nutritionally balanced diet."[15] Inmates also have the right to be notified which meals contain pork products, and have the right to avoid foods sanctioned by certain religious beliefs.

California also stipulates that "each warden shall ensure a library, law library, and related facilities are maintained for the benefit of inmates in their facility."[16] Indigent inmates in this state also receive welfare related to mail correspondence, receiving paper, envelopes and postage for up to five 1-oz. letters per week free of charge.

In California inmates may also participate in a handicrafts program, which allows inmates to produce items for sale with materials purchased by the inmates. This is a case of the ancient class process, where individuals produce and appropriate their own surplus. Inmate welfare in California includes the possibility of state loans to inmates who cannot afford to buy their own materials to produce handicraft items.[17] For the sake of brevity, handicraft production by inmates is not analyzed here.

Inmates in CA may also form associations, councils, and other organizations, with certain specified limitations. Once such a body has been approved and formed, the inmates who comprise it are provided with office space, furniture, access to typewriters and copiers, and other office supplies.[18]

Inmates also have the right to medical and dental care, when it is deemed urgent or medically necessary.[19] Inmates, if they request medical care, will be charged $5.00 per visit, unless it is an emergency, communicable disease, follow-up visit, or mental health visit. In addition, upon being incarcerated or transferred, and when being released all inmates receive a health screening, and are notified of any existing health problems. If indigent inmates require eyeglasses, artificial eyes, dental prosthesis, artificial limbs, orthopedic braces and shoes, or hearing aids, these are provided as part of the state welfare.

If inmates require mental health services, including medication, this is provided by the state. Here, the inmates do not have the right to refuse medication and treatment if it is deemed necessary by the authorities. Inmates do not have the right to mutilate or kill themselves, and if they are discovered doing this, emergency medical care will be provided. Again, inmates cannot refuse this form of state welfare.

Upon release from prison, inmates may apply for and receive a cash assistance loan, with variable repayment options. The interest rate of the loan is not specified.[20] Paroled inmates also receive food coupons, bus passes, and job placement services.

Even after death, an inmate may continue to receive state welfare. When inmates die, mortuary services are provided including cremation, transportation of the body, and other services. If no family claims the body, the state buries the deceased inmate.

Table 3.2 summarizes some of these two forms of welfare that inmates receive in California:

It may seem from this list of state welfare in the state of California that inmates there have more rights than those who are not incarcerated, who do not receive such things as "nutritious meals," clothing, personal hygiene items, medical and dental care, access to law libraries, stamps, and so forth if they cannot afford to pay. Of course, inmates have many of

Table 3.2 Provision of Commodities and Use-Values to Inmates

Direct provision of commodities		Provision of Non-commodity use-values	
1.	Clothing	1.	Food
2.	Shelter	2.	Laundry
3.	Heat, water, and other utility services	3.	Cleaning
4.	Necessary medical and dental care	4.	Grounds keeping
5.	Personal hygiene products	5.	Maintenance
6.	Personal correspondence products		

their rights revoked in prison, e.g. free association, freedom to own certain items, the right to vote is revoked in many states, etc. For the sake of argument, let's say that they do have more rights than Americans who are not prison inmates. Does this counter the argument that prison labor is a form of slavery?

Weiner (1999) has shown that slavery may exist where slaves have certain rights, exercise power, or even possess considerable fortunes. Each of these processes is distinct from the class processes which define the *SFCP*. However, the fact that inmates receive welfare while those outside prison do not may provoke anger and resentment on the part of the general citizenry, who do not receive the same level of welfare. The cost of state welfare to inmates may become a symbol of tolerating, even rewarding criminal behavior. Of course, welfare for inmates is inevitable within the structure of crime and punishment in the U.S. Since incarceration cuts inmates off from their previous means of subsistence, they must be provided with welfare if they are expected to live through their sentences.

Note that in California, the level of state welfare is fixed by the Department of Corrections, and is paid for by the approval of the Legislature. Title 15 details how elements of state welfare may be taken away from inmates, as discussed earlier, this would place inmate in position of receiving NCR_{seg}.[21] However, the overall or average level of state welfare is determined at the Department level, and is not altered by the warden or other officials on an individual basis. However, the Department of Corrections may make changes in the level of welfare, although the ability of the Department of Corrections to do so is limited by their budget, and hence by the state legislature.

REDUCTION OF STATE WELFARE

As noted above, the state welfare is equal to that which is needed to sustain inmates at the level which is determined by society at large. If societal ideas about crime and punishment change, and people come to believe that the level of state welfare is too high, then there will be pressure to reduce the state welfare. People may be particularly upset about welfare to inmates in a political climate where no one is seen as deserving welfare, not children, not single parents, not mothers, and certainly not criminals.

In response to the changing social mood, the Department of Corrections may develop policies which lower the value of the state welfare (NCR_{state}), forcing inmates to either participate in the *SFCP* or obtain income from some other source in order to maintain their level of income.

Sources of income may come from family or some other outside source, or may come from enslavement. Inmates already enslaved may seek to work longer hours, given that P_1 and P_2 remain constant, in order to maintain the same standard of living as before.

The magnitude of P_{slave} may even rise in response to the fall in NCR_{state}, possibly resulting in a greater number of inmates seeking to work in commodity and prison household production. If for some reason the number of jobs available is less than the number of inmates seeking to maintain their standard of living, the result may well be waiting lists and generally high levels of desire to be exploited as a slave. (See I.C.4.) This result can be observed in many prisons, as prison policy seeks to increasingly charge inmates for services that before had been provided free of charge as part of state welfare. This represents a reduction of state welfare, since inmates who cannot pay for the services will no longer receive them, lowering the cost to the state. An example is the practice of charging inmates for medical visits. Washington prisoners must pay $3 each time they seek medical treatment, California prisoners must pay $5 per visit.[22]

In 1995 Arizona passed a law allowing the state to charge inmates a "utility fee" of $2 a month, intended to make inmates pay for the costs of electricity for their television sets. Arizona Governor Fife Symington and Director of Corrections Sam Lewis, who instituted this and many other repressive changes to corrections were both forced to resign amidst widespread public outcry. Symington was convicted of fraud in a federal court, and Lewis was repeatedly ordered by judges to improve conditions in Arizona prisons, yet the changes remain.[23]

Because of the new charges that the inmates face, labeled $\sum c$, the expression for inmate income developed above would change as follows.

Table 3.3 Actual Income of Inmates by Class

Inmate Category	Actual Income with charges
1. *Slave Producers*	
a. Commodity production (*SFCP1*)	$\left[P_1 + NCR_{state}\right] - \sum c$
b. Non-commodity production (*SFCP2*)	$\left[P_2 + NCR_{state}\right] - \sum c$
2. *Subsumed Slaves*	
a. Commodity production (*SSCP1*)	$\left[SSCR_1 + NCR_{state}\right] - \sum c$
b. Non-commodity production (*SSCP2*)	$\left[SSCR_2 + NCR_{state}\right] - \sum c$
3. *Non-laboring inmates*	
a. General population	$\left[NCR_{state}\right] - \sum c$
b. Segregation	$\left[NCR_{seg}\right] - \sum c$

Note that $\sum c$, would not be a constant term, but would vary depending on what services the inmate used.

Inmates in most prisons are also charged for commodities purchased at the prison canteen, notorious in inmate lore for inflated prices. If prisons cut costs on food service, lowering the quantity and quality of the food served, inmates must purchase more of their food from the prison canteen.

The Department of Corrections in Texas was recently found to have fed the inmates cheap, pesticide-ridden, animal grade soybeans, which were so unfit for human consumption that they caused boils, vomiting, diarrhea, and a variety of intestinal disorders. In this case, money was siphoned off by a number of high-ranking officials, ultimately ending up in their own pockets. This scandal caused the ouster of the head of the Texas Department of Criminal Justice.[24] However, since these activities went against the established procedures of the Texas Department of Criminal Justice, they would not be labeled an official lowering of state welfare, which must be done through explicit department policies.

Not all inmates react to this lowering of state welfare by seeking enslavement. Some may seek to get money from their families, or from criminal associates outside prison. Others may seek to gain income from the black market within prison. Since not all inmates can profit from the black market trade, there will naturally be fierce competition to control the lucrative informal markets that exist for sex, drugs, and other illicit commodities. Though the full scope of these informal markets is outside the scope of this study, some of the effects of the competition over these markets are explored later in this chapter.

The reduction of the state welfare described above seems to be part of a punitive trend in corrections, and may results in a generalized lowering of the NCR_{state} in prisons. These measures which lower the state welfare payments are part of a nationwide movement to 'get tough' on criminals, which means punishing them more severely and taking away more of their rights and privileges. Since the NCR_{state} represents the value of the goods and services deemed necessary for inmate consumption, if the general feeling in society is that inmates do not require or deserve that level, then the legislature or the department of corrections may act to lower NCR_{state} for inmates, thus reducing the material quality of inmate's lives as a method of enhanced punishment, or to cut costs, or both.

The ways in which this affects enslaved inmates are more complex. Recall from equation 12 that $V_{slave} = (NCR_{state} + P_{slave})$. If policies are developed which lower NCR_{state} for all inmates, it is not necessarily the case that V_{slave} falls. It is possible that at the same time P_{slave} rises, perhaps to compensate enslaved inmates, to ensure their cooperation, or to provide an additional incentive to keep the intensity of labor high.

The preceding analysis has theorized the necessary labor of inmate-slaves. It may also be useful to consider the magnitude of these payments of abstract labor for a given prison jurisdiction. This is done in the following section.

PRISON HOUSEHOLD PRODUCTION

Inmates receive goods and services such as food service, laundry, cleaning, maintenance, and repairs. These items are produced by inmates within the prison, and production of these items is distinct from commodity production because the goods and services are produced for their own useful characteristics, or use-values, and are not exchanged in a market.

Although prison household production has many other unique features which distinguish it from commodity production, it has the same fundamental class process, that of slavery. The fact that markets do not exist for these products affects, but does not define the class process that takes place within this productive sphere. The following argument will discuss the appropriation of inmate slave surplus labor in prison household production; it will be shown that the warden of the prison appropriates the surplus labor in prison household production.

The production of prison household use-values by enslaved inmates consists of a number of different kinds of concrete labor, including the activities listed above. The production of these use-values is an economic necessity for any prison, since prisons are mandated to provide for the basic needs of the inmates, and most prisons do not have the financial ability to pay outside workers the prevailing wage to produce these goods and services.

PRISON HOUSEHOLD PRODUCTION AND STATE WELFARE

The part of state welfare that consists of the direct provision of commodities to inmates, such as clothing and medical care, will be termed $PROV_1$. It is assumed that this direct provision of commodities is purchased by the state at a price equal to its value. The total state welfare, $\dot{N}CR_{state}$, is equal to the abstract labor embodied in the both the commodities directly provided to inmates and the value of the use-values produced by inmate-slaves which go to inmates (W_2^i):

(13) $$\dot{N}CR_{state} = (PROV_1) + (W_2^i).$$

Let us examine the prison household use-values more closely. Only a portion of the total value of the prison household use-values goes to the inmates, the rest of the value goes to other groups, which are examined later in the chapter. In other words, the appropriator takes the slave surplus labor and distributes it to others, both inmates and non-inmates.

The total value of the prison household use values produced by inmates is equal to the embodied labor (C_2)—the value of the raw materials and depreciation on equipment used in production—plus the living labor—the necessary labor, or the portion of the labor time spent to reproduce the slave labor-power (V_2) and the surplus labor (S_2) of the inmates in $SFCP_2$:

(14)
$$W_2^T = C_2 + V_2 + S_2 .$$

A portion of the inmate population is enslaved to produce the prison household use values which are necessary to maintain the consumption needs of all the inmates and make up a part of the state welfare. It is far cheaper to provide welfare to the inmates by utilizing their labor to produce portions of the welfare, then it would be to purchase the commodities which would be needed to sustain the inmates.

The state provides to the inmates a set of commodities free of charge, including shelter (in the form of the prison building), medical care, clothing, and so forth. The state also provides the warden with the necessary raw materials, tools, equipment, machinery, and so forth needed to produce prison household use values. A portion of the use-values produced by inmates then goes to inmates—again, not in exchange for money or other items, but as welfare.

Suppose that the state was required to discontinue the use of slave labor in the production of prison household use-values and that the level of welfare remained constant.

This would mean that the state would have to replace the prison household use values with either a sum of money, or with a set of commodities, produced outside the prison, equal to the value of the use values which had previously been produced by inmates. In either case, the cost of obtaining the welfare is certain to rise.

DIVISION OF LABOR

Prisons do not generally require every inmate to perform the labor necessary for his or her own individual consumption. In other words, there is a division of labor. Some subset of the inmates are enslaved to provide prison household use-values for all the inmates in the prison. This subset usually consists of one-quarter to one-third of the total number of inmates.[25] In addition, there are further divisions of labor, where certain inmates specialize in laundry or food service, for example. One reason for these divisions of labor is that the prison authorities seek to minimize inmates' movement within the prison, to better control inmates' activities. Another may well be to make production more efficient, although this may not be a consideration in every prison. Yet another may be to actually use participation in the $SFCP_2$ as a kind of incentive for good behavior. Inmates may prefer enslavement to idleness—an irony of prison life discussed in Chapter One.

Consider the tasks within a hypothetical prison that incarcerates 1000 inmates, 250 of which perform prison household production. We will divide the prison household production into 5 areas, with the number of slaves that perform each task:

Let us assume further that the list in Table 3.4 includes the value of all the prison household use-values produced within the prison that inmates receive—that is, not including any commodities which may be part of the state welfare but are not produced within the prison. A particular prison may require some inmates to perform additional tasks, but this list will serve to illustrate the general point. We could further divide these tasks into two categories; A is production of use-values distributed to inmates as part of the state welfare, and B is production of use-values distributed to non-inmates who provide conditions of existence for the $SFCP_2$. The social labor embodied in the use-values in A and B is equal to W_2^T. The warden receives this flow of value and distributes it (in the form of the particular use-values which compose the value flow) in order to secure the conditions of existence of his or her position as the appropriator of prison household slave surplus labor.

Prisons generally do not recognize the distinction made above between performance and appropriation of surplus labor. Because a class analysis of

Table 3.4 Prison Household Production, Total

Task	# of slaves	A	B
1. Cleaning	25	Cleaning inmate facilities	Cleaning offices and staff facilities
2. Maintenance	25	Maintaining inmate facilities	Maintaining staff facilities
3. Food preparation	100	Preparing food for inmates	Preparing food for staff
4. Laundry	50	Laundry for the inmates	Laundry for the staff
5. Grounds maintenance	50	Grounds maintenance in the prison	Grounds maintenance outside the prison
Total	250		

prisons has not been available until now, observers of prisons see cleaning as cleaning, whether it is cleaning the warden's office or the inmate recreation area, and do not consider the appropriation of surplus labor. For the moment we will concentrate on A. We will consider B in the next section.

In the first area, cleaning, 25 inmate slaves clean all the facilities in the prison that inmates use. Let us call the value of this service CL_1. Let's assume that the clean facilities are equally used by all 1000 inmates of the prison. Thus, each inmates receives a sum of value equal to $\frac{CL_1}{1000}$. We can generalize this as follows:

Table 3.5 lists the components of the total value of prison household use-values provided to inmates, which is labeled

$$(15) \qquad W_2^i = \left(CL_1 + M_1 + F_1 + L_1 + G_1 \right).$$

As discussed earlier, because all the inmates receive state welfare, it is possible for the master, in this case the warden, to provide the inmate slaves with an actual master's provision, P_2, which is less than is needed to reproduce their labor power, V_2.

The way that the products that make up the state welfare are consumed by inmates is as follows. In the case of cleaning, consumption of clean cells, clean showers, clean hallways, and so forth takes place when the inmates use these facilities (We have already assumed, for simplicity, that all inmates use the common spaces equally).

Similarly, inmates consume the labor of inmate slaves who maintain the facility's plumbing, electrical systems, and make the necessary repairs to the building and furniture when they use any of these facilities, which

Table 3.5 Prison Household Production, Each Inmate's Share

Task	# of slaves	A	B	Each inmate's share
Cleaning	25	CL_1	CL_2	$\dfrac{CL_1}{1000}$
Maintenance	25	M_1	M_2	$\dfrac{M_1}{1000}$
Food preparation	100	F_1	F_2	$\dfrac{F_1}{1000}$
Laundry	50	L_1	L_2	$\dfrac{L_1}{1000}$
Grounds maintenance	50	G_1	G_2	$\dfrac{G_1}{1000}$

they must use for as long as they are incarcerated at that prison. Grounds maintenance is quite similar to this, although most of the grounds that are maintained are those that surround the prison, which inmates are not allowed to use. The only part of the product of these enslaved inmates' labor that is used by inmates is the maintenance of the prison yard and any other grounds inside the prison. One could make the argument that inmates "use" all the grounds that are visible to them as well, through the enjoyment of gazing at maintained lawns and so forth, but such enjoyment is probably minimal.

In the case of food preparation, consumption takes place in the centralized dining area. The exception to this is the inmates who are in administrative segregation. These inmates eat in their cells or in separate dining facilities. Another exception is when the entire prison is on 'lockdown,' which can take place for any reason, such as an escape attempt or a riot. Lastly, inmates consume clean laundry when it is delivered to their cells or when they pick it up, as the case may be in that particular prison.

APPROPRIATION OF SURPLUS-LABOR

It may seem that the inmates collectively receive the surplus labor they produce, shown in Table 2.5, Column A. If so, it would make prison household production a case of the communist fundamental class process ($CFCP$) rather than the $SFCP$.

Although inmates consume the products of their own or other inmate-slaves' labor, this is not a case of the $CFCP$. The $CFCP$ entails some kind of collective process where inmates meet and make decisions about the surplus labor they collectively performed. While this process of collective appropriation may take place in certain limited settings, e.g. possibly in the case of gangs, it does not occur in the area of prison household production. A collective appropriation of surplus labor must be supported by distributions of surplus labor to secure the myriad cultural, economic, and political conditions of existence which support the $CFCP$. These distributions do not take place in U.S. prisons; inmates are not in control of such distributive processes, because they do not receive the products of their own slave surplus labor.

The product of inmate slaves' labor is appropriated by the warden of the prison. The warden is able to appropriate the surplus labor of inmate slaves in prison household production because of the political, cultural and economic processes operating within prisons, detailed in Chapter Two.

Politically, inmates are subject to the authority of the warden, and must obey his or her directives or face certain penalties. The warden has the legal right to compel inmates to labor as slaves, and the head of the department of corrections, who owns the labor-power of the inmates, delegates authority to the warden to appropriate slave surplus labor.

In terms of cultural processes, inmates are seen as despicable criminals who deserve whatever punishment they may receive; various processes in prison forge a new identity for inmates—that of a slave. Many in society believe "prison labor" to be beneficial to the inmates, and do not see it as enslavement.

Economic processes within prison also secure the warden's position as appropriator. The inmates need for income leads many to enslavement in the $SFCP_2$. In prisons where the $P_2 = 0$, this obviously does not apply. The warden controls the inmates consumption of state welfare, thus the reproduction of slave labor-power takes place within the relationship of master to slave. Although the warden must provide the state welfare to the inmates according to the policies of the department of corrections, wardens can punish inmates in various ways for violating prison rules, including not working. As noted above, one form of punishment involves placing an inmate in segregation, where he or she receives a state welfare at a lower level.

Thus inmates' consumption of state welfare occurs, to some extent, at the discretion of the warden. While the warden cannot legally reduce the state welfare below that level stipulated in NCR_{seg}, the warden can control the manner and time of consumption.[26] For example, the warden, through delegation of authority to prison guards, controls inmates' movement, and thus their consumption of clean spaces. The warden controls when inmates shower, and the location of meals (this could be in cells in the case of a lockdown). The warden similarly controls the laundry and access to the grounds at all times, thus controlling inmates' consumption of clean clothing and outdoor spaces.

In short, the warden is designated, through the above processes, as the slave master of the prison, in much the same way as the appropriators of surplus labor on plantations in the Antebellum south were designated as slave masters. Note that the warden is not the appropriator for slave-produced commodities, only for prison household use-values.

THE MASTER'S PROVISION IN PRISON HOUSEHOLD PRODUCTION

The level of the master's provision in prison household production may be determined by department of corrections policy, or may be left to the discretion of the warden. For example, in the federal prison system, the level of the master's provision in prison household production depends on the level of education, skill, and productivity of the inmate slave. Certain tasks are considered higher skill tasks, and thus slaves who perform them are paid a P_2 that is higher than slaves performing low-skill tasks. As mentioned above, it is common for P_2 to be far less (in relative terms) than P_1. Both P_1 and P_2 are in money form.

The warden of the prison receives a budget from the department of corrections to run the prison and pay the various expenditures necessary for its operation. Part of the budget goes to obtaining the raw materials necessary for the production of state welfare, labeled C_2 above. Another part of the budget goes to all the inmates in the form of commodities produced outside the prison, such as clothing or soap. Another part of the budget must be used to provide slaves with P_2.

Because inmates may be enslaved in prison household production yet not directly produce surplus there, a part of the budget must also go towards paying them. These inmates are thus subsumed to the prison household production process and are labeled subsumed slaves. These subsumed slaves do not receive P_2, since their labor does not directly produce the surplus. Instead they receive $SSCR_2$, as detailed in Table 2.1; the $SSCR_2$ payment is also in money form, and is seen by prison authorities as the same as P_2. In other words, because prison authorities do not perceive that some inmate-slaves directly produce surplus, while other inmate-slaves perform labor that does not directly produce surplus, they do not see the distinction that we have drawn here between P_2 and $SSCR_2$. For this reason, the two are equal: $P_2 = SSCR_2$.

This subsumed class payment from the warden to the subsumed slaves must come from the surplus produced by the slaves who directly produce surplus in prison household production. However, since the surplus in prison household production is in the form of use-values, while P_2 and $SSCR_2$ are in the form of money, the warden faces a potential difficulty: where to get the money? The answer is from the state, which provides the warden with a budget, enabling the warden to pay for P_2 and $SSCR_2$.

In some jurisdictions, both P_2 and $SSCR_2$ are zero. In others, P_2 is positive in order to motivate the slaves to provide a greater number of prison household use values or a better quality of use values, if that is of concern to the warden.[27] On the other hand, it may benefit the warden to seek reduce P_2, so that there is more money available in the budget for other purposes. The level of P_2 is generally determined by the state department of corrections, however the warden may be able to influence department policy through formal and informal relationships with the political powers within the department of corrections, or with the outside correctional board, if one exists in that state.

THE REVENUES AND EXPENDITURES OF THE WARDEN

According to the Marxian class analytical theory used here, every fundamental class process is both supported and undermined by an infinite number of subsumed and non-class processes that take place within a given social formation. The appropriator of surplus labor must distribute it to secure the conditions of existence of the fundamental class process. This means that the appropriator of surplus labor must make payments to other groups—termed subsumed classes—which provide conditions of existence for the revenue he receives in the form of surplus labor.[28]

At the same time an appropriator may have to make other payments, and may receive income flows, for reasons that are not directly related to the performance and appropriation of surplus labor. These revenues and expenditures are termed non-class.

Let us consider the value flows which go to the warden as revenue, and the expenditures which he must make in order to secure his conditions of existence. The warden appropriates surplus labor from slaves, which appears as a class revenue. The warden must also distribute all of, or some portion of, this surplus labor to individuals who are subsumed to prison household production. The sum of these various distributions of surplus labor are termed subsumed class payments ($SSCP_2$).

While the $SFCP_2$ generates output in the form of use-values, these are not sold, and therefore are not in money form, though they do have value in terms of social labor. However, the warden is (in most jurisdictions) obligated to pay inmates a master's provision of P_2 and $SSCR_2$, which are in money. The warden is also obligated to provide all inmates with welfare, of which part is in the form of commodities ($PROV_1$), which, of course, also must be paid for in money. This is a potential dilemma, for where would the warden get the money to pay the sum? The answer is the state. The warden qua master receives aid from outside the slave system in the $SFCP_2$ to secure his class and non-class conditions of existence.

In class terms, the warden receives 4 non-class revenues from the state, in the form of the state budget for the prison. The warden receives a non-class revenue so that he may purchase commodities necessary for inmate welfare, labeled NCR_{PROV1}. Another portion enables the warden to pay the staff salaries, insurance, and other costs of the prison that are not related to inmate welfare, labeled NCR_e. The warden uses a part of NCR_e in order to provide slaves and subsumed slaves with P_2 and $SSCR_2$. Thus the warden is able to meet his monetary needs through these two non-class revenues.

Another portion of this budget is labeled NCR_v, which exists due to the welfare to all inmates, including those in the $SFCP_2$. This allows the warden to provide inmate slaves in the $SFCP_2$ with P_2 rather than V_2, so the warden receives an amount equal to the total difference between the master's provision and the actual master's provision:

(16) $$NCR_v = \dot{V}_2 - \dot{P}_2.$$

Lastly, the warden receives a non-class revenue due to the difference between the means of production employed in the $SFCP_2$ and the price and quantity of said means of production:

(17) $$NCR_C = C_2 - \left(\Phi_C \cdot uv_C \right),$$

where Φ_c is the price of the means of production, and uv_c is their number. Φ_c is effectively zero for the warden, since he receives these means of production from the state, so equation 17 becomes: $NCR_c = C_2$. Thus the warden's revenue is:

(18) $$R_{warden} = S_2 + NCR_{PROV1} + NCR_e + NCR_C.$$

The warden is obligated to make certain expenditures. In order to appropriate surplus labor, the warden must secure the conditions of existence of the $SFCP_2$ by making a series of subsumed class payments, $SSCP_2$, which are discussed in more detail below. Since the warden is given the responsibility for administering state welfare to the inmates, the warden must make an expenditure of $Y_{welfare}$ to buy the commodities that inmates receive. In addition, the warden must pay the various non-welfare related costs of running the prison, labeled Y_e. Finally, the warden must provide the inmates with use-values such as cooked meals, cleaning, laundry services, etc. The value embodied in these use-values is labeled W_2^i. This duty of administering of the state welfare is the result of the aforementioned social, economic, and other processes which overdetermine the level of state welfare. Equation (19) summarizes the warden's expenditures.

(19) $$E_{warden} = SSCP_2 + Y_{welfare} + Y_e,$$

We expect the following equations to hold:

(20) $$S_2 = SSCP_2 \,,$$

since by definition, the surplus must be distributed to secure the conditions of existence for the slave class process; furthermore, since we assume that non-class revenues (NCR) are equal to the non-class payments needed to obtain them (Y), then

(21) $$NCR_{PROV1} = Y_{PROV1} = PROV_1 \,, \text{and}$$

(22) $$NCR_e = Y_e \,,$$

which means that we assume that all the money received from the state actually goes either to the inmates in the form of commodities, or toward prison expenses.[29] Equation 21 means that we can rewrite equation 13 as:

(23) $$\dot{NCR}_{\text{state}} = \left(Y_{PROV1} + W_2^i\right),$$

which shows the total state welfare from the warden's perspective.

If equations 20–22 hold, then the question of whether the warden's revenues equal his expenditures depends on whether or not the following is true:

(24) $$NCR_C + NCR_V = W_2^i \,.$$

In other words, it depends on whether the non-class revenues from the state are sufficient to produce the use-values which form part of the state welfare. This is largely an empirical matter which does not affect the theory developed here, and hence will be left to other researchers to determine. If equations 20, 21, and 24 hold, then

(25) $$S_2 + NCR_{PROV1} + NCR_e + NCR_C + NCR_P = SSCP_2 + Y_{PROV1} + Y_e + W_2^i \,.$$

To summarize, the warden uses the use-values produced by enslaved inmates, together with commodities purchased from outside the prison, to fulfill his responsibilities to administer to inmates the welfare provided by the state and uses non-class revenues from the state to provide enslaved inmates with P_2 and $SSCR_2$ in money form. If the warden fails to meet his or her responsibilities to the mandate of the state department of corrections, including the delivery of the specified items which make up inmate welfare, he may lose his job, losing also the ability to appropriate inmate slave surplus labor.

In terms of the subsumed class payments the warden must make, we will discuss three general recipients. The first is the prison staff, the second is inmate slaves in the production process, and the third is inmates outside the production process. Of these, the first is discussed below, and the second and third in the next section.

The subsumed class payment the warden makes provides benefits to himself or herself and the rest of the correctional staff and guards working at that prison. Some of these benefits may be official, for example, the guards contract may include meals provided by the prison, or the benefits may take the form of unofficial perks, such as car washes, shoe shines, cleaning, laundering of uniforms, maintenance of staff facilities, or other services.[30] Consider Tables 2.4 and 2.5; the labor performed by inmates in $SFCP_2$, which the warden uses to provide benefits to guards and staff, appears in column B in each table. The value of these goods and services represents the magnitude of the subsumed class payment to staff, labeled $SSCP_{staff}$:

(26) $$SSCP_{staff} = [CL_2 + M_2 + F_2 + L_2 + G_2] \ .$$

The above distribution of slave surplus labor secures an important political condition of existence of the warden's appropriation, which is a motivated staff. This is essential for the warden to maintain control over the prison. Of course, the official and unofficial benefits which the warden provides to staff may not be enough to ensure his total control over the prison. Guards and staff members may break the rules of the prison for various reasons, and some of these illicit activities may undermine the control of the warden over the prison. For example, the state of Texas recently introduced a law banning smoking in all state prisons. The wardens of Texas prisons then were mandated to uphold this ban, making cigarettes another form of contraband. Since inmates still have the desire to smoke, and indeed cigarettes are a form of currency in most prisons, but because the prison canteen can no longer sell them, a strong incentive emerges for guards to sell cigarettes to inmates. This can undermine the warden's political control over the prison, because if inmates are able to violate some of the prisons rules, they may seek to violate other rules, which more directly uphold the slave class process—for example, inmates may refuse to work, make mistakes on the job, or steal materials, any of which would endanger or reduce the slave surplus labor.

Notice that the warden may be able to gain from using inmate slave surplus labor to provide the staff with these benefits. The warden may be able to reduce direct expenditures on staff by using inmate surplus labor. For example, it may be possible for the warden to pay staff members lower wages due to the staff members receipt of meals or other services while on the job. It may be the case though, as in the case of state welfare to inmates, that the state department of corrections policy rules this out.

In addition to the distributions of surplus labor described above, the slave class process in prisons is also supported by subsumed class positions within the population of inmates. Inmates occupying subsumed class positions are considered subsumed slaves—while these inmates do not directly produce surplus, they provide conditions of existence necessary for surplus labor to take place.

The distributions of prison household surplus labor to staff may result in most or all of the surplus being depleted. This means that the surplus left over for other purposes may be small. Hence, for the warden to secure other conditions of existence, he or she must seek to obtain them at reduced cost. The warden may accomplish this by using inmates—subsumed slaves—to secure other conditions of existence. The warden is able to obtain these inmate-slaves' services for less than the cost might otherwise be due to the state welfare that all inmates receive. Also, the warden may be able to make informal arrangements with inmates to provide their services in exchange for certain favors from the warden, the wardens' bending of certain rules, and so forth, thus obtaining conditions of existence for less.

First, we will consider distributions of surplus to subsumed slaves who are involved in the production process. Second, we will consider distributions of surplus to inmates who are not involved in the production process, but who nonetheless secure crucial cultural and political conditions of existence for the slave class process within prisons.

SUBSUMED CLASSES IN THE PRODUCTION PROCESS

The slave subsumed classes directly involved with production are slave managers and administrators. Marx notes that managers occupy a dual role, both cooperative and supervisory[31]. The former is productive labor, since it involves a useful coordination of different activities that results from a division of labor. The latter is unproductive, since it does not directly produce surplus, though it may involve the expansion of relative surplus through supervision. In prisons the managers are in some cases a correctional staff who are experts are placed in charge of a given department, for example, plumbing. Since this area requires special licenses, it is usually occupied by a professionally trained plumber. However, in most prisons, this person must rely on experienced inmate slaves to informally train and manage the other slaves. These experienced inmates may occupy multiple class positions. They may occupy a slave fundamental class position and a slave subsumed class position depending on their specific activity, or even at the same time. Such is the position that all managers occupy, due to the dual nature of management.

To continue with the example from plumbing, inmate slaves who are designated by the staff plumber to serve in subsumed class positions may train other slaves—thus providing a condition of existence for plumbing maintenance to take place. These inmate slaves may also relay information to the prison authorities about the competence of their fellow slaves, for example, letting the staff plumber know which slaves deserve to stay in the plumbing shop, and which should be reassigned to another area.

These inmate-slave managers, like many of the slave subsumed class positions in prisons, are generally occupied by so-called "trusties"[32]—the lowest security level inmate, who have the highest level of privileges, and are sometimes even allowed to leave the prison for various purposes. The existence of different levels of privileges is often an important tool in maintaining control over the prison by dividing inmates against each other.

Other areas of prison household prison production also have managers, such as the kitchen, which is typically the largest single area of prison household production. The kitchen is very important and usually involves about 10% of the total inmate population (40% of the inmate slaves in the example above). The laundry, maintenance, grounds maintenance, and other areas of prison household production may also have slave managers at a variety of levels of responsibility. Subsumed slave administrators perform tasks such as keeping records about their area of production, acting as a liaison to the prison authorities, as well as tasks such as ordering and storing materials.

All the slaves who occupy these subsumed class positions, receive a distribution of slave surplus labor, which is needed to reproduce the ability of these subsumed slaves to perform labor. Because of the state welfare, the warden can reduce the size of the subsumed class payment, as detailed above. In fact, the warden may even be able to reduce the subsumed class payment to zero.

Generally in the literature on prison labor and within the prison itself these subsumed slaves are considered to be 'working inmates' just like the inmates who directly perform surplus labor—rarely are inmates seen as slaves within this literature. No distinction is made between a fundamental class position and a subsumed class position. However, in a class-based approach such as the one employed here, such a distinction is important. Since prisons generally categorize inmates as working or non-working, each of the subsumed class payments to inmates securing the managerial and administrative conditions of existence discussed above would be the same as the P_2:

$$(27) \qquad\qquad SSCP_{manager} = SSCP_{adm} = P_2,$$

where $SSCP_{manager}$ = the subsumed class payment to inmate managers, and $SSCP_{adm}$ = the subsumed class payment to inmate administrators.

The equality described in equation 27 is not theoretically necessary; there are typically levels of pay within P_2, so subsumed slaves may receive a higher money income than slaves in the $SFCP_2$, but this is generally seen as owing to their greater level or responsibility, experience, etc., since the class status is not recognized.

Examining these subsumed class processes reveals an interesting and sometimes overlooked theoretical point: that class conflict may exist between slaves. In this case, there is tension and possible conflict between slaves in the $SFCP_2$ and slaves subsumed to it. These tensions are often exacerbated in prisons by differences in the amount of money granted and differences in the amount of power wielded by different kinds of slaves.

SUBSUMED CLASSES OUTSIDE OF THE PRODUCTION PROCESS

We now turn to those subsumed inmate slaves who are not directly involved in the production process. First we will consider inmate slaves whose labor provides the cultural conditions for the $SFCP_2$, are found in the area of officially-sanctioned activities such as peer counseling and religious services. This subsumed class receives a subsumed class payment labeled $SSCP_{culture}$. These inmate slaves urge other inmates to accept and seek to fit into the established order of things in prison, to take individual responsibility for one's actions, and not challenge the rules or practices of the prison. This creates a series of cultural messages which seek to affirm the economic and political structures in prison, including the slave class process in both prison industries and prison household production.

Because these inmates are outside the production process, they are understood by the warden and other prison authorities as being non-working, even though they provide conditions of existence for the $SFCP_2$. This means that these inmates do not receive a subsumed class payment equal to the master's provision, P_2. This also means that these inmate slaves do not receive any money. Instead, these inmate slaves receive subsumed class distributions that are often quite low. Again, the influence of the state welfare plays a role. In the absence of the state welfare, slaves would have to receive enough of a distribution of surplus to enable them to meet their consumption needs. Because these needs have to a large extent been met by the state welfare, the warden can secure their cooperation with a far smaller distribution of surplus.

Several examples may be found in a revealing prison documentary entitled *The Farm: Life at Angola Prison* (1998). When new inmates arrive at the Louisiana State Penitentiary at Angola, they are addressed by an inmate, Ashanti Witherspoon, who urges them not to get involved with the 'negative' side of prison life—gangs, drugs, and violence—and instead take part in the many different legitimate activities available at Angola, such as work, clubs such as the debate team or the CPR team, the infamous Angola prison rodeo, etc. Scenes from a sermon at the prison church at Angola focus on the need for individual repentance rather than systemic change.

Inmate slaves who perform these non-class cultural or religious activities no doubt do so for many complex reasons. Some of these may be related to personal or spiritual development, or other reasons that we may regard as quite positive. This analysis is not meant to demean any of these activities or the inmate slaves who perform them—many inmates have written of profound, life-changing experiences as a result of participating in religious and cultural programs in prison. This analysis merely shows the complex role of these institutions in supporting the slave class process as a system, and is not meant to implicate any particular individual.[33]

It may also be the case that the same religious and cultural processes simultaneously play a role in undermining the slave class process. Inmate organizations can play a dynamic role in facilitating communication and organization among inmates, and have sometimes been important in inmate movements to reduce or eliminate exploitation in prison and generally advocate for better conditions.[34]

As discussed above, these subsumed class positions are maintained through distributions of surplus labor from the $SFCP_2$. As shown above, the entire mass of use-vales produced by inmates in Column A goes to inmates, leaving only the use-values in Column B. However, this says nothing about how the use-values are distributed. The warden may promise an inmate such things as more or better food, a favored cell location or cell-mate, other goods and services produced by inmate slaves in addition to the inmate's normal allotment of state welfare, or a positive note in the inmate's record, which may lead to early release.

The second subsumed class of inmate slaves are those who perform labor which secures the political conditions of existence of the slave class process in prison household production, facilitating the exercise of political control by the warden and the correctional staff over the inmate population

as a whole. (See I. C. 1.) These political subsumed class processes are critical for the running of any prison, especially as prisons become more vola-
tile due to overcrowding and increasingly poor treatment of inmates.

Distributions of surplus to secure political conditions of existence for
the slave class process are paid to gang leaders, informants, and rapists.
For now, we will mainly be concerned with understanding the relationship
between these political subsumed classes with the slave fundamental class
process. The effects of both the fundamental and subsumed class processes
will be discussed in Chapter Four.

Gangs occupy a contradictory position in prison. On the one hand,
they may serve a useful function—if the warden can secure their cooperation, gangs have effective internal hierarchies which control the behavior of
all members of the gang. Gangs also have the political power to command
the use of violence to serve various ends, such as intimidating other inmates
or controlling the market for illicit commodities in prison.

On the other hand, gangs are organizations of inmates, and their political power may at any time threaten the prison system.[35] Prison authorities often act on both sides of this contradiction, recognizing the power
and potential usefulness of gangs, and at the same time fearing them and
attempting to undermine and control them.

Wardens seek several things from gangs. First, their cooperation with
the prison system. Second, their role in enforcing order among their members, which generally means that violence is restrained to other inmates, not
directed at guards or other staff. Third, the warden or correctional officers
may call on the gang to perform certain tasks, such as disciplining inmate
troublemakers who refuse to follow orders, threaten or harm guards, etc.

In exchange the warden and the prison staff may give the gang
such things as placement in certain cells or areas in the prison, perhaps
the overlooking of the possession of certain contraband items, or implicit
permission to engage in such black market activities as prostitution and
drug dealing without interference. This may allow the warden to obtain the
gang's services for a lower payment of surplus labor than would otherwise
be possible.

Unless the gang fulfills the tasks outlined by the warden, they will lose
the privileges and/or revenue they enjoy—perhaps another gang will get it.
Thus, for the gang, simply allowing them to sell drugs may be as good as a
direct payment of money or goods.

While activities such as selling drugs and prostitution are illegal and
against prison rules, they are tolerated out of the necessity of "brokering"
power with the inmates. The warden may believe that drug sales are inevitable in prison, hence he may seek to gain a condition of existence for his or

her appropriation of inmate slave surplus labor from the sales that would happen anyway. In addition, the warden may recognize that inmates can take over nearly any prison if they choose, and that they are only governed with their tacit consent.

The warden may also use rivalries between gangs as a way of undermining the political power of gangs, hence reducing or eliminating their potential threat to the prison. Prison officials are known to perpetuate violent struggles between gangs, which are often sparked by disputes over the control of illicit economic activity in prisons. There are many documented cases of correctional officers intentionally celling rival gang members together, or releasing rival gangs into the yard at the same time and so forth. At many California prisons, such activities are so commonplace that they are called 'cockfights' by the guards, who, far from intervening in the conflicts, instead place wagers on the outcome and sometimes even videotape them for later viewing. Although such accusations are typically made of the guards, it is hard to believe that the warden would not know about, and hence, implicitly or explicitly allow these activities.[36]

Prison informants, or "snitches" are very important to the maintenance of control, because much of the information about inmate activities is not observed by guards. Informants provide information to the prison staff about inmate activities such as political organizing that the prison staff can use to single out and punish individuals and more effectively crush any resistance movements.

In exchange for these services, prison informants receive rewards such as additional privileges, being forgiven for committing some disciplinary infraction, or they may receive commodities such as books, magazines, clothing, or cigarettes. Parallel to the case of prison gangs, prison informants receive a subsumed class distribution which is equal to the value of the items they receive, whether it is commodities or privileges. This payment is labeled $SSCP_{snitch}$.

The final group is prison rapists. These nefarious individuals sexually assault other inmates. To understand the context in which they function and the role they play, it is necessary to briefly consider the phenomenon of rape in prison. Authors such as Parenti (1999), Scacco (1980, 1982) and Rideau (1992) have argued that rape in prison functions as a form of internal oppression of the inmate population. Inmates are divided into groups based on whether they are the initiator of or victim of sexual assaults. Inmates who are physically strong or affiliated with gangs sometimes forcibly obtain sex from weaker, unaffiliated inmates, who may be forced to the bottom, so to speak, of the prison hierarchy.[37]

If a portion of the inmates' energy is engaged in either raping or being raped, it stands to reason that inmates will do less to resist their captors.

The phenomenon also may serve the function of a convenient outlet for the anger of some violent inmates, a response to the daily humiliations of prison life.

Parenti provides shocking details of one example of an inmate rapist providing political conditions of existence for the *SFCP* in the case of Eddie Dillard.[38] Dillard, while incarcerated for assault, kicked a female correctional officer, and as punishment was housed with Wayne Robertson, an inmate in the Corcoran prison in California so well-known for being a sexual predator that he was called the "Booty Bandit." Robertson brutally tortured and sodomized Dillard for several days, and Dillard brought suit against the California Department of Corrections. During the trial, the details of Robertson's unofficial relationship with the correctional officers came to light. Robertson's "job," as Parenti puts it, was to take a given prisoner who caused problems for the correctional officers and go to work "battering their head, smashing their nose, tearing open their rectum, and then abusing and ridiculing them for days on end until the victim was reduced to the status of a psychologically broken, politically servile 'punk.'"[39] In exchange for this, Robertson was provided with a subsumed class payment, in the form of tennis shoes and extra food. Notice that in this case, even though the direct evidence was against the correctional officers rather than the warden or the head of the department of corrections, the suit was brought against the department of corrections, which points to the ultimate responsibility of the warden as the representative of the department of corrections.

How common such arrangements are, and the ultimate level of participation of the warden is very difficult to know. If the warden is not aware of such arrangements, then the warden was not making a distribution of the surplus that he or she appropriated, and this is a case of the correctional officers acting alone, rather than a condition of existence for the $SFCP_2$. However, if the warden had knowledge of the arrangement, then given that the warden bears a share of responsible for the inmates, he or she must either approve of the arrangement or be powerless to stop it. The latter seems unlikely.

These political subsumed classes also point to the ease with which inmates may be enslaved in the $SSCP_2$, perhaps for short periods of time, and perhaps without recognizing that they are in fact providing conditions of existence for slavery. However, whether their participation is recognized or not, these subsumed slaves still play a role to support the $SSCP_2$, though they may, at the same time, undermine the $SSCP_2$.

To summarize, the warden makes a series of subsumed class payments in order to secure the conditions for the $SFCP_2$. The warden makes these subsumed class payments out of the surplus labor he appropriates in the $SFCP_2$. The argument above has discussed some of these subsumed class payments, as a way of illuminating the class processes that occur in prison household production. The following list is not intended to be exhaustive, but provides a set of conditions of existence that seem relevant and important to prison life. Thus, we can write the wardens' class revenues and expenditures—the surplus labor and subsumed class payments, respectively—as follows:

$$(28) \quad S_2 = SSCP_{staff} + SSCP_{manager} + SSCP_{adm} + SSCP_{cultural} + SSCP_{gang}$$
$$+ SSCP_{snitch} + SSCP_{rape}$$

CONCLUSION

The preceding chapters have provided the first analysis of how surplus labor is performed, who appropriates the surplus labor, and the conditions which surround such appropriation in U.S. prisons. These chapters build on an established body of work within Marxian theory which constructs the performance and appropriation of surplus labor as the basis of a theory of slavery, creating a class-based theory in contrast to a property-based or power-based theory of slavery. This makes it possible to understand how slavery can exist in social sites where property and trade in human beings as chattel is lacking.

These chapters show that one of the key aspects of prison life is a form of slavery called the slave fundamental class process. Using a Marxian analysis, these chapters demonstrate how and why many inmates (but not all) are slaves who perform a surplus for masters both inside and outside prisons. These inmates are enslaved due to a combination of specific laws, rules, customs, traditions, ways of thinking, and economic forces that together compel them to produce surpluses for masters in a manner that is quite similar to what has occurred in other shameful periods of human history, such as the sugarcane fields of the Caribbean, the mines of Ancient Rome, or the workshops of feudal China. The result of this Marxian analysis is to throw into sharp relief the fact that, despite the Civil War waged to eliminate slavery in the U.S., slavery and its horrors continue today for a significant and growing number of U.S. citizens.

The inevitable class contradictions that emerge from a process where surplus labor is performed and appropriated can now be understood in terms of their impact on prisons. One of the features of prisons which has been illuminated by this approach is the provision of state welfare to inmates. The state plays an important role in prison life, in that state prison expenditures on such things as prison buildings, roads, and grounds, salaries for officials, food, raw materials, etc., help to create the necessary conditions for prison slavery. We have seen these state expenditures shape the slave class process, allowing the master to lower the actual master's provision far below the value of slave labor-power.

Although the state welfare forms an important condition of existence for prison slavery, it exists in contradiction to other processes which support prison slavery. For example, the cultural processes surrounding prison slavery, the objectification and dehumanization of inmates, coupled with the dishonor and shame of being an inmate, also may have an impact on the level of the state welfare. It is possible that these cultural processes lead the public to have less tolerance for inmates, and to support policies which reduce the level of state welfare. This seems to describe the current social climate.

If the welfare is reduced, it is possible that the actual master's provision will be raised, to economically push inmates into slavery, or to compensate the inmates who are enslaved, to keep them productive by granting them a far higher standard of living then that received by inmates. However, this raising of the actual master's provision would impose additional costs on the masters, which may produce a crisis for the *SFCP*.

It is also possible that the same cultural dynamic results in a fall in the actual master's provision, perhaps lowering it to zero, as has occurred in certain states. This may lead to all sorts of tensions within the prison. Inmates who are enslaved may feel that they are getting a far worse deal than the inmates who receive the same standard of living, but are not slaves, which may lead to conflict. Inmates may resent the state charging fees for certain services, and may be angry about being economically pushed into slavery as the only way to obtain necessary services such as medical care. Thus inmates may be driven to a collective effort, such as unionization, which may threaten the *SFCP*. Currently, such organized activity by inmates is rare.[40]

In some jurisdictions, this cultural process has resulted in the removal of programs that directly stem from state welfare, as well as freedoms and opportunities that are unrelated to welfare. One example of the latter is the recent legislation outlawing weightlifting equipment from certain prisons. Other pieces of legislation forbid common prison pursuits such as smoking or possession of pornography. These are restrictions on the inmates which directly stem from the idea that inmates have it easy.

Even if the level of state welfare were to remain constant, it may lead to tensions and at times produce violence among inmates, as well as between slaves and the prison guards who are also slave subsumed class officials and the warden who is the slave master. For example, we have seen that the state welfare and the master's provision combine to provide several different income levels to inmates. When inmates are enslaved, they often receive a higher income than inmates who are not slaves, a difference equal to P_{slave}, the actual master's provision.

Recall that the $SFCP_1$ may provide slaves with a significantly higher level of income (between 2 and 10 times higher) than the $SFCP_2$. Because of this large income differential, masters may be able to exert economic power over their slaves. Slaves may be kept in line by the ability of masters to prevent them from receiving the higher income level of $SFCP_1$, ensuring high productivity and low rates of theft among the slaves there. Masters may also be able to use selective criteria for enslavement within the $SFCP_1$, knowing that there is high demand from the inmates to receive the higher income level that prevails there. It is common for masters to demand that slaves have a clean disciplinary record, that is, they must carefully follow all prison rules, or at least not get caught breaking any. Typically any disciplinary infraction would make a slave ineligible for the $SFCP_1$, though not necessarily the $SFCP_2$, depending on the rules of the particular institution or jurisdiction.

Inmates who have such disciplinary infractions may be angry at the slaves in the $SFCP_1$, and may have a desire to take away a slave's higher income, in much the same fashion as inmates will try to engage in a conflict or entrap in some form of rule-breaking an inmate who is known to be due for parole, to take away his eligibility for parole. This tension could manifest itself along class lines, between non-slaves who would actually prefer being enslaved, due to the higher income level of the slaves (and perhaps due to other reasons as well, discussed in Chapter Four), or between slaves in the two areas of production, $SFCP_1$ and $SFCP_2$. Slaves in the $SFCP_2$ may feel that they work just as hard as slaves in the $SFCP_1$, yet receive a far lower income. These slaves may accuse the slaves in the $SFCP_1$ as being "sellouts" or "snitches"—both incendiary terms in prisons, where an attitude of rebellion against the authorities is often cultivated, and cooperation with prison authorities, especially in the form of getting other inmates in trouble, can lead to severe conflict.

Slaves in both areas may also feel that they deserve more than they currently receive. Other inmates are able to sit around all day, yet receive the same basic food, clothing, and shelter. Slaves may demand, and are sometimes granted, some sort of special consideration from the prison authorities, such as a special housing unit, away from the general population of inmates, or simply the recognition of being a "trustworthy" inmate. Such recognition has a long and often sordid history in prison, where inmates who earn the term "trusties" have sometimes been given positions of responsibility, even significant power over other inmates. One example is the "trusty-shooter" position from Parchman prison labor farm in Mississippi. During the 19th and early 20th century, about 20% of the inmates at Parchman were designated trusty-shooters, and were given rifles, along with the job of watching the other convicts. Oshinsky writes,

> Once chosen, a trusty became an unpaid member of the prison staff. He got better food and quarters than the regular convicts, and did not have to stoop all day in the fields. He could move freely about the camp, hunt and fish in his spare hours, and spend some extra time with his wife, a lover, or a prostitute brought in from a nearby town . . . Shooters escaped more often than regular convicts because their opportunities were better, and stories of their quick tempers and questionable killings became the stuff of legend throughout the South.[41]

Most prisons still have a version of the trusty system in place (though today no inmates are ever armed) in that there are different security levels, where an inmate at the highest security level has the most restrictions, while an inmate at the lowest security level has the most freedom. Some inmates may use the freedom gained from a low security designation to obtain power over other inmates, perhaps settling old scores, or demanding some sort of payment from other inmates, or using their position to indulge in other illicit activities. The division of inmates into separate categories, with different privileges, is a time-honored method of dividing an unruly populace into warring factions, where it can more easily be governed.

This chapter has examined a few of the divisions between productive and subsumed slaves, and revealed how differences in class position among the slaves can lead to violence within the prison, as the warden uses subsumed slave classes such as managers, administrators, gangs, snitches and even rapists to provide him with some of the economic, cultural, and political conditions of existence for the *SFCP*. Some of these subsumed class processes are profoundly disturbing, revealing the horror and brutality that are commonplace in prisons.

Prison slavery adds a powerful economic motivation to this process of division, creating class conflict between slaves in the $SFCP_1$ and the $SFCP_2$, between productive and subsumed slaves, between inmates and slaves, and between inmates who are not slaves. In sum, the class and non-class dynamics that produce different levels of income routinely lead to theft, tension, and conflict in prison, which has sometimes led prison authorities to separate inmates into different areas of the prison.[42] This separation of the inmates by class does not necessarily solve the underlying problem, and may even exacerbate it in all sorts of unpredictable ways. Supporters of "prison labor" argue that when inmates are working, they are more manageable, and there are fewer assaults of staff and fewer inmate "disturbances," i.e. riots. The analysis presented here suggests that if this is so, it is the result of the successful division of inmates along class lines, pitting slaves against non-slaves, subsumed slaves against productive slaves, and so forth. Given these social, economic, and political divisions which spring from the slave class process, it is not surprising that prisons are full of violence.

Some may respond to this analysis by arguing that prisons are intrinsically violent, and there is no way to reduce the tensions and conflicts of the prison which lead to violence. Such a view is at odds with the epistemological position employed in these pages, in which nothing is seen as intrinsically or essentially given, but rather that everything, including human behavior, is the complex result of many different processes. The variations in violence that exist in different prisons suggest that the context of prison life plays a significant role in overdetermining the level of violence. An underlying assumption of this work is that prison life can be understood, and once it has been understood, changed for the better. It is hoped that studies of prison life can now be more sharply focused to understand how the class dimension of prisons affects the events which take place there, as well as the effects of the prison on American society.

Chapter Four

The Production of Commodities in Prison

INTRODUCTION

This chapter analyzes the specific dynamics related to the production, appropriation and distribution of surplus labor by inmates enslaved in the $SFCP_1$ producing commodities for both state and private masters. The goal here is provide a detailed theoretical analysis of prison commodity production, using the value analysis of state welfare produced in Chapter Three and the theory of the slave fundamental class process developed in Chapters One and Two. I hope that the concrete examples of the class analysis will add depth to the reader's understanding of prison slavery.

In any numerical study a potentially infinite number of assumptions must be made about what to count and how to count it. In this chapter we have sought to make some of these assumptions explicit, but others will remain implicit, for the simple reason that we cannot possibly count all the assumptions that must be made in the process of quantifying a complex social process. This is a particular problem when the theory or theories used to guide the collection of data are class-blind, as is generally the case with the data that exists for prisons. In this case, there is an additional difficulty of taking existing data, with its numerous contingent assumptions, and reinterpreting it in class terms. All quantitative and theoretical works have this problem, though few acknowledge it explicitly. Despite the problems, it is hoped that this chapter will both elucidate the theory developed thus far, and show its application.

THE MASTER'S PROVISION IN COMMODITY PRODUCTION

Many factors participate in overdetermining the magnitude of P_1, the actual master's provision in commodity production. Such factors include department of corrections policies, the customs and traditions of prison life, skills, education, the productivity of labor, the political organization of inmates, the history of inmate organizing, rioting and resistance by inmates, outside movements for prison reform, and so forth. This study focuses on one set of factors participating in this complex process of the determination of P_1, which is the value of slave labor-power and the state welfare.

As discussed in Chapter Three, the level of the state welfare is determined socially, through the mechanism of the laws and statutes which apply to the treatment of prisoners in a particular jurisdiction, and the economic, cultural, religious and other sorts of processes that overdetermine these laws. The state furnishes the department of corrections with a budget, mandating the department to ensure, among other things, that inmates receive the stipulated amount of state welfare. The state welfare allows the master's provision to fall to a level far below the quantity of social labor needed to reproduce the slave labor-power. However, the level that P_1 actually falls to depends on several factors, among them state and federal law.

The state department of corrections may place certain limits on P_1. In Texas, Arkansas, and Georgia, as noted previously, the level of P_1 is set at zero. Other states, such as Florida, limit only P_2 to zero. However, P_1 depends on more than department of corrections policies. For example, there is a federal program which mandates the level of P_1, and supersedes any state law or department of corrections policy, taking effect when there are partnerships between state agencies and private enterprises. The program is the Private Sector / Prison Industries Enhancement Certification Program (PS/PIEC, often called simply PIE)—a federal program exists due to a 1979 law that allows for private industry to make bids for inmate labor-power, creating the conditions for partnerships between the state and private enterprises.[1]

The PIE Act stipulates that inmates involved in commodity production which features the involvement of private enterprises must pay a P_1 equal to the level of the federal minimum wage, but the department of corrections may deduct, at their discretion, up to 80% of this payment. The law also requires the following:

1. Inmates must be paid at a rate that is not less than that paid for similar work in the locality as determined by the state Department of Economic Security or its equivalent;

2. Written assurances must document that non-inmate workers will not be displaced by the program;

3. Benefits typically made available to non-inmate workers by the state or federal governments must be made available to inmate workers;

4. Inmate participation must be voluntary;

5. Victim Compensation Program contributions must be from 5% to 20% of gross wages;

6. The total of deductions form inmate pay cannot exceed 80% of total pay

7. Organized labor and local private industry must be consulted before startup.[2]

The PIE Act partly reverses laws made in the early 20th century which restricted the market for prison-produced commodities; these laws restricted the scope of the $SFCP_1$. The PIE Act was designed to lift some of these restrictions; for example, the law allows private industries which use prison labor to sell to the federal government in contracts exceeding the $10,000 limit to which state programs are subject, while it also lifts the ban on interstate commerce that exists for state programs. The various partnerships between the state and private industry that the PIE Act makes possible are discussed in detail in this chapter, while the history of restrictions of prison slavery is recounted in Chapter Five.

Within the limits of the policy of the department of corrections, and when private enterprises are not involved, the level of P_1 is generally determined by a state agency that is charged with the organization and maintenance of prison commodity production within that state. In California, this state agency is called the Prison Industry Authority (PIA). The PIA is regulated by the Prison Industry Board. According to the PIA website, the role of the Board is as follows:

> As mandated in Penal Code Section 2800–18, the Board, among other things, sets general policy for PIA, oversees the performance of existing PIA industries, determines which new industries shall be established, and appoints and monitors the performance of the General Manager.[3]

In California, there are no specific limits on P_1 set by the department of corrections. Thus the ability to determine P_1 is given to the PIA.

As mentioned above, if inmates produce commodities in a production process which involves private enterprises, then the policy of the department of corrections is superseded by federal law, and the level of P_1 cannot fall below the minimum wage. This means that there are several different levels of P_1, depending on whether private enterprises are involved or not. Let P_{PIE} represent the master's provision within commodity production involving private enterprise, and let P_s represent the master's provision for commodity production without the involvement of private industry, so that $(P_{PIE}, P_s) \in P_1$. Let $\sum d_{PIE}$ represent the sum of deductions from P_{PIE} made by the department of corrections. Since the maximum deduction is 80%, the minimum amount of money income an enslaved inmate would receive in this form of production would be $1.30 per hour. Thus the actual income for inmates directly enslaved in commodity production involving private enterprises is:

$$(29) \qquad Y_1^A = \left(P_{PIE} - \sum d_{PIE}\right) + NCR_{state},$$

while those inmates who are subsumed slaves to the $SFCP_1$ involving private industry receive an income of

$$(30) \qquad Y_1^A = \left(SSCR_{PIE} - \sum d_{PIE}\right) + NCR_{sta}.$$

Again, we'll assume that, in general $P_{PIE} = SSCR_{PIE}$, since there is no distinction made between slaves and subsumed slaves within any state or federal jurisdiction.

Table 4.1 shows the total payments to inmates as part of the PIE program, from December 1979 to June 2001.[4] While the PIE program gives correctional departments the authority to deduct up to 80% of the legally mandated master's provision, P_{PIE}, on average the deduction is less than the maximum, at 54% of gross pay.

State agencies and departments of corrections may stipulate that there be different levels of P_1 to reward higher levels of productivity, skill, or education.[5] For example, the PIA in California sets a range for P_s of between

Table 4.1 Total PIE Payments to Inmates, Less Deductions

Total gross pay to inmates $\left(\dot{P}_{PIE} + \dot{SSCR}_{PIE}\right)$	$197,619,245
Contributions to victims' programs	-$18,510,801
Room and board deductions	-$50,127,654
Family support deductions	-$11,717,213
Taxes withheld	-$26,695,997
Total Deductions $\left(\sum d_{PIE}\right)$	-$107,051,665
Total net pay to inmates $\left((P_{PIE} + SSCP_{PIE}) - \sum d_{PIE}\right)$	$90,567,580

$0.30 and $0.95 per hour. However, the income which inmates receive will be lower than this, as inmates may face deductions from P_s for court-ordered restitution and fines, payments to cover room and board, and other fees which jurisdictions may impose. Let $\sum d_s$ represent the deductions made from P_s. Thus, the level of income for inmates involved in commodity production which does not also involve private enterprises is:

(31) $$Y_1^A = \left(P_s - \sum d_s\right) + NCR_{state}$$

It is nearly always the case that $(P_{PIE} > P_s)$. This may create strong demand on the part of the inmates to participate in the $SFCP_1$ involving private industry. Inmates may see this as the best of a very limited set of choices. To be clear, inmates do not possess the ability to freely choose whether or not to work, for their slave labor-power is owned by the head of the department of corrections. However, in some jurisdictions, prison industries are undeveloped, so that there are not enough jobs to force all inmates to work. In federal prisons, for example, all inmates are enslaved, but they can choose enslavement in the $SFCP_1$ or the $SFCP_2$.[6] The fact that the master's provision can be 2—4 times greater in the $SFCP_1$ leads to a long waiting list. Federal Prison Industries, also known as UNICOR, the agency which oversees the $SFCP_1$ in the federal system, may be able to take advantage of this situation to obtain the most 'motivated' workers in commodity production, who will doubtless be the most pliable when it comes to workplace discipline. Of course, this sorting process would leave a larger proportion of less motivated workers in prison household production, but this is apparently not a concern for Federal Prison Industries.

The above allows us to provide more detail in our categorization of inmate income levels. Table 4.2 incorporates the above discussion into Table 3.3 from Chapter Three.

The literature on prison labor uniformly understands the actual master's provision (P_{slave}) to be wages which go to inmate workers, who are often understood to be much like other capitalist workers. Remarkably, even critics of prison labor, who allege that inmates are enslaved, consider the payments to inmates to be wages, albeit very low wages. Perhaps this is a consequence of overlooking the concept of surplus labor, and instead falling back on other analytical traditions which take exploitation as a given and seek only to reduce it to an acceptable level by raising wages.[7]

This study understands wages to be the price of the commodity labor-power that results from a free market for labor-power, where individuals who own their labor-power agree to sell it for a particular wage to an employer. Much of the Marxian tradition sees wages as the essence of the

Table 4.2 Actual Income of Inmates by Class, Including All Deductions and Charges

Inmate Category	Actual Income (Y_A)
1. *Slave Producers*	
a. Commodity production (*SFCP₁*)	
- Involving private industry	$\left[\left(P_{PIE} - \sum d_{PIE}\right) + NCR_{state}\right] - \sum c$
- State industry only	$\left[\left(P_s - \sum d_s\right) + NCR_{state}\right] - \sum c$
b. Prison household production (*SFCP₂*)	$\left[P_2 + NCR_{state}\right] - \sum c$
2. *Subsumed Slaves*	
a. Commodity production (*SSCP₁*)	
- Involving private industry	$\left[\left(SSCR_{PIE} - \sum d_{PIE}\right) + NCR_{state}\right] - \sum c$
- State industry only	$\left[\left(SSCR_s - \sum d_s\right) + NCR_{state}\right] - \sum c$
b. Prison household production (*SSCP₂*)	$\left[SSCR_{ncp} + NCR_{state}\right] - \sum c$
3. *Non-laboring inmates*	
a. General population	$\left[NCR_{state}\right] - \sum c$
b. Segregation	$\left[NCR_{seg}\right] - \sum c$

capitalist mode of production. Such a position is not taken within these pages, for that would suggest that a characteristic of markets, a form of economic distribution—specifically the market for human labor-power— would be definitive of a class process, which occurs at the point of production.

As argued in Chapter Three, the master's provision is distinct from a wage. To assume inmates receive a wage implies that they can choose to sell or not sell their labor-power as they see fit, which does not occur precisely because the labor-power of all the inmates is owned by the head of the department of corrections, making it slave labor-power. Hence enslaved inmates do not receive wages, but receive a master's provision.

THE PRODUCTION OF SURPLUS-VALUE BY SLAVES

Before we can understand the value (W) produced by inmates, we must say a bit about value theory employed here. In Marxian theory, value is equal to the socially necessary abstract labor time (SNALT) embodied in a commodity. This SNALT takes two forms, the embodied labor (C) which consists of the value of the fixed capital (tools, equipment and raw materials) that is used up in the production process, and the living labor, which, in capitalist production, is divided into variable capital (V, the cost of the labor-power purchased by the capitalist) and surplus value (S, the value produced by workers above and beyond their pay, which Marx also refers to as unpaid labor). Hence the value of a commodity can be described as

$$(32) \qquad W = C + V + S.$$

If slaves produce commodities, the value of the commodity is still given by the amount of socially necessary abstract labor time embodied in it, the sum of the embodied labor (not necessarily performed by slaves, hence there is no slave subscript) and the living labor performed by slaves. As discussed above, V_{slave} represents the quantum of socially necessary abstract labor time embodied in the goods and services needed to reproduce the labor power of the slave. Thus any labor performed by slaves above this is surplus value, labeled S_{slave}. Notice that the use of the term V_{slave} is not the same as the capitalist V, denoting that the capitalist paid the worker the value of his or her labor power. The V_{slave} term does not indicate that the labor-power of the slave was purchased by the master, for as we have already discussed, the labor-power of the slave is in fact owned by the master. Thus the above formula, although it reflects a different class process than capitalism, can also be used to understand the value of commodities produced by slaves:

$$(33) \qquad W_{slave} = C + V_{slave} + S_{slave}.$$

As discussed earlier, in prisons the value of the goods and services needed to reproduce the labor-power of slaves is termed V_1 for slaves in commodity production and V_2 for slaves in prison household production. At this point we are only concerned here with V_1, having analyzed prison household production in Chapter Three. We will use the term W_1 to indicate the value of commodities produced by slaves in the $SFCP_1$, C_1 to indicate the value of the embodied labor, and S_1 to indicate the surplus value. We can thus rewrite the above expression as:

$$(34) \qquad W_1 = C_1 + V_1 + S_1.$$

The slave surplus value that slave masters appropriate is distributed to secure various conditions of existence for the continuation of the $SFCP_1$. In general, we can say that the magnitude of the surplus value is equal to the sum of these distributions of surplus, or subsumed class payments, labeled $SSCP_1$, although the equality is neither assured nor theoretically necessary:

$$(35) \qquad\qquad S_1 = SSCP_1.$$

Thus inmate-slaves in commodity production produce both the value necessary to reproduce their own labor-power (V_1) and they also produce a slave surplus above and beyond that. As we have shown, slave masters take advantage of state welfare to provide the inmate-slave with a payment P_1, lower than V_1.

THE MARKET FOR SLAVE-PRODUCED COMMODITIES

Appropriators of inmate-slave surplus value cannot realize the surplus value they appropriate without selling the commodities in a market. Depending on the circumstances of the market, prison appropriators may be able to realize both the surplus and additional gains beyond it. These gains are considered non-class revenues, since they are related not to the surplus value produced, but to factors not directly related to class.

   If the market is competitive, the prison appropriator must sell at the competitive price, which we will assume is equal to the market unit value, the total value divided by the number of use-values (uv) produced. However, since the competitors in the marketplace are largely capitalist firms which must pay the prevailing wage outside prisons, labeled V_c, and hence appropriate a surplus equal to S_c, while the prison appropriator grants the slaves a master's provision of V_1, and appropriates slave surplus value equal to S_1. If we assume that $V_c > V_1$, that is, the socially constructed level of sustenance for workers outside prison is greater than that for enslaved inmates, and if the intensity of labor is the same, we may find that the prison slavemaster can obtain a greater amount of surplus value than the capitalist competition, due to a higher rate of exploitation in prisons:

$$(36) \qquad\qquad \left(\frac{S_1}{V_1}\right) > \left(\frac{S_c}{V_c}\right).$$

The prison slavemaster's gains from lowering the master's provision to P_1 is conceptualized as a non-class revenue, and is labeled NCR_w, and is equal to the difference between P_1 and V_1. Hence the class and non-class revenue flowing to the master would be

$$(37) \qquad\qquad (S + NCR_w).$$

In a non-competitive market, where the prison commodity has only a small share of the market, the prison appropriator may be able to gain by lowering the price of their commodities below the market unit value in order to obtain a greater share of the market. If the price of the commodity is now Φ_s, say that the difference between the price and the market unit value is the difference between P_1 and V_1. This would not threaten the conditions of existence of slavery occurring in prisons, because the cost of production of the slave commodities is less than it would be due to the state welfare. To summarize:

(38) $$\Phi_s < \left(\frac{W}{uv}\right), \text{ and}$$

(39) $$(\Phi_s \cdot uv) = C + P_1 + S_1.$$

Notice that in equation (38) the magnitude of the slave surplus is unchanged, even though the price is below the value of the commodity.

If the market is non-competitive and the prison commodity has a significant portion of or all of the market, it may be possible for the slave-master to raise the price above the market unit value of the commodity, resulting in a price of Φ_s^M :

(40) $$\Phi_s^M > \left(\frac{W}{uv}\right).$$

This results in an additional source of revenue to the slavemaster, a non-class revenue due to the monopoly power he enjoys in the market, labeled NCR_M:

(41) $$\left(\Phi_s^M \cdot uv\right) = \left[(C + P_1) + (NCR_w + NCR_M + S_{slave})\right]$$

Many jurisdictions grant to prison slavemasters in commodity production a monopoly for whatever goods they produce by requiring that the state buy commodities produced in prison first, and can only be exempted from this requirement if the needed commodity is not produced in prison, or the quality is lacking. One examples of this is Federal Prison Industries, which has a 'mandatory source' requirement, meaning that all federal agencies must seek to obtain commodities from Federal Prison Industries, and can only buy elsewhere if FPI doesn't produce the item. The state of California has a similar requirement that California state agencies purchase items from the Prison Industries Authority. Some critics of prison commodity production have charged that the price of prison commodities is higher than the value, that the mandatory source requirement grants Federal

Prison Industries monopoly power in many markets.[8] If this is the case, then Federal Prison Industries has additional non-class revenue to use for purposes such as expansion of operations, investment in new technology, and so forth, as detailed above.

APPROPRIATION OF SURPLUS-VALUE

Appropriation of the total product produced by inmates in commodity production depends on the organization of the prison industry. Appropriation of inmate-slave surplus value is done either by a state agency or by a private enterprise. There are 2 forms of state appropriation and 3 forms of private appropriation (each one is discussed separately):

1. State Appropriation
   a. State Enterprise Model
   b. Customer Model

2. Private Appropriation
   a. Employer Model
   b. Manpower Model
   c. Privatized Prison Model

STATE APPROPRIATION

All 50 U.S. states have departments of corrections. Generally, appropriation of inmate slave surplus value is done by a separate agency, either within the department of corrections, or a semi-private corporation set up by the state to administer prison industries.

The Department of Corrections of California established the Prison Industry Authority (PIA) to do the following:

> Develop and operate manufacturing, agricultural, and service enterprises that provide work opportunities for inmates under the jurisdiction of the Department of Corrections.

> Create and maintain working conditions within enterprises, as much like those which prevail in private industry as possible, to assure inmates assigned therein the opportunity to work productively, to earn funds, and to acquire or improve effective work habits or occupational skills

> Operate work programs for inmates that are self-supporting through the generation of sufficient funds from the sale of products and services to pay all its expenses, thereby avoiding the cost of alternative inmate programming by California Department of Corrections.[9]

The PIA is mandated to use inmate slave labor-power to produce commodities, and then to sell these commodities, using the proceeds to pay its own expenses. In other words, PIA is designated as the official appropriator of inmate slave surplus value in the state of California. State agencies in each state have similar mandates as the PIA to appropriate the surplus value of the enslaved inmates.

Although the state agency is the appropriator in this kind of commodity production, note that the slave labor-power of the inmates is owned by the head of the department of corrections, who delegates the authority to the warden and then to the rest of the prison staff that directly compels enslaves the inmates. Thus there is a separation of ownership and direct control over the production process. Such a separation also exists in the modern corporation, which is generally owned by its many stockholders but is actually run by the management, who may own some stock, but are not the owners in the sense of having actual property titles to the corporation's assets.

The largest example of a state-sponsored corporation designed to appropriate the surplus from slave commodities is Federal Prison Industries, which was incorporated in 1934 to administer prison industries in the federal prison system.

The state enterprise model is by far the most widespread form of surplus appropriation that exists in prisons in the U.S. In order to elucidate its features, we will consider the revenue and expenditures for a sample state appropriator. It is hoped that this empirical sample will provide a concrete example that will clarify the theory developed thus far.

The state of Florida has a semi-government, semi-private entity[10] called PRIDE ("Prison Rehabilitative Industries and Diversified Enterprises") which is in charge of producing commodities using prison slave labor, appropriating the surplus and realizing the surplus value. PRIDE is organized as a nonprofit corporation, and hence pays no taxes, even though, unlike most nonprofits, it appropriates an enormous mass of surplus value.

Before delving into the details, a note on terminology is in order. As noted in Chapter Two, terms such as P_1, V_1, NCR_{state}, and others are defined as the *individual* master's provision, value of slave labor power, and state welfare, respectively, while $\dot{P}_1$ is the aggregate master's provision in the $SFCP_1$, $\dot{V}_1$ is the aggregate value of slave labor power in the $SFCP_1$, and N_{PRIDE} as the number of inmates enslaved in PRIDE. Thus $(NCR_{state} \cdot N_{PRIDE})$ is the total state welfare going to slaves in PRIDE, while $\dot{NCR}_{state}$ is the aggregate state welfare to Florida inmates.

In 1998, PRIDE produced a mass of commodities with the total sale price of $81,220,930. Inmate slaves were paid a total master's provision $(\dot{P}_1)$ of about $1.9 million, which is less than the total value of slave labor-power $(\dot{V}_l)$. As shown in general terms in Chapter Three, PRIDE takes advantage of the state welfare to pay inmate slaves less than the value necessary to reproduce their labor-power. This allows PRIDE to obtain what is understood here to be a non-class revenue, labeled NCR_{PRIDE}, which is equal to the difference between the total master's provision and the total value of the slave labor-power:

(42) $NCR_{PRIDE} = \dot{V}_l - \dot{P}_l$.

Assuming that price is equal to value,[11] the total price of the mass of commodities produced by PRIDE is equal to:

(43)   Total sales $= C + \left[\dot{P}_l + NCR_{PRIDE} \right] + S_{slave} = W.$

The magnitude of can be calculated by considering the total value needed to reproduce the slave's labor power, which we will consider to be the total spending on inmate food, depreciation on living quarters, clothing, and all the other spending on inmates that directly reproduces their labor-power, plus the master's provision:

(44) $\dot{V}_l = \dot{P}_l + (NCR_{state} \cdot N_{PRIDE}) = \dot{P}_l + NCR_{PRIDE}$

According to the Florida Department of Corrections Annual Budget Report, the cost of incarcerating an inmate is $50.06 per day, or $18,272 per year.[12] However, not all of this can be considered state welfare. Welfare only includes the items that inmates directly consume, not every expenditure made in corrections, the same way that not every government expenditure can be considered a form of welfare. For example, the costs of administration does not affect the size of inmate welfare, but is necessary to administer the prison. Similarly, insurance may protect the department of corrections against risk and liability, but is not a part of the welfare that goes to inmates.

As the Table 4.3 shows, security is the largest single cost. Security includes several variables: including the cost of security technology, equipment, maintenance, and the cost of salaries of correctional officers, which is the largest cost category. Security includes both confining the inmates, which can hardly be considered welfare, and protection of inmates from each other. It may be argued that the latter benefits inmates, in the same manner that the establishment of a police force that enforces laws fairly benefits citizens of a nation. However, policing is not normally considered a form of welfare to individual citizens, rather, it is a cost of the government.

Table **4.3** Florida Department of Corrections Annual Budget Report, Cost of Incarceration, 1999–2000

Category	Spending	% of total
Administration	$31,387,160	2.7
Insurance	$20,670,208	1.8
Security	$653,069,754	56.3
Food	$79,956,609	6.9
Medical	$226,076,801	19.6
Clothing / Laundry	$17,000,530	1.5
Education	$34,227,928	2.9
Physical plant	$79,712,172	6.9
Inmate services	$18,685,630	1.6
Total Spending	$1,160,786,792	100
Total Cost of State Welfare	**$455,659,670**	**39**
Inmate Population (June 30, 1999) = N	68,599	--
NCR_{state}	$6,642	--
Average P_1	$418	--
Average income per commodity-producing inmate, not including deductions and charges *	$7,060	--

* We are assuming that all inmate-slaves are productive, i.e. that none occupy subsumed class positions. This is unlikely, but the limitations in the data make this assumption necessary.

The shaded portions of Table 4.3 are not included in the cost of inmate welfare. Thus the total welfare to each inmate per year is = $6,642.

If we take the total number of inmate-slaves in PRIDE and multiply by the state welfare to each inmate slave, we total non-class revenue flowing to PRIDE due to the state welfare:[13]

$$(45) \qquad NCR_{PRIDE} = (2,534)*(\$6,642) = \$16,831,755.$$

Note that this non-class revenue is not a direct payment from the state to PRIDE. PRIDE seems to be quite proud, so to speak, of the fact that they operate purely out of their own surplus appropriations, without receiving any direct payments from the state. PRIDE does receive indirect subsidies, in the form of a complete tax break and the freedom to pay a price of labor-power that is far less that the value.

The total master's provision, $\dot{P}_1$, is \$1,869,346. Therefore the total actual income of slaves in commodity production is:

$$(46) \ \dot{Y}_1 = (\ \dot{P}_1 + \dot{NCR}_{state}) = \$18,701,101.$$

Let us consider the revenues PRIDE receives; from the sale of slave commodities, PRIDE receives a sum of money equal the total value of the commodities, W, assumed to be equal to the number of goods sold times the price of the goods. As in equation 34, the value produced by PRIDE can be represented as $(C_1 + V_1 + S_1)$. PRIDE has three sources of revenue; the first stems from its appropriation of the slave surplus labor, S_1, and is therefore considered a class revenue, while the second is the non-class revenue resulting from the state welfare, NCR_{PRIDE}. The third source of revenue consists of the repayment of loans made by PRIDE, loans which apparently were made without specification of repayment or interest, as detailed in PRIDE's annual report.[14] While this revenue source is zero for the period being analyzed, it is labeled NCR_{loans} to note that it is a potential future revenue stream. Table 4.4 provides the magnitudes of each of these sources of revenue for 1998.

In order to appropriate surplus labor from inmate-slaves, PRIDE must secure its various conditions of existence, paying for costs not directly related to production, but necessary in order to remain the appropriator of inmate-slave surplus. These costs are considered subsumed class payments, labeled $SSCP_{PRIDE}$. These terms includes the costs of administration, marketing, advertising, security, promotion, and others.

PRIDE may also have to bear certain costs in order to maintain the conditions which result in the flow of non-class revenue from the state welfare. These costs are labeled Y_{PRIDE}. This may include such activities as monitoring state law, keeping in touch with lawmakers, arranging tours

Table 4.4 PRIDE Revenues, 2000

Revenues	
Sales $= W = (C_1 + V_1 + S_1)$	\$81,220,930
Slave Surplus Value (S_1)	\$6,866,156
NCR_{PRIDE}	\$16,831,756
NCR_{loans}	\$0
Total Revenue	**\$81,220,930**

Source: PRIDE Enterprises Annual Report, 2000. http://www.peol.com/about.htm

of prison production facilities to show lawmakers, media and others that prison slavery is beneficial and should continue. PRIDE does not provide much detail about its costs, so it is not possible to separate which costs are subsumed class payments and which costs are non-class payments. Finally, PRIDE gains a non-class revenue from interest on loans, which requires the loan of a principal, labeled Y_{loans}. Table 4.5 provides the magnitudes of these expenditures.

The following expression summarizes the argument presented above, showing PRIDE's revenues (left-hand side) and expenditures (right-hand side) in class terms:

(47) $S_1 + NCR_{PRIDE} + NCR_{loans} = SSCP_{PRIDE} + Y_{PRIDE} + Y_{loans}.$

Note that while Table 4.4, 4.5 and Equation 50 present an equality between PRIDE's revenues and expenditures, this equality is not theoretically necessary.

PRIDE does not recognize the difference between revenue obtained from the slave fundamental class process (slave surplus), and revenue obtained from non-class processes such as the deviation of the master's provision from the value of inmate necessary labor (NCR_{PRIDE}). As one can see from Table 4.4, the slave surplus value is about $6.9 million, but far more significant is the $16.8 million in non-class revenue. If PRIDE did not receive this non-class revenue, it would be unable to make all of its current expenditures. In other words, the state of Florida indirectly subsidizes a semi-private enterprise which exists in order to appropriate inmate slave surplus labor.

The rate of exploitation, defined as (S_1/V_1), is 0.384. For purposes of comparison, consider that Moseley (1982), (1991) has found that the U.S. rate of exploitation is between 1.00 and 1.40 for the period 1944–1979. This means that the rate of exploitation of prison inmates is considerably

Table 4.5 PRIDE Expenditures, 2000

Expenditures	
Constant Capital (C_1)	$56,464,734
Master's Provision (P_1)	$1,869,346
Loans (Y_{loans})	$3,030,656
Subsumed class and non-class payments ($SSCP_{PRIDE} + Y_{PRIDE}$)	$19,856,194
Total expenditures	**$81,220,930**

Source: PRIDE Enterprises Annual Report, 2000. http://www.peol.com/about.htm

It may also be useful to consider the surplus in relation to the master's provision, since P_1 is so much less than V_1. If we do so we find that $(S_1/P_1) = 3.67$; while this number is not a rate of exploitation as defined by Marx, it does reflect the magnitude of the surplus value produced by slave labor relative to the master's provision that PRIDE must pay to secure the reproduction of slave labor-power. This figure is far higher than the rate of exploitation facing workers outside prisons. Since a large disparity between the master's provision and the value of the necessary labor exists, this number may more accurately describe the subjective feeling of exploitation in prison, as much as any number can.[15]

Another measure which may be relevant is the slave surplus value added to the non-class revenue PRIDE receives due to state welfare relative to the master's provision,

(48)
$$\frac{\left(S_1 + NCR_{PRIDE}\right)}{P_1} = 12.68$$

this measure captures more clearly the gain to PRIDE of exploiting inmate slave labor relative to the direct cost they must bear, revealing how much PRIDE profits from the combination of slave labor and state welfare.

As the preceding has shown, PRIDE appropriates slave surplus labor from inmates and benefits financially from state welfare payments. The same can be said for state agencies like PRIDE in other states or in the federal prison system. Analyses of these and other jurisdictions can be completed by using the methodology developed in this study.

As noted above, it is possible for a state prison system to act in partnership with private enterprises to produce commodities under the PIE program. Under this law, the state may make contracts with private companies whereby the prison provides to a private enterprise a finished product at a previously negotiated wholesale price. This is known as the "customer model."[16]

Since the state agency is the first receiver of the inmate slave commodities, it is the appropriator of the slave surplus labor. The private enterprise takes the commodities and sells them, assuming a subsumed class position providing the master (the state agency) with the important condition of existence that is the realization of surplus value, i.e. taking the commodities and transforming them into money form. Let us assume that the commodities are sold at a retail price (Φ_{retail}) equal to their value.

(49) $(\Phi_{retail} \cdot uv) = W_1 = [C_1 + P_{PIE}] + [NCR_w + S_1].$

Note that because P_{PIE} is equal to the minimum wage, NCR_w would be very small, perhaps even zero. The private enterprise acts as a merchant, obtaining profits from the difference between the wholesale and the retail price. Hence, the wholesale price which the private enterprise pays is below the value of the commodity. The difference between the wholesale and the retail price is the portion of the inmate slave surplus labor distributed from the appropriator, in this case the state agency. This distribution of slave surplus labor is a subsumed class revenue, a revenue which flows to the merchant to secure a condition of existence of the *SFCP*, the transformation of commodities into money.

(50) $$(\Phi_{retail} - \Phi_{wholesale}) = SSCR_{merchant}.$$

Presumably, the state agency would only make this distribution of its slave surplus labor to this private enterprise if the private enterprise was deemed more likely to succeed at marketing the commodities than the state agency, which could use that portion of the slave surplus to pay a sales staff, print catalogs, maintain an office, take orders, and complete the various other tasks involved in selling commodities. In addition, the profits of the enterprise may also be distributed to shareholders as dividends, to advertisers, to lenders, and to other groups providing the firm with necessary items to receive the above distribution of slave surplus value. The sum of these expenditures made to procure the $SSCP_{merchant}$ is labeled $X_{merchant}$.

In the customer model, the role of the private enterprise is not one of direct appropriation of slave surplus labor. In other words, in this particular arrangement of production, the private enterprise does not exploit the slaves in the Marxian sense; rather it is the state agency which exploits the enslaved inmates.

Since the a private enterprise is involved here, the state agency must pay, by law, a master's provision greater than or equal to the minimum wage, and then is permitted to make deductions from it. As noted above, the payment to the slaves is $\left(P_{PIE} - \sum d_{PIE}\right)$.

PRIVATE APPROPRIATION

There are three forms of appropriation of slave surplus value in which private enterprise is the appropriator: the manpower model, the customer model, and the privatized prison model.

In the manpower model, inmates work for private companies on-site (in the prison) and the state agency charges the private enterprise a "burden rate" for the use of inmates' slave labor-power. Typically this is set at the minimum wage, the lowest level of P_1 enslaved inmates can receive under PIE rules. The private enterprise is now the first receiver of the inmate slave surplus labor. The private enterprise owns the commodities that inmates produce, and is obligated to pay a master's provision of P_{PIE}. As noted above, the state agency makes deductions from this amount, gaining an amount equal to $\sum d_{PIE}$. Because the PIE rules allow for a deduction of up to 80% of the value of P_{PIE}, the prison gains from increases in P_{PIE}.

This situation is very similar to a slave rental market, in which masters obtain a revenue by selling the slave labor-power that the master owns to another party. Thus, the price of the slave rental ($\Phi_{slave\text{-}rental}$) is equal to the price the firm must pay to gain access to it, P_{PIE}.

$\left(P_{PIE} - \sum d_{PIE}\right)$ represents the actual master's provision that slaves receive in the $SFCP_1$ involving private firms in the manpower model. In the manpower model the private firm is an appropriator of surplus value, whether the firm produces a good or service. For example, slaves may perform labor by making telephone calls in which they enter reservations for a firm which then sells the service to an airline as a commodity.

In the manpower model the state agency owns the factory and other elements of the constant capital used in production, and pays the workers directly. The private enterprise has flexibility in this arrangement; rather than hiring its own workforce, the enterprise can outsource production.

The private firm benefits in several ways from this arrangement. First, they obtain revenue from the surplus value they appropriate from the enslaved inmates, labeled S_m. Second, they obtain a non-class revenue in the form of free rent, for the enterprises are normally not charged for the use of prison space, and the use of machinery and equipment that may be owned by the state agency. This non-class revenue is labeled NCR_{rent}. Third, the private firm benefits by a regulatory environment that is significantly less restrictive that that which prevails outside prisons. For example, the Occupational Safety and Health rules which may increase costs for appropriators outside prisons by mandating certain acceptable levels of toxic materials, requiring the purchase of certain safety equipment and so forth, do not apply to prisons. In addition, prison workers get neither breaks, nor workman's compensation in case of an accident. Hence these firms are able to obtain a non-class revenue by producing in the lax regulatory setting of the prison; this is labeled NCR_{laws}. One way in which the private firm does not gain is through the state welfare. Because the firm must pay slave-rental price for the labor-power of the slaves equal to an amount the firm would pay for the labor-power of a capitalist worker outside prison, the firm is not able to benefit from the state welfare.

The firm may also need to make expenditures in order to receive these class and non-class revenues. The firm must pay to obtain the conditions of existence for their appropriation of S_m, possibly including such payments as interest, dividends, managerial and executive salaries, administrative costs, and marketing costs. These are considered subsumed class payments, and the total of them is labeled $SSCP_m$. Since the non-class revenues largely result from the legal structure of prison slavery, these expenditures may include tracking state and federal law, lobbying for changes to the law, and so forth. These are labeled Y_m. To summarize, a productive enterprise producing in prison under the manpower model would have the following revenues (right-hand side) and expenditures (left-hand side):

$$(51) \qquad S_m + NCR_{rent} + NCR_{laws} = SSCP_m + Y_m.$$

In the employer model the private company directly enslaves the inmates. As in the manpower and customer models, the enterprise pays the inmates a master's provision of P_{PIE}. However, in the employer model the enterprise owns the equipment used in production, and engages in the management and supervision of the inmate slaves.

The prison merely provides the space and makes available the slave labor-power. Again, the prison is able to make deductions of $\sum d_{PIE}$ from the master's provision .

In the employer model the private enterprise appropriates the slave surplus value that the prisoners produce. In this model the firms revenues and expenditures would be much like those of the firm in the manpower model; we will use the subscript *emp* to mark this as the employer model:

$$(52) \qquad S_{emp} + NCR_{rent} + NCR_{laws} = SSCP_{emp} + Y_{emp}.$$

Of the three forms of appropriation involving a partnership between state agencies and private enterprises, the employer model is by far the most frequent, with 1,586 inmates working under this type of appropriation in 1998. The customer model is second most common, with 430 inmates in this structure. The manpower model is quite rare, only found in South Carolina and Tennessee, with 385 inmates in total. This means that out of the 2,399 inmates participating in the PIE program in 1998, 1,971 are in the position of having their surplus value appropriated by private companies.[17] This makes private appropriation a small share of the total, but the PIE program is growing rapidly—the number of inmates participating in PIE programs has increased 200% during the 1990's—and might well become more important in the future.[18]

The final kind of private appropriation is the privatized prison model, where a private corporation has obtained a contract from the state to administer a privately owned prison, in which prisoners perform productive labor. The products of inmate labor are appropriated by the board of directors of the firm which owns the prison.

When a private prison firm is the appropriator of inmate slave surplus labor, the head of the department of corrections in that jurisdiction is still the owner of inmate slave labor-power. Since the head of the department of corrections has the final authority to grant contracts to private prison firms as well as the final responsibility for the inmates, the ownership of slave labor-power is still in his or her hands.

The private prison slavemaster becomes the appropriator of both the $SFCP_1$ and the $SFCP_2$, much like the warden of a public prison was at an earlier period in prison history, which will be discussed in more detail in Chapter Four. The private slavemaster obtains two surpluses: S_1 and S_2. As in equation 25, he also benefits by receiving the same four non-class revenues from the state that the warden of a public prison receives. In addition, the private slavemaster receives a non-class revenue equal to difference between P_1 and V_1, labeled $NCR_{private}$. Thus the total revenue flowing to the private prison slavemaster is:

$$(53)\ R_{private} = (S_1 + S_2) + (NCR_{PROV1} + NCR_e + NCR_C + NCR_V + NCR_{private}).$$

Turning to the expenditure side, the private prison is now responsible for providing the inmates with the items which make up the socially-determined level of state welfare, along with the expenses of the prison, as seen in equation 25. The private prison master must also make the subsumed class payments necessary to appropriate his surpluses, labeled $SSCP_1$, and $SSCP_2$. In addition, the private prison slavemaster makes a payment of, perhaps consisting of marketing and promotion of the idea of private prisons, lobbying lawmakers for legislation favorable to private prisons, and so forth, to secure the continuance of $NCR_{private}$. We can summarize the expenditures of the private prison master as:

$$(54)\qquad\qquad E_{private} = SSCP_1 + SSCP_2 + Y_{PROV}.$$

Private prisons generally offer to run the prison for less than what the state would pay to run a public prison, meaning that they offer to accept a total non-class revenue of which is reduced from what it would have been had the prison been public. Private prisons typically begin by analyzing the budget for a given prison, or the average cost of incarceration, and make a deal to accept a lower sum.

The private prison must then reduce its own expenditures, within the legal limits of state welfare which exist in that particular jurisdiction. Since the law is often quite clear on what elements of welfare must be given to inmates, the private prison often reduces costs by reducing the Y_e term; since security is the largest single item in that category, which is itself mostly the salaries of the correctional officers, private prisons can cut their expenses by lowering the salaries of its correctional officers, through hiring non-union workers. Some critics charge that private prisons provide inmates with a lower level of state welfare than public prisons do, exploiting ambiguities in the law or counting on a lack of enforcement of the law.[19]

CONCLUSION

This chapter has provided a detailed account of the enslavement of inmates in commodity production. It was shown that the production of commodities in prisons is quite complex, with five different forms of production and appropriation of surplus value, involving different 'partnerships' between the state and private enterprises. A numerical example of the most common of these forms (state enterprise) was provided for the State of Florida, to show how the class categories developed here may be employed to understand state enterprise appropriation of inmate slave surplus labor. It is hoped that this concrete example provides the reader with a more thorough understanding of the theory, as well as of the class structure of slavery in prison commodity production.

Some critics of prison labor have argued that the involvement of private enterprises in prison slavery means that there will be more of a focus on the maximization of profits and less focus on rehabilitation and education of inmates. The history of prisons lends little support to this claim. For much of the 19th and into the early 20th century, state-run prison labor programs were often brutally exploitative and did little to rehabilitate inmates. There seems to be no particular reason to believe that the state will exploit enslaved inmates any more or less brutally than private enterprises. Moreover, from the Marxian perspective employed here, it matters less what the actual rate of exploitation of these slaves is, than the fact that they are enslaved. Would it have mattered much in terms of the horrendous effects of slavery if the state had owned the cotton plantations of the Antebellum south?

This chapter has shown that the largest revenue a typical state enterprise receives is the non-class revenue which is the result of the state welfare. This suggests that prison industries typically rely on the state welfare in order to continue to enslave inmates. As argued in this chapter, the state indirectly subsidizes these state entities.

Building on the analysis of Chapter Three, it stands to reason that if state entities and private enterprises rely on the current level of state welfare in order to meet their expenditures, if the level of state welfare falls, these appropriating bodies may face a crisis. Inmates who are enslaved in commodity production may grow angry that their standard of living has fallen, and demand that the master provide them with a higher P_1 so that they can regain their former level of consumption. If the master raises P_1, he lowers his profits. Some masters have enough of a revenue stream to survive such a lowering, but others may not.

Chapter Five
The History of Prison Slavery in the U.S.

INTRODUCTION

So far we've developed a class analytical theory of slavery used to understand labor in U.S. prisons. Slavery exists in U.S. prisons, although it is of a different form than our common conception of slavery in such sites as the Caribbean or the American south during the Antebellum period. Inmates are enslaved due to the unique structure of the production and appropriation of surplus labor, including the cultural, political, economic, and physical forces which overdetermine this class process.

In Chapter Three, we discussed the importance of the state in prison life, through the state's provision of welfare to all inmates. The state welfare allows the masters in each area of production to grant the slaves a master's provision that is far lower than it would otherwise need to be to reproduce the slave labor-power.

The conclusion of Chapter Three sketched a few of the consequences of slavery and its interaction with welfare, showing a few of the class contradictions of the *SFCP* in prison, such as the conflicts between enslaved inmates and non-slave inmates, between slaves in different areas of the *SFCP*, between inmates who are subsumed slaves and those that produce surplus, and so forth. The class dimension of prison can be understood in addition to the many other processes that lead to violent tensions within prisons, adding detail to the study of prison life.

Chapter Four showed how commodities are produced in prison in each of the different 'models,' which specify different roles for the state and private enterprise in the production and appropriation of slave surplus value. Unlike other contemporary analyses of prison commodity production, the analysis presented here constructs neither an essentially positive nor an essentially negative view of the role of private enterprise in prison commodity production. The main point of this study is to provide an analysis of the class processes which occur in U.S. prisons and the implications of these class processes. As the preceding work has shown, most of slave surplus labor performed in prisons is appropriated by state agencies. There is no *a priori* reason to believe that private enterprises will be more or less exploitative, though the slave class process may well differ depending on the particular circumstances of each production process.

It is likely that the economic drive to increase profits may lead to increases in the rate of exploitation which make the *SFCP* more brutal that it would be without the influence of the market for commodities, just as it often has in other forms of the *SFCP* throughout history that involved commodities, such as the production of sugar, cotton, indigo, tobacco, gold, and salt. However, since state agencies and private enterprises both produce for the market, this tendency would occur in both models of prison commodity production.

One of the contributions of the class analysis of prison labor presented here is the fresh perspective it provides into the history of the modern prison in the U.S. In the following section we consider the history of prison slavery in the 19th and 20th century, providing a new understanding of the interdependent relationship between prisons and the overall society of which they are a part.

THE MODERN HISTORY OF U.S. PRISONS: A CLASS PERSPECTIVE

The detailed class analysis of prisons undertaken thus far enables a different understanding of prisons, prison history, and the relationship between prisons and American society. During the twentieth century, U.S. prisons saw a dramatic shift in the amount of state welfare granted to inmates, as well as changing social, political, economic conditions which dramatically altered the scope and context of prison slavery. As the result, certain forms of the *SFCP* were transformed or abolished, while other forms of the *SFCP* were increased. At the same time other important changes took place, such as a massive increase in both the number of people incarcerated and the prevalence of incarceration in society, a skyrocketing of prison costs, and all sorts of changes in the relationship between prison and society at large. A brief discussion of these trends and their relationship to the class processes in prisons may create a sense of perspective for the theoretical work done in the preceding three chapters; hopefully, such an exposition will give the reader a better understanding of prisons and the class dynamics which overdetermine prison life.

Let us begin at the end of the 19ᵗʰ century, a time when a vastly different social and political climate prevailed, in which prisoners were seen as deserving of a very low level of consumption, perhaps quite close to subsistence. Descriptions of prison life from the time reveal desperately poor conditions, involving routine deprivation in terms of food, clothing, and other necessary items.[1] Thus, we conclude that the level of state welfare was far lower than it is today.

At the end of the 19ᵗʰ century, like today, inmates were enslaved. Although many of the circumstances of prison life were quite different from the modern prison setting, the class and non-class structure of prison labor was consistent with the description of the modern prison depicted in Chapters One and Two. Inmates were obliged by political, economic, cultural, and legal forces to engage in labor, and all the fruits of their labor were appropriated either by state officials or private enterprises; these forces rendered the ability of the inmates to work as slave labor-power, which was owned by the department of corrections in the jurisdiction where they were caged. This ownership of the enslaved inmates' labor-power allowed prison officials to rent inmates to private enterprises, who would then appropriate the slave surplus labor. One way that the different sociopolitical climate of the 19ᵗʰ century affected prison slavery, was to reduce the value of inmate-slave labor-power below the value of labor-power among capitalist workers, so that $V_{slave} < V_{capitalist}$.

During this time, there was a high rate of enslavement of inmates in prisons, mostly in the production of commodities. In 1885, for example, 94% of the inmate population was enslaved in either the $SFCP_1$ or the $SFCP_2$, whereas in 2001, an estimated 36% of the inmates are enslaved, as discussed in Chapter One and shown in Table 5.2 below.[2]

The combination of a low level of state welfare and a high proportion of enslavement made for a very different set of revenues and expenditures for prison slave masters. This period lasted until about 1940, when a series of new laws lowered the number of inmates enslaved significantly. As is the case today, in the late 19ᵗʰ and early 20ᵗʰ century there were several different forms of prison commodity production, involving various kinds of partnerships between state entities and private enterprises. For the sake of brevity, we will not cover these forms in detail here; let us assume, for simplicity, that the warden of the prison appropriates slave surplus from both the $SFCP_1$ and the $SFCP_2$, a situation similar to that of private prison slavemasters today.

The warden slavemaster's revenues would be S_1 and S_2, representing the surpluses appropriated, as well as the non-class revenues from the state:

NCR_{PROV1}, NCR_e, NCR_C, NCR_V, and NCR_W, as seen in equations 37, 53, and 54. Thus the warden's revenues in the pre-1940 period would be:

(55) $R_{pre\text{-}1940} = (S_1 + S_2) + (NCR_{PROV1} + NCR_e + NCR_C + NCR_V + NCR_{private})$.

The pre-1940 warden also faced a set of expenditures similar to that faced by the private prison slavemaster of the current era (with the exception of the $Y_{private}$ term):

(56) $$E_{pre\text{-}1940} = (SSCP_1 + SSCP_2) + (Y_{PROV1} + Y_e + W_2^i).$$

Equation 55 shows that there is, potentially, a very high level of revenue flowing to wardens—this revenue is understood here to be due to a combination of surplus labor appropriation and non-class revenue, but was understood differently, in terms other than class, by state prison authorities within the department of corrections in each state. Some states observed this possibility, due especially to the large surpluses produced in the $SFCP_1$. The states consequently lowered their non-class payments to the prison; in some cases, all four non-class payments were lowered to zero, meaning that the warden's revenue would be effectively reduced to:

(57) $$R_{pre\text{-}1940} = (S_1 + S_2).$$

This means that the prison is 'self-sufficient,' or that no state money is needed to provide for prison costs, including inmate welfare. History records some examples, such as Auburn and Sing-Sing prisons in New York in 1828 and Parchman Prison Farm in Mississippi in 1915, which maintained its self-sufficiency until the early 1970's. Parchman farm even delivered large money payments to the state.[3] Many states sought out this situation; those unable to attain self-sufficiency were able to reduce the total state expenditures on prisons significantly, often by a third, and in many cases by two-thirds.[4] This situation did not last in any state; the following will provide a class explanation for why the self-sufficient prison was only rarely attained in the U.S. and did not endure to the modern era.

One implication of this reduction in state prison expenditures is that the master's provision must be increased so that it equals the value of slave labor power:

(58) $$NCR_w = (\dot{V}_1 - \dot{P}_1) = 0 \therefore \dot{V}_1 = \dot{P}_1;$$

(59) $$NCR_v = (\dot{V}_2 - \dot{P}_2) = 0 \therefore \dot{V}_2 = \dot{P}_2.$$

This means that the master's provision was actually raised for all slaves to a level equal to the value of slave-labor power: $P_1 = P_2 = V_{slave}$. However, in this era neither the master's provision (V_{slave}) nor the subsumed class payment to subsumed slaves ($SSCR_1$ and $SSCR_2$) was paid in money, but rather, in goods and services, some produced outside the prison ($PROV_1$) and some produced inside the prison (W_2^i).

Even though the flow of revenue from the state has ceased, the warden still faces the requirement, perhaps for a combination of legal and moral reasons, to deliver commodities to slaves in the $SFCP_2$ and slaves subsumed to the $SFCP_2$ and to inmates who were not enslaved; in addition, he must purchase means of production for the $SFCP_2$, and pay other prison expenses.[5] All of these payments must be in money form, but the only source of money that the warden has is S_1, since S_2 is not in money form, but in use-values. These money payments must come from the surplus; there is no other source of money available. This is a problem for the warden, for by definition the entire surplus must be spent in securing the conditions of existence which make the production and appropriation possible. For example, the distribution of a portion of S_1 to the state may provide political, legal, and cultural conditions of existence to the warden, for example, causing legislators to look favorably at prison production, preventing them from issuing any laws which would make the warden's appropriation of surplus more difficult, and producing support for the $SFCP_1$ among citizens, since it is seen as productive.

Thus, any payment from the surplus which does not secure conditions of existence would threaten the slave class process by creating an inequality; the warden's revenues and expenditures for the self-sufficient prison have become insufficient:

(60) $$(S_1 + S_2) < (SSCP_1 + SSCP_2).$$

A tension arises between the requirement of delivering welfare to non-slave inmates as a sort of gift, like charity, and the very survival of the warden as a slavemaster. The warden may attempt to reduce the difference between his revenues and expenditures by enslaving all the inmates, or by reducing the welfare gift to the non-slave inmates to zero. This may be successful economically, but may be socially or morally unstable, for it inevitably occurs that some inmates are not physically capable of working, and to enslave them would result in their death, while of course to not give them welfare would also result in their death. Both of these were common tendencies in 19th century prisons, particularly in the south.[6] When scrutinized, this situation was seen as morally unacceptable by the standards prevalent in society, and hence pressure was brought to bear to prevent the death of these inmates, which would involve increased welfare and decreased enslavement, which would lead to inequality (60) arising again. This was the case in Parchman prison, where a 1972 court decision resulted in significant reforms, raising welfare and reducing levels of enslavement, due to the position by the judge that Parchman farm violated modern standards of decency and that "conditions and practices [had] become so bad as to be shocking to conscience of reasonably civilized people."[7]

The warden may also seek to reduce other prison costs by, for example, using inmates as guards. These inmates thus become subsumed slaves, since their labor secures a condition of existence for slavery, while at the same time reducing the need for expenditures on guard salaries, since these inmates were unpaid. If these subsumed slaves, or 'trusty-shooters' as they were called on Parchman farm, where this practice had a long tradition, were to kill an inmate who attempted to escape, the trusty-shooter would receive credit for his sentence and may be even be freed. Of course, this solution has its own contradictions, including an extremely high mortality rate among inmates.

Another way to solve the problem of inequality (60) would be to increase the surplus, although this may also cause the subsumed class payments to rise, as nothing comes for free. Increased exploitation leads to other contradictions, which must be negotiated by other uses of the surplus. However, some contradictions may take time to emerge, or may not threaten the *SFCP* with an immediate crisis, such as a failure to set aside a portion of the surplus to purchase new and improved equipment and machinery. Nonetheless, slavemasters sought to expand the surplus through far longer working days and a more intense work pace than is generally the case today in prisons. To take one example, inmate-slaves on Parchman farm worked from sunrise to past sundown with a 30 minute break for lunch; a hard work-rhythm was established through call and response songs and the creation of an assembly-line gang labor system similar to what was employed in the Antebellum era. These inmate-slaves had a quota of 200 lb. of cotton per day.[8]

Though some wardens attempted to solve the problems and contradictions presented by inequality (60) by engaging in the brutal policies such as those undertaken by Parchman farm, none were ultimately successful. Cultural and political shifts would also make it far more difficult for wardens to run self-sufficient prisons, meaning that the non-class revenues from the state were raised significantly. One of these shifts affected the proportion of inmates who were enslaved in prisons.

PATTERNS OF ENSLAVEMENT

Enslaving a high proportion of inmates (as close as possible to 100%) is very important for wardens who are driven by various forces to maintain a self-sufficient prison. However, the proportion of inmates enslaved fell during the 20th century, due to pressure from organized labor and capitalist manufacturers outside prisons who were in competition with the $SFCP_1$ in the same market. A series of laws were passed which effectively reduced the number of inmates who could be enslaved, by limiting the market for prison commodities. Labor unions argued that free capitalist workers should not be forced to compete with slaves in the same market; manufacturers also resented the competition in the marketplace from prison commodities. Both sides united their criticism by labeling prison production "slave labor," though the reasons for this charge were rarely articulated, and never in terms of surplus labor.

The first of several acts limiting prison labor was Roosevelt's Executive Order 325A in 1905, which prohibited the use of state prisoners as a slave labor supply for federal contracts, although federal inmates could still be used for federal contracts. This was followed by the Hawes-Cooper Act (1929), which severely limited interstate commerce in prison commodities by granting the authority to the states to place nearly any restrictions on the trade of such goods. The Ashurst-Summers Act (1935) made it mandatory to label "prison-made" goods as such; the Walsh-Healey Public Contracts Act (1936) limited any federal contractor with a contract of over $10,000 from using inmate-slave labor, and finally, the Prohibitory Act (1940) banned all prison commodities from interstate commerce.[9]

Limiting the market for prison commodities had the desired effect of reducing the scope of commodity production in prisons. Figure 5.1 shows one of the effects of the decreased market for prison commodities: a steadily dropping rate of enslavement of inmates in the $SFCP_1$.

As the number of slaves in $SFCP_1$ dropped, so did the total number of inmates enslaved; it was not possible for prison authorities to increase the number of inmates enslaved in the $SFCP_2$ by much beyond 35%, due to the simple fact that only a certain number of use-values are needed by inmates, given a certain level of state welfare and value of slave labor-power.[10] Even if they could increase the number of inmate-slaves in the $SFCP_2$, this would not help the warden to obtain the money necessary to pay prison expenses, purchase commodities, etc., and still make his other subsumed class payments.

In some cases, the number of inmates enslaved in the $SFCP_2$ was raised even though it meant productivity would necessarily fall—with only a limited need for use-values and a limited supply of productive inputs.

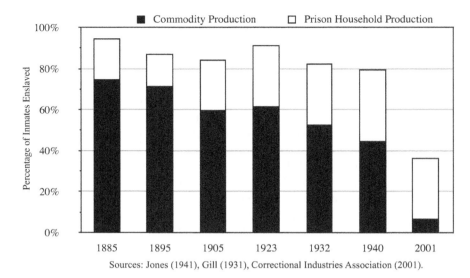

Sources: Jones (1941), Gill (1931), Correctional Industries Association (2001).

Figure 5.1. Percentage of inmates enslaved, 1885–2001.

However, it is also possible to use fewer slaves in the $SFCP_2$ by raising productivity there, however this is likely to occur only if there is a need for slaves in the $SFCP_1$.

As the number of non-working inmates rose, prison slavemasters found it impossible to continue to provide welfare gifts to non-working inmates. The following table shows the real value of commodities produced in the $SFCP_1$ over time, both per slave in the $SFCP_1$ and per inmate.

Notice that although the productivity of each inmate in terms of total value produced divided by total number of slaves in the $SFCP_1$, has fluctuated over this period; if we consider the value produced per inmate in the entire prison population, we see that productivity per inmate has dropped considerably. These numbers indicate the difficulty of providing welfare gifts to non-slave inmates without additional sources of revenue, resulting in a worsening of the crisis written in inequality (60).

The legislative changes discussed above did not abolish prison slavery altogether, but merely limited the market for prison-produced commodities. This means there was little, if any effect on the $SFCP_2$. One effect was to reduce the $SFCP_1$, another was to shift production away from certain production models and towards others. Despite what we assumed above, that the warden appropriates both S_1 and S_2, it was sometimes the case, as today, that private firms appropriated S_1. The changes in the law made it far more difficult for private enterprises to profit in the newly-restricted market

Table 5.1 Value Produced by Inmates, 1885–2001

Year	Total Value	Value per inmate in $SFCP_1$ per year	Value per inmate in total population per year
1885	$459,346,637	$14,888	$11,237
1895	$374,238,520	$9,742	$6,899
1905	$648,652,583	$12,676	$7,539
1923	$751,970,866	$14,517	$8,872
1940	$696,105,748	$8,335	$3,630
2001	$1,800,887,541	$21,080	$1,248

Note: these numbers are based on the assumption that the price of commodities is equal to their value; the numbers above abstract from the amount of means of production used. Sources: Gill (1931), Jones (1941), Correctional Industries Association (2001)

for prison commodities. Many private enterprises ceased their appropriation of S_1. In addition, some of these production forms were abolished, such as the practice of convict leasing. This shift in appropriation largely went from private to state, with state agencies increasing production of commodities for purchase and use by the state itself, as such commodities were, for the most part, the only kind allowed by 1940. In this situation, commodities are produced by one part of the state and sold to another part of the state, which is still common today. For example, from 1923 to 1940, the total number of commodities produced for state use went from $24 million to $47.6 million, in constant 1940 dollars. However, this increase in production for state use was not enough to prevent the total number of prison commodities from falling; during the same period the total value of commodities produced in prisons fell from $63 million to $57 million, again in 1940 dollars. This depicts a shift of the appropriation of slave surplus value from the private sector to the public sector.

This shift in appropriation means that the state became the primary beneficiary of the slave surplus value, rather than the private enterprises. To some extent, this represents the removal of a subsidy that had before been provided to the private enterprises who took advantage of both the state welfare and the cultural, political, and economic forces which produced a low value of slave labor-power to become prison slavemasters and profit thereby.[11]

In 1979 new legislation was passed which began to reverse the historic trend of decreasing enslavement within the $SFCP_1$. This is the PIE legislation discussed in Chapter Four, which lifted some of the restrictions on the market for prison-produced commodities and allowed for a greater degree of private sector involvement in prison slavery. Consequently, since 1979 there has been a general growth of the $SFCP_1$. However, since the number of inmates has grown rapidly during the same period, the total proportion of inmates enslaved has remained low by historical standards. Although the private exploitation of inmate-slaves has grown since 1979, private appropriation is currently a small part of the $SFCP_1$. Most slave surplus value is appropriated by a state agency.

CHANGING LEVELS OF WELFARE AND THE GROWTH OF THE PRISON POPULATION

Another trend occurring during the 20th century is a general rising of the level of state welfare provided to inmates. This trend developed in part due to increased public outcry over conditions in prisons, including high rates of mortality, disease, filthy living conditions, and brutality. Popular books such as Robert Burns' *I Am a Fugitive from a Georgia Chain Gang*, which was made into a Hollywood film in 1932, dramatized the brutal exploitation of prison labor, including the deplorable conditions.[12]

Public awareness of prison conditions led to a changing social climate, which in turn led to a number of prison reforms, including the abolition of certain forms of prison slavery. These forms of labor included, firstly, the chain gang, where inmates were generally enslaved by the state, doing road work and other outdoor labor in chains, overseen by armed guards. Secondly, the convict lease system, in which a private firm was the master, renting inmate-slaves from the state through a competitive bid. Although these kinds of prison slavery had long been considered acceptable—from around the Civil War to about the 1920's (although some states did not officially abolish chain gangs until about 1945), they were now seen as brutal, oppressive, and backward.[13] This change was part of a movement to create humane prisons, which included the view that inmates deserved a higher standard of living, that no human being should be subjected to the filth, brutality, and assorted hardships that were prevalent in prisons at the time.

People were also appalled at the level of corruption that took place in prisons, where kickbacks, bribes, and general theft of public funds were widespread. There was a general demand for an end to the corruption and a reform of the most notorious prisons in the prison system. One result was an overall increase in the amount of welfare provided to inmates, as a way of ensuring a decent and adequate level of consumption in prison—based, of course, on a new understanding in American society of both the conditions that actually prevailed in prison, and what they ought to be. This new understanding also led to an increase in the value of labor-power of the enslaved inmates, because, as argued in Chapter Two, many of the same social, cultural, economic, political and other processes that regulate the level of state welfare also shape the value of slave labor-power, though the two are not the same.

Although the change occurred unevenly over different prison jurisdictions, society's notions about what constituted acceptable treatment of inmates did change. Consequently, the laws and practices regarding the amount of goods and services inmates would be given were changed, resulting in an increase in the state welfare for all inmates, and an increase in the value of labor-power for enslaved inmates.

The number of enslaved inmates steadily fell, decreasing the surplus, particularly in commodity production; at the same time, the level of welfare steadily rose, increasing the magnitude of the crisis faced by prison slavemasters and bringing about the resulting transformation of the prison system. Prison slavemasters could no longer continue to pay these increased welfare gifts from their shrinking surplus in commodity production, and were forced to rely on dramatic increases in non-class revenue from the state, which were part of a series of prison reforms taking place from the 1930's to the 1970's in prisons throughout the U.S.

At the same time another trend was taking place in the U.S. prisons system: a significant increase in the number of inmates incarcerated. As new laws were instituted in the wake of the Civil War to criminalize common behavior among the freed slaves, such as loitering in the street with less than $5, gathering in a crowd of more than three without the supervision of a white person, breaking curfew, appearing in public with a white woman, and so forth, the prison population saw its first rapid increase in U.S. history. Many authors have described this process of regaining control over the freed African American slaves through the imposition of harsh new laws. Inevitably, these laws also trapped some poor whites within their net.[14] Incarceration of African American slaves before the Civil War was relatively rare—the slaves' status as chattel did offer some protection from incarceration.[15]

In the North, new laws were instituted to control both the influx of African Americans as part of the Great Migration to the Northern cities of the late 19th and early 20th centuries, and also to control immigrant and poor working class populations in the swelling urban ghettos of the time, where economic deprivation resulted from unemployment, poverty, discrimination against immigrants and other minority groups, often leading to criminal activity. The history of the 20th century is one of rapidly expanding incarceration, particularly in the second half of the century. Figure 5.2 shows the change in the number of people behind bars in the U.S.

These numbers show massive increases in incarceration, but at the same time other demographic shifts were taking place, including population growth and immigration, which make it necessary to consider the number of persons incarcerated relative to the total population, or the rate of incarceration. The rate of incarceration did increase dramatically, with most of the increase concentrated in the second half of the 20th century. The rate of incarceration remained relatively stable in the period 1939 to 1963, between 136 (per 100,000 persons) and 114, with a low of 100 occurring between 1945 and 1946, but after that the rate of incarceration escalated sharply, for a total increase of 376% since 1945, as shown in Figure 5.3.

The large increase in the rate of incarceration shows that the number of people behind bars increased at a far more rapid rate than the overall population of the U.S. This measure also reflects the increasing burden that incarceration places on state budgets. Economic growth in the U.S. during the 20th century was matched by increases in spending in the state and federal budgets. Nonetheless, such large increases in the number of persons incarcerated relative to the total population are reflected in increased burdens on the state, as more inmates combined with more state welfare per inmate led to larger costs for departments of corrections. Both the increase

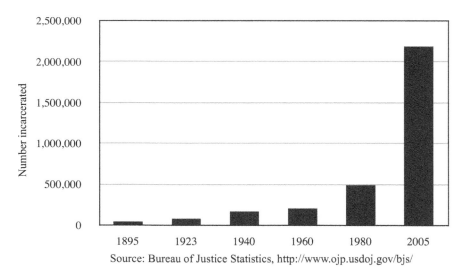

Source: Bureau of Justice Statistics, http://www.ojp.usdoj.gov/bjs/

Figure 5.2 Incarcerated population in the United States.

in the absolute number of people incarcerated and the increase in the rate of incarceration provoked dramatic changes in prison administration.

To some extent, rising costs of incarceration were seen as acceptable, for during the period from the 1930's to the 1970's there was a belief that prisons would be perfected through science, so that in the future, the cost of incarceration would be lower, since inmates who had served their time would be reformed, while at the same time crime would be reduced through the deterrent effect of the modern prison. Criminologists sometimes refer to the period characterized by this view as the "Treatment Era."[16] During this period, the level of state welfare was quite high, as prisons undertook an ambitious program including higher levels of consumption than what had been provided in prison in the past, educational, therapeutic, and vocational training programs were also provided by the state.

An important reason for this change was also the increasing political activity of inmates and their advocates. Inmates increasingly challenged the prison system through the courts, demanding their rights much more intently than in the past. Many inmates began to view themselves as political prisoners rather than merely criminals, based on the perspective that the poverty, unemployment, racism, and other forms of oppression which shape law enforcement and incarceration are political. Increasing political activity by inmates, including books, both by inmates and about them, led to greater visibility of inmates and prisons, which in turn led to a greater concern with inmate treatment, including the level of welfare in prisons

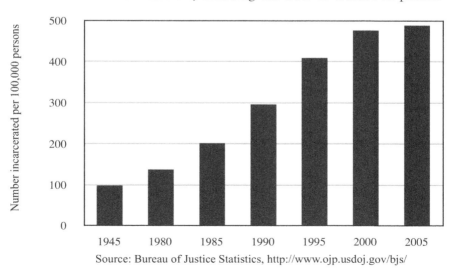

Source: Bureau of Justice Statistics, http://www.ojp.usdoj.gov/bjs/

Figure 5.3 Rate of incarceration, 1945–2005.

and the kind of programs which would help inmates to overcome criminal behavior.[17]

The Treatment Era view of prisons was shaped by the ascendancy of modern liberalism. As Keynesian economic policies were designed and implemented to regulate the overall economy, the idea of the state as the steward of society reached wide currency. The prison was an extension of this idea, where the power of the state reached its apogee. Rather than allowing prisons to be minimally-managed environments where the survival of the fittest was the only real rule, prisons were gradually transformed toward the ideal of order, regimentation, and rehabilitation. Punishment was seen as counterproductive, and criminality was more often viewed as a societal failure rather than an individual one. Prisons mirrored the modern welfare state, with large sums going to inmate education, rehabilitation, therapy, and other programs. During this time work reached a low point, where the majority of inmates did not work, and where prison labor played a far less significant role politically, economically and culturally than it had in the past in many prisons.

The conservative attack on liberalism played a major role in the end of the treatment era, and the transformation of the prison system toward a far more punitive focus. Conservatives argued that we don't know what causes crime, but we do know how to incapacitate criminal offenders: isolate them from society in prison. Conservatives argued that prisons 'coddled' criminals with easy sentences that did nothing to deter criminal behavior. An important part of this ascendant conservatism was an attack on the welfare state, through an attempt to discredit transfer payments to the impoverished. Hand in hand with the attack on welfare was an attack on idle prisoners. Increasingly, arguments appeared which asserted that inmates should work, on moral as well as economic grounds.[18] The success of these arguments was part of a new build-up of the $SFCP_1$, although as history shows it has not yet reached anything close to its former level in terms of the proportion of inmates enslaved.

PRISONS, CLASS, AND RACE

Another major trend in the 20th century is the struggle for racial equality; this struggle has shaped, and been shaped by, prison slavery in many ways. Many authors have argued that racism is rampant in U.S. prisons.[19] Others have argued that severe racial biases exist in law enforcement and the court system. Others have shown that the criminal justice system is biased against those with low incomes, who not only cannot afford adequate defense attorneys, but are disproportionately targeted by law enforcement and given harsher, longer sentences than those with high incomes.[20]

The class analysis of U.S. prisons put forth in these pages provides a new perspective from which to view these claims, allowing us to construct a new relationship between class processes involving the production and appropriation of surplus labor, and the various cultural, political, social, and physical processes which overdetermine the modern construction of race.

The above has shown that enslavement in prisons exists for approximately 36% of the current incarcerated population of about 2 million people. Prisons are disproportionately populated with African Americans and other people of color. As noted in Chapter One, though African American males are just 8.3% of the U.S. population, they are 64.4% of the incarcerated population.[21] Although inmates are not enslaved on the basis of race, one cannot ignore the confluence of escalating incarceration of African Americans and slave exploitation.

Racist notions of criminality and the history of slavery in the U.S. no doubt play a role in making enslavement of many African American men socially acceptable. Race may also have been a factor in the decline of the treatment era, which occurred at a time when the struggle for civil rights took a militant turn, with Black Muslims, Black Panthers, and other radical and militant groups becoming increasingly organized and active within and without prisons.[22] Events such as the race-related prison riot at San Quentin, the kidnapping, brainwashing and trial of Patty Hearst by violent revolutionaries, the bloody prison uprising at Attica in 1971, the killing of students at Kent State by the National Guard, the riots marring the Democratic National Convention in 1968, and other events marked the era as a time of violent revolutionary activity, in which race played a significant role.[23] Many young activists at the time argued that prison would be the source of the revolution that would bring down capitalism, racism, and imperialism.[24]

Some authors have persuasively argued that there are important linkages between racism and rising levels of incarceration occurring in the 20th century. The civil rights struggle of the 1950's and 60's, with increasing visibility, militancy, and sympathy of rising numbers of people, especially young people, signaled the success of movements to undermine the political, economic, and cultural conditions of existence of racism. Contemporary historians have focused attention on how reactionary forces within the U.S. government reacted to these movements, such as the FBI Counterintelligence Program (COINTELPRO) which actively sought to infiltrate, disrupt, and destroy movements which were considered to be revolutionary, including a large number of African American groups which organized to end racism. Marable (2000) argues that the FBI and other government agencies used entrapment, assassination, planting of evidence, and other strategies to neutralize individual leaders and organizations.[25] Lusane (1991) argues that the legal and cultural changes of the 1980's which produced the War on Drugs—itself part of a massive increase in incarceration during the 1980's—was partly a response to the threat of movements which sought to end racism.[26]

The destruction of these movements led to a re-securing of the conditions of existence of racism. In terms of economic conditions of existence, there was rising desperation and poverty in the inner city, leading to increased crime, drug addiction, and other problems. Culturally and politically, the 1980's produced a new wave of intolerance, led by President Reagan and other conservatives who sought to dismantle the civil rights legislation and affirmative action, effectively increasing racism by arguing that it no longer existed, hence the laws which were designed to contain racial injustice were no longer needed.[27]

Racism has transformed the prison population, dramatically increasing it through the incarceration of vast numbers of African American males and Chicanos.[28] This has fed into the re-creation of a modern aspect to racism, which is its association with criminality. While the argument that race ultimately determines criminal behavior can be traced back to the American eugenics movement of the early 1900's, such ideas had faded from the bounds of polite conversation and acceptable discourse by the 1970's. With books such as *The Bell Curve* (1994), and *Crime and Human Nature* (1985), the argument that criminality is nearly synonymous with 'nonwhite' status was given new vigor, finding a receptive audience in a society with a rapidly escalating fear of crime.[29]

Racism is a powerful social force supporting the rise of incarceration and the enslavement that follows it. Racism has led to tolerance for the escalating use of incarceration as a punishment for all kinds of crimes, even non-violent crimes of poverty and desperation, such as low-level thefts, drug use, and so forth. The association of criminality with blackness has led to a certain amount of social acceptance of high rates of incarceration for African Americans.

Prison slavery may also act to increase racism, as class conflicts among slaves, between slaves and inmates, and between inmates and prison authorities are expressed along racial lines. One example is the prison strikes, unionization efforts, and other mobilizations of the 1970's and 1980's organized in part by Black Muslim prisoner organizations. These attempts to address some of the horrors of prison slavery—as well as other brutal aspects of prison life—were undermined by prison authorities who exploited racial and other sorts of divisions between inmates.

* * * *

As we have seen, the class dimension of prison life has been affected by the various changes in the prison system over the course of the 20th century. As changes in incarceration rates, demographic trends, laws, the social context of imprisonment, and economic events, have occurred, prison slavery has gone through several transformations, from widespread enslavement at the turn of the 20th century, to a dramatic reduction of enslavement during the mid-20th century, with certain forms such as convict leasing and chain gangs being abolished, to the current, tentative buildup of slavery at the end of the 20th century and beginning of the 21st.

The common thread in these changes is the brutal exploitation of inmates as slaves. Early in the 20th century, people reacted to the horror of prison slavery and demanded the abolition of certain of its excesses, such as leasing and chain gangs. Unions fought successfully to curtail prison slavery, fearing the competition. As the rate of incarceration rose, increasing costs dramatically, while at the same time the public became increasingly aware of what is taking place behind the walls, the prison was transformed, seeking a humane, impersonal face while continuing to exploit inmates as slaves, but in a different form. Rather than being subjected to the traditional forms of hard labor, such as road building, quarrying stone, farming, and so forth—all public forms of labor often done specifically to humiliate inmates—now inmates performed modern factory labor. While the scale of such production was smaller than the prison industries of the past, it steadily increased throughout the 1970's until today. At the same time the prison system expanded tremendously, leading to massive overcrowding. The practice of placing two inmates in one small cell became commonplace as state budgets were strained to accommodate the massive inflow of new inmates. States began to more vigorously promote prison slavery as the way out of their dilemma—politically, the fear of crime made it undesirable for a politician to appear soft on crime, but economically, few states could pay for their addiction to incarceration, so the answer became the expansion of prison slavery.

The preceding section has focused on the effect of social, economic, and cultural changes on prison slavery. Next we will consider the effects of enslavement on the enslaved, and how prison slavery affects society in general.

Chapter Six
Consequences of Prison Slavery

THE CONTRADICTORY NATURE OF PRISON LABOR

We do not assume that the specific tasks which are done by inmate-slaves are essentially negative or destructive to inmates or society. Rather, it is presumed that prison labor, even if it is slavery, has many contradictory effects and consequences. Depending on an observer's point of view, the effects of prison slavery may be seen as positive or negative. It is my own view that prison slavery is, on the whole, unfair and exploitative; prison slavery runs contrary to American ideals of justice, freedom, and basic human rights. For these reasons, a transformation of the class processes in prison away from exploitation would be positive for both inmates and society. However, other observers may see the situation differently, seeing reform and rehabilitation rather than exploitation and enslavement.

Thus we have two related problems—one is that different observers may see the same processes as positive or negative, as according to their point of view. Second, each observer may attach different weights to these positive and negative features, so that on balance, one observer finds the practice to be more positive than negative, while another finds the reverse. Of course, these issues plague all quantitative discussions which seek to weigh the "pros" and "cons" of a given social process, so the lack of a definitive assessment of prison slavery should not be seen as exceptional.

In arguing that prison labor is slavery, we do not imply that inmates should not work. Marxian theory focuses on the role of exploitation in shaping society; writers in the Marxian tradition argue that exploitation is often to the detriment of human development and happiness. Marxian theorists argue that eliminating exploitation may ultimately benefit everyone in society.[1] However, this does not imply that no one will have to work, or that surplus labor will not be performed. What it does mean is that the labor process, and class processes that are involved in it, are transformed, so that those who produce surplus labor are also those who appropriate the surplus labor.[2]

Prison is a setting which involves deprivation. Prison deprives inmates of liberty, of the freedom to move about, associate with family and friends as one chooses, of privacy, of personal property, of hetero-sexual relationships and physical intimacy, of control over ones' person, of ones' independence, and sense of oneself as a self-sufficient being, of the autonomy necessary to create a meaningful existence. A major part of creating a meaningful existence is ones' work.[3]

If a person's ability to do work, to be productive, to create something of value, is taken away, then he or she is deprived of something important, perhaps even necessary. The individual is deprived of the ability to become self-actualized, to learn about his or her own abilities, perhaps achieving excellence in them—through this process a person matures and develops. It is a great cruelty to deprive people of work, for the simple reason that work is never inherently one thing, it is never simply "toil and trouble," as Adam Smith famously argues, but is also development and fulfillment.[4] Labor is a complex, contradictory totality. In an evocative passage, Marx discusses Smith's negative view of labor:

> 'Thou shalt live by the sweat of thy brow!' was Jehovah's curse that he bestowed upon Adam. Adam Smith conceives of labour as such a curse. 'Rest' appears to him to be the fitting state of things, and identical with 'liberty' and 'happiness.' It seems to be far from Smith's thoughts that the individual, 'in his normal state of health, strength, activity, skill, and efficiency,' might also require *a normal portion of work*, and of cessation from rest. It is true that the quantity of labour to be provided seems to be conditioned by external circumstances, by the purpose to be achieved, and the obstacles to its achievement that have to be overcome by labour. But neither does it occur to Smith that the overcoming of such obstacles may itself constitute an exercise in liberty, and that these external purposes lose their character of mere natural necessities and are established as purposes which the individual himself fixes. The result is the self-realization and objectification of the subject, therefore real freedom, whose activity is precisely labour . . . Really free labor, the composing of music for example, is at the same time damned serious and demands the greatest effort . . . Instead of speaking of a sacrifice of rest, one might speak of a sacrifice of laziness, of lack of freedom, of unhappiness—in fact, *the negation of a negative condition* . . . Work is a positive, creative activity. [5]

The above passage seems directly relevant to prisons, where inmates are given copious amounts of "rest"—especially in the highest security areas of the prison—and this clearly does not result in the "liberty" or "happiness" for the inmate. The passage seems to suggest that it is reasonable to conceive of inmates as being alienated not only by their participation in prison slavery, but by their inability to engage in labor. Recall that in many American prisons, there are waiting lists for employment in prison slavery, especially in commodity production, where the master's provision is far higher in relative terms than in prison household production. We should not interpret inmates' apparent desire to work and to be productive, as a desire for enslavement per se.

While it is cruel to deprive people of work, it is also clearly cruel to force people to work, to make them work at tasks they hate, or at tedious, repetitive tasks that dull the senses and the mind of the worker. Prisoners have often been subjected to these forms of labor historically, such as the endless staircase, the crank box, and other forms of pointlessly hard labor. Inmates have also been subjected to industrial labor processes that are mindlessly repetitive, so that they learn no useable skill that could allow them to compete with free workers as the result of their enslavement.

Prisons have engaged in both forms of cruelty described above—forcing inmates to perform hard labor as slaves, and taking away inmates' opportunity to labor. This leads to a contradiction where inmates are alienated by becoming inmate slaves, if such an option is available—recall that in some jurisdictions, all fit inmates are subject to enslavement. If inmates are enslaved, they are alienated from the products they produce, from themselves as autonomous beings, and from others through the class conflict that arises between producers and appropriators (in this case, slaves and masters). If inmates are not enslaved, they are alienated by being cut off from the ability to be productive, to achieve self-actualization through work.

A scene from the classic prison film *Cool Hand Luke* (1967) illustrates the dual nature of labor in prison. The film shows the inmates working on a road, in the blazing southern heat, under the watchful gaze of armed guards. The inmates normally work as slowly as possible. One day an inmate, Luke Johnson (played by Paul Newman), begins to work hard, and some of the other inmates quietly try to get him to slow down, as it makes them look bad. He refuses, and the others must keep pace. He is smiling and laughing, talking about building the whole road in a day; clearly, he is enjoying the process of his "hard labor." The other inmates begin to join in, and together they establish a hard, but enthusiastic rhythm of work. The guards are clearly uncomfortable; they are used to their captives being dispirited, not energetic, but there is nothing the guards can do to prevent it—the inmates are doing exactly what they were told to do. They accomplish their goal, and are flushed with the joy of their success. They took a form of labor which was intended to subjugate, and made it their own, excelling in it for the pure physical satisfaction of swinging a pick and lifting a shovel, as well as the satisfaction of accomplishing a goal. In the process, the work becomes their pleasure rather than their torment, and they are enervated by the feeling of self-determination that they gain. This illustrates the complexity of any labor process, and the ultimate subjectivity of labor. However, this illustration should not be read as a denial of exploitation and alienation.

Marx argues that labor performed under exploitative conditions may be alienating, producing in the individual an estrangement from himself and others. Yet preventing an individual from working at all is also alienating, for it keeps the individual from developing her capacities, from truly knowing herself as a human being. Prison labor has this contradiction but it has rarely been addressed as such.

It is precisely this same contradiction of labor that is seen in the phrase "Arbeit macht frei" (work makes one free) which some anonymous Nazi penned above the entrance to Auschwitz concentration camp. Perhaps this phrase was merely designed to make the captives believe that if they worked hard they would be released. Perhaps it is intended to encourage those trapped within the camp to lose themselves in work, as a means to freedom within.

Contemporary prison managers speak of advantages of an inmate work force. Inmates are always on time, they take no vacations, and the best of them work with a passionate intensity that is unmatched by free workers.[6] This suggests that inmates' freedom can only be realized through an utter absorption into the work itself, where concentration is focused on the task at hand, and incarceration vanishes. The wretchedness of prison—the oppressive rules, the deprivation, the daily dehumanization—may serve to create more efficient slaves.

Perhaps because of the politics surrounding prison labor, those entering the debate over its effects on society have not seen both the positive and negative aspects of prison labor. Those who are supportive of prison labor stress only the positive aspects. Those who argue against prison labor tend to stress only its negative aspects.[7] To say that prison labor is contradictory, involving both positive and negative aspects, does not doom us to irrelevance. On the contrary, we are liberated from the various dogmas too often present in the debate over prison labor and slavery.

Arguing that labor is contradictory, that it involves both positive and negative aspects, does not prevent us from seeking to reduce the negative aspects and increase the positive aspects—on the contrary, an admission of complexity allows us to be more honest about the prospects of improving the conditions of labor, including both the class and the non-class dimensions of labor.

THE CONTRADICTORY EFFECTS OF PRISON SLAVERY ON ENSLAVED INMATES

Thus far, we've mostly been focused on the relationship between the producers and appropriators of surplus labor in prisons. We will now turn to the relationship between prison slavery and the society as a whole. We will begin by considering the various effects of prison slavery on inmates. We expect that each inmate may be affected by enslavement in a unique way, and that the effects will always be a mix of positive and negative.

Several writers have argued forcefully that prison labor has positive effects on inmates. These arguments echo the position of much of the mainstream penological literature. While there are many critics of prison labor, they tend to be outside the mainstream, as it is represented by most major journals, books, testimony before Congress, and so forth.[8]

Reynolds (1996), for example, views prison labor in such an overwhelmingly positive light that he even defends the 19th century practice of convict leasing. Most historians view convict leasing as a shameful and barbaric enrichment of a few private entrepreneurs that came at the expense of tremendous cruelty to inmates, high mortality rates, corruption, and fraud. In fact, no serious historian of convict leasing offers a defense of the practice. In criticizing Oshinsky's view that convict leasing "would disgrace the South," Reynolds argues that the rate of incarceration in Mississippi was about the same as the nation as a whole. This is a spurious comparison, for what is at issue is not the overall rate of incarceration, but the rate of *exploitation* of the inmates, the comparison between the surplus and the necessary labor inmates performed, and the question of whether or not this exploitation resulted in the inmates receiving substantially worse overall treatment. Since Reynolds does not use the concept of surplus labor, he has no way to evaluate the claim that inmates are exploited (as slaves or otherwise) and so he points to the irrelevant rate of incarceration.

Reynolds (1996) also argues that prison labor reduces inmate idleness, and gives inmates a means to financially pay restitution for their crimes as well as reduce the cost of their incarceration to taxpayers. Many state agencies charged with prison industries argue along similar lines, claiming that prison labor reduces security problems in prisons, due to inmates being less idle, and therefore fewer conflicts break out. Some of these conflicts result in violence, which may endanger correctional employees.[9]

The argument that prison labor may aid the security of an institution does not conflict with the argument that prison labor is a form of slavery. It simply hints at the contradiction of labor discussed above, namely that the denying a healthy individual the ability to engage in productive activities, including labor, can be as great a cruelty—albeit a different kind of cruelty—as enslavement or some other form of exploitation. Additionally, it is in principle quite difficult to know whether in fact enslavement of inmates results in less violence within the prison.

As discussed in Chapter Two, it may be that slave exploitation does not reduce violence in correctional institutions. In other words, while prison slavery may indeed solve the problem of inmates being bored and cut off from labor (a potential venue of self-development), it may also encourage violence, as class conflicts between inmates, correctional officials, and slaves resulting from prison slavery may take the form of violence. The fact that slaves must be separated from non-slaves in many prisons due to repeated conflicts attests to this.

Many advocates of prison labor have argued that participation by inmates in what is seen here as prison slavery reduces the likelihood of inmates returning to prison after their release from prison, in other words, the likelihood of inmate recidivism. The implication is that prison slavery plays a role in rehabilitating inmates. Many of these arguments are anecdotal, but some studies have been done looking at the relationship between prison slavery and the rate of recidivism. One study, due to its prominence in the literature, deserves further discussion here: the "Post-Release Employment Program" (PREP) study, co-authored by Saylor and Gaes (1992), (1995).

Saylor and Gaes find a positive relationship between prison slavery and lower recidivism, based on a study of some 7,000 inmates who were released from the federal prison system over several years. As noted in Chapter One, most researchers who have studied the relationship between prison slavery and recidivism have found no clear relationship between the two.[10] Thus the findings of Saylor and Gaes deserve some scrutiny.

There are three clear methodological flaws in the Saylor and Gaes study. The first is the use of an unusual definition of recidivism. Most studies define recidivism as the proportion of inmates released from prison who violated parole or committed a new crime (these are not the same) and were returned to prison within a given length of time, e.g. one year. These studies do not distinguish between an ex-convict who commits a crime one month after release from one who commits a crime 9 months after release. In both cases, the individuals have clearly returned to criminal behavior. Some studies do consider differently parole violations, and actual crimes.

Saylor and Gaes define recidivism as *survival time*, or the number of days released inmates last before being arrested and convicted for a violation. The authors find that survival time is increased by nearly 20% by participating in what is here understood as the *SFCP*. This finding suggests the authors would define as favorable, for example, the case of an inmate who commits a crime 36 days after being released as compared to an inmate who commits a crime 30 days after release. The latter case is a 20% increase in survival time, but by any reasonable measure, both should certainly be considered failures at rehabilitating the inmates, as both clearly undertook criminal behavior soon after being released. Is it possible that Saylor and Gaes make this unusual departure from the literature in order to conclude that prison slavery rehabilitates inmates?[11]

The second methodological problem with the Saylor and Gaes study concerns the way inmates are placed into groups. In an experiment involving a population, any experiment which seeks to determine the effect of a particular cause on the population must form two groups, an experimental group, which is exposed the cause, and a control group, which is not. Saylor and Gaes' experimental group contains inmates who were enslaved in the $SFCP_1$, or who received occupational training.[12] The problem is that the inmates are not placed in the groups randomly. Rather, the inmates must apply for a "job" as a slave in commodity production. The inmates must not have any disciplinary infractions. As Maguire et al. (1988) argue, this introduces *selection bias* into the study, for the most obedient inmates are selected for prison commodity production, leaving out the more troublesome inmates. It seems likely that the inmates who are approved for enslavement in commodity production are more likely to be those who have made an internal decision to rehabilitate themselves, and hence these inmates may well have a longer survival time. Since there is a selection mechanism, it is possible that this selection mechanism is responsible for any differences between the groups. Of course, whether the 'rehabilitation' of the freed inmate-slaves stands up to the economic pressures of life as an ex-convict over the long term is a separate question.

Since Saylor and Gaes use data from the federal inmate population, it is quite likely that the inmates in the control group participated in the $SFCP_2$, as it is mandatory for all able-bodied inmates who are not in high security areas of the prison in the federal system to work. The number of inmates deemed unfit for labor is 10%. Thus, the Saylor and Gaes study does not directly deal with the effects of prison slavery per se, but only the effects of prison slavery in commodity production. This issue results from

Saylor and Gaes' lack of consideration of class. Because they see only commodity production as "prison labor," they miss the effect of enslavement in
the $SFCP_2$.

The final methodological flaw in this study is its essentialism. The
study posits an essential relationship between participating in prison commodity production and increases in survival time (which is then read as a
success at reducing recidivism). Other elements of prison life, or of inmates'
personal lives are ignored, including the class dimension. No doubt one
reason these other dimensions of inmates' lives are ignored is because statistical regression analysis becomes impossible with too many independent
variables, particularly if there is some relationship between them.

It seems clear that an inmates' participation in prison slavery may
increase or decrease the rate of recidivism, depending on how 'recidivism'
and 'participation' are defined. The focus here is on the class processes
occurring in prison and the effects this may have on the larger society, of
which the question of recidivism is only a tiny part. The above concerns
are noted here only as an illustration of the complexity of the relationship
between prisons and society, and the pitfalls of seeking to attribute a simple,
unidirectional causality between prison labor and the social readjustment,
rehabilitation or reform of inmates after being released.

Many prison labor advocates, including the appropriators of prison
slave surplus labor, argue that prison labor teaches inmates the value of
a hard day's work, and hence it builds character, or gives inmates good
work habits that will then help them to adjust to the labor market outside
prisons. No research that I am aware of has attempted to test any of these
propositions, nor is a coherent argument advanced for why enslavement
should make those enslaved enjoy labor rather than teaching them that
labor is something one is always forced into, something to be despised and
avoided by any and all means, including criminal activity. No doubt different individuals learn different lessons from being enslaved.

Similar to the issue of the effect of prison labor on recidivism, this
argument posits that prison labor contains an essence, which is that it will
always unambiguously transform inmates into disciplined workers. This
perspective is different from that developed here, which sees every process
as having a variety of contradictory effects.

Reynolds (1996) argues that prison labor provides a method for
inmates to pay part of the cost of their own incarceration, while a portion
of their labor may also go towards compensating victims or society at large
for the damage done by their crimes. Many states have followed Reynolds'
argument and have instituted a victim fund, where a portion of the master's
provision granted to inmate-slaves is placed.[13] Some inmates complain that

money is deducted from their master's provision even if they committed a crime where no one was victimized, such as drug possession or sale, prostitution, tax evasion, and so on.

Deductions from the master's provision may also be used for room and board payments, which may be used to offset the cost of incarceration. In some cases, the money collected from the deductions from the master's payment goes into the state's general fund. While using a portion of inmate slave labor to pay victims of crime may be positive and warranted for some cases, certain crimes (such as murder) are beyond restitution. This may introduce a measure of inequality into the process of restitution.

Paying for one's incarceration is a troubling paradox, a punishment that is, in a sense, doubled. First in the coin of deprivation, then in the coin of labor. These critics tend to view incarceration as a failure of society to provide adequate employment for all persons, therefore when inmates are forced to pay for their own incarceration, it is a case of punishing the victim.[14]

It is impossible to say that either the individual or the society at large is wholly responsible for criminal behavior, as many complex factors shape and relate both individual choice and societal structures. With that said, it may be quite positive for some individuals to be able to work to pay restitution, as a way of repenting for their crimes. However, it seems likely that any positive rehabilitative "penance" would only occur if the inmate chooses to undertake such labor.

This is a complex issue, for although financial restitution may be fitting for certain crimes, such as theft or fraud, money alone cannot ameliorate the suffering that criminal victimization causes. Criminal acts cause a breach in trust; voluntary restitution may be part of a healing of that breach.

It is not my intent to argue against restitution as a method of rehabilitation for inmates and an attempt to heal the damage that criminal acts cause. However, it is certainly not the case that restitution can only occur through enslavement. The desire for justice, for repentance, should not be used as a cover for slavery. In fact, the fact that restitution is part of a regime of prison slavery may well undermine its salience as a form of repentance.

In the introduction to Chapter One, it was argued that prison slavery and the exploitation which occurs therein may lead to inmates becoming angry, which may be expressed in the form of violent crime. It was argued that inmates are subject to the stigma of incarceration, which limits legitimate job opportunities for former inmates, which may lead to their participation in criminal activity, where a variety of class processes take place.

Prison slavery may produce a unique form of alienation in inmates. In order to examine this thesis, we must consider the concept of alienation more closely. In a famous section of *The Economic and Philosophical Manuscripts of 1844*, Marx argues that the system of wage labor and private property produces alienation in three forms. First, there is alienation in the form of a separation of the worker from the object he has created, which is appropriated by another as a commodity. Thus the producer is separated from the product of his labor. The worker must psychologically separate himself from the activity in which he is engaged. Second, there is alienation in the sense of the labor process itself becoming purely instrumental for the worker. That is, labor is not performed either for the joy of the activity in and of itself, nor for the immediate need which it fulfills, but in order to receive a wage, with which the worker can then proceed to buy commodities which fulfill his or her needs. Third, there is alienation in the sense of workers being separated from the appropriators of their labor, that the interests and desires of workers may be altogether different from those who benefit from the surplus workers produce. This is one source of class conflict between the producer of surplus labor and the appropriator.[15]

Marx's concept of alienation has had a wide influence, affecting such fields as anthropology, philosophy, economics, political science, sociology, and history. Marx's argument is not focused so much on how individual workers *feel*, but a tendency, a kind of general description of a process that occurs in modern societies. Though Marx does not make this argument in this work, it seems consistent with Marx's overall epistemological framework to conclude that alienation is one process among many, that may well be counteracted or increased by other forces in society. Though Marx does not refer to slavery specifically, it seems likely that enslavement produces alienation for the same reason that wage labor does. In fact, the alienation of enslavement may be more severe, due to the different social, economic, and cultural processes which overdetermine it.

Sociologists sometimes use a different concept of alienation than that described above. One such concept defines alienation as a subjective feeling of powerlessness, vulnerability, isolation, loneliness, lack of support, or despair. Others describe the concept as one of normlessness, in the sense of an ambiguity about what individual behavior is considered appropriate. This may lead to a feeling of self-estrangement, where the individual feels separate from himself.[16]

Although this concept of alienation is substantively different from Marx's use of the term, focusing more on the individual psychological dimension than on structural forces and economic processes, it is reasonable to say that the two are connected. For example, the alienation produced by prison slavery may produce feelings of powerlessness and despair in inmate-slaves. It is likely that the alienation Marx describes is more acute in prison, for the simple reason that inmates are alienated from the appropriators of their surplus labor by the fact that the appropriators are not inmates. In the case of prison household production, the warden is the appropriator, and the warden is a figure who bears substantial responsibility for the caging of the inmate-slaves.

It could also be the case that slave exploitation creates in the inmates a kind of objectification which is particularly painful since instances of the slave class process are relatively rare outside prisons. It may be, in other words, that through the unique exploitation in prisons, the inmate is transmogrified into a non-person, a dehumanized object, merely a criminal.

In one study, Silberman (1995) considered the relationship between alienation and violence in prison. Alienation was measured by inmates' level of agreement with these survey statements:

I sometimes do things I don't like to do just to get along with other inmates.

I sometimes do things I don't like to do just to get along with the staff.

The staff runs this institution and there is little the inmates can do about it.

If they, try hard, most inmates can make parole before mandatory release.[17]

Notice that in the statements above, there is no mention of labor, or the workers feelings about those who appropriate their surplus labor. This is purely a measure of how powerful or in-control the individual inmate feels, based on an Internal/External Scale developed by a psychologist and a sociologist.[18]

Silberman found that prison inmates who have a greater level of alienation also have a greater level of expressed hostility toward staff and correctional officers. The highly alienated, hostile inmates were also found to be over twice as likely to have assaulted another inmate than the less alienated, less hostile inmates.[19] Silberman concludes that alienation (again, defined as a subjective feeling of powerlessness) is "one of the most important contributors to violence among inmates."[20]

Though Silberman lays considerable stress on alienation as a cause of prison violence, he has little to say about what may cause the feeling of powerlessness, and does not directly consider inmates' participation in prison slavery. In practical terms, it may be impossible to separate kinds of alienation and their sources with any precision. Individuals themselves may not know exactly why they feel a particular feeling or even why they undertake a given action. No doubt there are many reasons why inmates may feel alienated or powerless.

Inmates may feel alienated by their explicit separation from the rest of society, both physically, due to their confinement in a prison, and discursively, due to their categorization as a separate and reprehensible kind of person, a criminal. If it is the case that alienation is related to crime and violence within prison, it would make sense that such a relationship would also be present outside prisons, for people outside prisons may also be alienated by being separated from themselves and others due to their production of commodities, or due to class conflict owing to their exploitation, or in the psychological sense because they feel powerless to change their lives.

One of the main predictors of violence is violent behavior in the past. If inmates' enslavement produces alienation, which then tends to lead to violent acts, this may represent patterns of behavior that repeat after inmates are released from prison. As Chapter Two has shown, inmates receive substantial state welfare, which forms their subsistence while incarcerated. This state welfare is intertwined with the caging of the inmates. Although it is legally required that inmates be provided with a minimum level of subsistence, the warden is designated as the provider of this subsistence, and may place inmates in a lower category of state welfare, by placing them in segregation.

Welfare is support by the state. The granting of state welfare to inmates plays into socially constructed (and gendered) notions of what it means to receive support from the state, or from another person more generally. The receipt of such support is generally associated with a state of childhood, motherhood, old age, or infirmity. Receiving state welfare is not in accord with the social understanding of manhood prevalent in the U.S., which involves strength, independence, and self-reliance. A large part of this construction of maleness involves the ability to be financially self-reliant.

Male inmates may feel emasculated by receiving state welfare. These inmates may be tortured by the very consumption that is guaranteed to them. They may greatly desire employment, even if it involves enslavement. Thus we have a seemingly contradictory result—that inmates often want to work, they want to maintain a self-image of productivity, hard work and self-sufficiency, even if their sustenance is still largely paid for by the state welfare payments and the labor of other inmates. As a result, it may the case that in prisons not working is subjectively worse than being enslaved.

As prisons have become increasingly expensive to operate throughout the 20th century, the level of resentment of many citizens about the position of inmates has risen. Although most inmates feel the pain of incarceration, they still receive substantial state welfare. Prisons have often been understood as punishment due to the taking away of a person's liberty. While taking away certain aspects of individual liberty—the freedom of mobility, freedom of association, and so forth—prison may actually enhance other aspects of individual liberty. Inmates are in one sense liberated from many economic concerns: inmates will have a roof over their head, clean clothes, and three meals a day regardless of what they do. They have a measure of security in their basic needs being met that is difficult to find in American society outside prisons.

As prisons have grown in size and expanded the number of services they offer, as well as expanding the level of security and the number of people behind bars, the costs of the prison system have skyrocketed, and begun to seriously compete with other social services, like schools, maintenance of roads and infrastructure, etc., the level of anger has risen, and along with it calls to make the inmates work to offset the costs of incarceration. This process has acted to rapidly expand prison slavery.

At the same time, the presence of state welfare causes a greater level of anger at inmates, as if it were their fault that this bizarre situation exists that seems so alien to the rules of American life, that in attempting to punish an individual, we may well raise that individuals standard of living. Even if that particular individual was materially better off before entering prison, their standard of living remains above that of millions of poor people in America—all those who go to sleep at night hungry, cold, without proper clothing or shelter.

Enslaved inmates may also be angry about their enslavement. Evidence of such sentiments is not difficult to find—there are many accounts of prisoners refusing to work, speaking out, rioting, and going on strike, always at great personal cost, as most of these "troublemakers" will spend periods in segregation, where they will live with a lower level of state welfare; they may have time added to their sentences; or they may be transferred to other prisons far from friends and family. One inmate, working in furniture production, stamped the inside of cabinets with the message: "This product produced by slave labor." He was eventually caught and spent two months in punitive segregation in solitary confinement.[21]

Most inmates are not willing to make such extreme personal sacrifices for their beliefs. Indeed, many inmates prefer not to think about their own exploitation, as a way of avoiding getting angry about a situation which they feel powerless to change. Psychologists have shown that there are two common responses to the anger which is often caused by oppressive situations. One is to turn one's anger outward, towards the perceived cause of the oppression. Another is to turn one's anger within, perhaps by accepting the oppression as penance for a guilty conscience, or in the hope that it will somehow be beneficial in becoming a better person. The latter path accepts the situation as legitimate or at least unchangeable, and seeks to adapt to it, while the former seeks to change the situation.

Both of these approaches have the possibility of turning into violence. In the case of turning the anger outward, it is straightforward that one might violently confront the oppression directly and seek to end it. The second approach, turning the anger within, can lead to violence if one is not successful in adapting to the situation. One often denies the reality to which one cannot adapt, that seems outside one's control, insisting that nothing is wrong, even when it is, trying to put it out of one's mind. Yet the oppression is unchanged, and the anger still exists. One often blames oneself for not being able to deal with the situation, considering oneself weak, and coming to hate one's weakness. Often this is acted out in self-destructive actions such as drug and alcohol abuse, self-mutilation, purposefully engaging in dangerous activities, depression, suicide attempts, and other behaviors which are all quite common among inmates—particularly inmates in solitary confinement.

Another path that the anger may take is towards others regarded as weak, because they are reminders of one's own despised weakness. Thus anger directed within quite frequently is eventually directed outward, though usually towards a substitute for the true target. This may well be one reason why there is so much violence within prisons, much of it directed at those who are seen as low on the prison hierarchy—sex offenders, homosexuals, snitches, anyone who refuses to fight, etc. An atmosphere of violence naturally breeds more violence, as inmates seek to protect themselves from threats. Thus the tendency within every prison for inmates to produce homemade contraband weapons.[22]

It is difficult to make generalizations about the large, complex, and ever-changing inmate population in the U.S. Not every inmate becomes filled with rage during their prison sentence. It could be a very small minority—but it does seem to be common response to prison life, especially from young people. At any rate, this kind of reaction need not come from every inmate to have a profound effect on the prison. A small number of enraged individuals can create an atmosphere of fear and tension in an entire prison. A prison is a small world. Once a violent atmosphere has been created, it is difficult to change, especially when many correctional officials see no problem with inmate-on-inmate violence. Some encourage it by setting up conflicts between rival gangs.[23]

If prison life and the violence within it shapes inmates, the next question is, what is the effect on society as a whole? The most obvious connection is that most of these inmates will be released into society, with the alienation and violent habits they learned in prison. These inmates may well commit violent acts. Many will not, preferring to abandon the habits that may well have been necessary to survive prison but are less helpful outside prison. Those that do act violently may well do so in ways that are unlikely to be reported as crimes, such as domestic violence towards a lover, wife, or children. Thus they may become a part of an epidemic of domestic violence that is admittedly largely committed by men who have never served time. It is clear in the case of domestic violence that patterns of behavior are often formed in the children who so often witness or experience the abuse. These patterns tend to repeat in the schoolyard and later in life. Inmates are only part of a larger story, and the slave class process is only one experience of the many that shape inmates' lives, but the ranking of factors in terms of their significance is not the aim here. Indeed, such a ranking of factors by importance is impossible, due to the number and complexity of the factors involved.

Prison slavery is unique among other forms of the *SFCP* throughout history in that it often exists within, and perhaps creates, a violent and sustained climate of resistance on the part of those enslaved. Compared to prisons, Antebellum slavery carried on with relatively low levels of violence on the part of the slaves as well as the masters.[24] Of course, this does not excuse the horrifying exploitation and brutality that did take place in the American south, nor is it meant to provide a comfortably revisionist view of American history. It merely shows that the *SFCP* in prisons is unique in producing violent resistance, even when the odds of success are very low.

Inmates revolt for many reasons, from anger over crime policy, to parole policy, to education, religious freedom, and so on. However, a constant theme of prison uprisings in the 20th century has been prison labor. Inmates have attempted to form unions under the most extreme conditions of observation and resistance from the administration.[25] Inmates have staged strikes, walkouts, sit-ins, even performed organized self-mutilations. In a famous case in Louisiana, a group of 37 inmates all severed their Achilles tendons to protest work conditions and brutality within LSP at Angola, crippling themselves to draw attention to their protest.[26] Riots and disturbances at prisons from San Quentin, CA to Attica, NY have involved the conditions of labor.

Prison slavery (and its unique conditions of existence) combines with other social and political processes in prison to produce an atmosphere of extreme violence. It remains to be seen how this atmosphere of violence inside prisons affects the larger society outside prisons.

PRISON SLAVERY AND AMERICAN CULTURE

One mechanism of transmitting the violent culture of U.S. prisons to the outside society involves the unique subculture of the prison and its particular relationship with the larger culture taking place around it. Of course the two influence each other in many complex ways.

Prison occupies an important cultural space, as seen in the many movies, television shows, books, and other cultural expressions feature prisons. Prison icons like jailhouse tattoos, gang signs and prison slang have gained much more visibility in recent years. Prison clothing has had a profound influence on Hip-hop clothing—the baggy pants, slung low on the hips originally referred to the ill-fitting state issue that inmates received, and the lack of a belt—for security purposes—meant the pants often rode low. During the 1990's prison culture had such an influence on U.S. culture that the orange jumpsuits became a fashion statement.

Sociologists refer to the process of American culture being influenced by the prison subculture as "prisonization."[27] An important reason that prison has become such an important cultural icon is through the same process of objectification of criminals that forms a condition of existence for slavery in prisons. Criminals are seen as less than human, as monsters or beasts.

We are exposed to thousands of messages that teach us to fear and hate criminals. Many people list fear of crime as one of their primary concerns, even in rural areas where actual crime rates are low. The media, through heavy coverage of violent crime, feeds such fears.[28]

At the same time criminals are often presented as heroic figures who rebel against society's arbitrary rules, thus playing into a common theme in American cultural iconography: the rugged individual. Films like *The Wild Ones*, and *Rebel Without A Cause,* literature like Kerouac's *The Open Road*, and many others have focused on the rebel or outlaw who heroically defies society's rules and laws in order to find true freedom and self-expression.[29]

American culture has an important place for rebels. This almost guarantees that anyone who is consistently and prominently represented as a model of what *not* to do, will in fact become a model for the behavior of many people—especially young people. Thus the cultural process of objectification that forms a critical condition of existence for slavery within prisons, and hence is intimately connected to the *SFCP*, leads to violence in society through the antithesis of the construction of the criminal—the romanticization of the outlaw—and the emulation of the heroic outlaw's personality and violent way of life. The founder of the notorious Crips gang writes that when he was a kid, prison had a strong allure—he saw prison as a "gladiator school" where a man could go to prove his toughness against other men.[30]

The cultural process of objectification that serves as a condition of existence of slavery at the same time undermines prison slavery by leading to violence both inside and outside the prison walls. The way we conceive of prisons and construct the meaning of the term "criminal" supports prison slavery, causing us to turn our back on slave exploitation. This may actually lead to more violence than the prison system itself seeks to prevent through deterrence and incapacitation of offenders.

LEGITIMACY AND SOCIAL ORDER

One effect of prison labor concerns the effects on inmates, another effect is more broad, and focuses on the perceived legitimacy of society, and the relationship between this sense of legitimacy, and crime. In the construction of a social order, certain forces uphold it, and what forces undermine it. Slavery, being contrary to contemporary notions of freedom, justice, and human rights, tends to undermine the legitimacy of the social order that supports and seeks to increase the enslavement of inmates in U.S. prisons.

Inmates are subjected to a form of labor universally viewed as unfit for human beings, on moral grounds. No contemporary theorist argues that slavery is morally acceptable, rather it is condemned by all, and viewed as an evil system that is a backward, primitive, vestige of a more brutal era in history. It is seen as a shame to American history.[31] The consensus on slavery is reflected in international law and agreements which forbid slavery.[32] Indeed, freedom from slavery is regarded as a basic element of human rights.

For slavery to be acceptable for inmates while it is clearly unacceptable for others, one is obliged to conclude one of the following:

1. Prison labor is not slavery.

2. Inmates do not deserve the same moral consideration due to other human beings.

The former would be in contrast to the argument developed thus far, perhaps obtained by using a different understanding of what is slavery than that which is produced here. This is the path taken by most proponents of prison labor. As argued in this study, to overlook or attempt to describe prison labor as something other than slave exploitation is simply not tenable if one is cognizant of the economic, political, and social forces which shape prison life. However, most proponents of prison slavery prefer instead to consider only the features of prison labor which seem positive. In general, the literature on prison labor does not clearly explain what is slavery, and hence cannot systematically show why prison labor is or is not slavery. Nor do most arguments on prison labor make any attempt to unravel the various social, economic, cultural, and political processes that shape prison life and the labor process.[33]

The latter conclusion, that inmates deserve slavery, would be in contradiction to established U.S. law and practice, which views inmates as having the same rights of citizenship as do non-inmates. In the eyes of the law, then, inmates are as human as non-inmates. As this study has argued however, inmates are frequently demeaned by a culture that sees criminality as more than the breaking of the law. Criminals are seen in this discourse as beasts, as animals, as monsters, terms which seek to place the criminal outside the circle of humanity, constructing him or her as utterly alien.[34] Some criminals have committed acts which anyone would describe as monstrous, but to uniformly place all inmates in the same category as those who have committed the worst violent offenses is essentialism, the belief that those who have broken the law all share the same evil criminal essence.

A proverb says, "Let the punishment fit the crime." Would the punishment of slavery be a fitting one to all of the crimes that lead to incarceration? Perhaps people would agree that violent crimes like murder, rape, assault, and so on deserve harsh punishments. Perpetrators of such violent crimes, however, are the minority in today's prisons.[35] Do non-violent drug users deserve the same punishment as rapists? What about people who have committed petty theft? Do individuals who turn to crime in large part due to poverty and desperation deserve enslavement for their economically-motivated crimes? Are these criminals really monsters?

A proponent of punitive slavery might reply that no one made the person commit the crime, they chose to do so, and hence they ought to be held accountable. This seems sensible. People must be responsible for their choices. However, such reasoning would lead us to support the institution of voluntary slavery, where an individual could sign a contract which would enslave him, perhaps for a certain time period. He would then be obligated to follow his master's commands for that time period, much like indentured servitude. Should we allow individuals to choose to enslave themselves, perhaps in exchange for money? Does the fact that we currently do not give individuals the right to make this choice mean that we infringe upon individual liberty?

Over the last several hundred years, systems of crime and punishment in Europe and the Americas have changed significantly. Corporal punishment, public executions, and public shaming were all commonplace in the 17th century. Incarceration often involved torture, exposure to disease, malnourishment, and severe abuse by other inmates and guards. Over time, corporal punishment and the public aspects of punishment have been replaced by incarceration, which has been modified and reformed continually, to reduce and place limitations on the pervasive abuse of inmates. One of the guiding principles of this reform process has been the idea of society's standards of decency, our shared ideas of what constitutes acceptable treatment of a person being punished. As society has developed and the rule of law has replaced the use of brute force to protect individuals, the notion of constitutes, for example, "cruel and unusual punishment" has changed. In the late 18th century, a public whipping would be considered an acceptable punishment for a crime. In the 21st century, that is no longer the case.

Perhaps this change in punishment in the result of a more defined idea of international human rights. Perhaps it reflects progress toward a more just world, where cruelty and barbarity are no longer tolerated. The Geneva Convention on the Treatment of Prisoners, which prohibits signatories from engaging in torture, and the International Slavery Convention of 1926, which prohibits signatories from enslaving people, are examples of this process of definition of human rights in an international context.[36]

For whatever reason, we have deemed many corporal punishments morally and socially unacceptable. Similarly, slavery is the one form of labor that we have seen fit to outlaw—in fact, it is the only form of labor that is specifically mentioned in any Constitutional Amendment. In large part this also reflects society's changing moral standards.

As we have shown, there is ample reason to reject both conclusions that prison labor is not slavery and the conclusion that inmates are deserving of slavery. This means that the practice of enslaving inmates is not legitimate. For if prison labor is slavery, and if inmates deserve the same right to not be enslaved as other people, then there is no justification for prison slavery.

There is an important connection between the perceived legitimacy of the prison system and its authority to make and enforce rules. In other words, it may be the case that individuals comply with rules they feel are legitimate, even if they disagree with the rule, or it is against their individual self-interest to comply with it.

In his analysis of the causes of violence in prison, Bottoms (1999) argues that the level of violence in prisons depends on the level of social order in prison, or the creation of a system of rules and practices which lead to orderly compliance.[37] Bottoms argues that prisons establish a social order through three basic methods. The first of these describes individual *instrumental* or goal-oriented behavior. Here compliance would be based on the set of incentives or disincentives that surround certain behaviors, based on the model of an individual as a rational actor. Second, individuals may comply due to *constraints,* perhaps on their person, or restrictions of access to their goal, or based on structural constraints. This refers to actual limits on individuals, so that their compliance with rules is based on their inability to break these rules.

Finally, compliance may be based on what Bottoms calls the *normative* dimension, that is either individual normative acceptance of a given rule or based on the perceived legitimacy of the rule. If individuals believe in a given law or norm they do not require incentives or constraints to follow it. An example would be attending church—individuals do this not because they are forced to or because they are given incentives to do so, but as an expression of the belief that going to church is the right thing to do.

On the other hand, individuals may accept norms because of their legitimacy rather than an acceptance of the norm per se. For example, an individual may follow the law not because she agrees with it, but because she believes that the law is legitimate, for example, because it was created in a manner that the individual believes in, such as by democratically elected representatives.

Thus the question of what determines legitimacy is a key issue for explaining why individuals follow rules, especially in the case where they could realize a gain from non-compliance, and where no structural constraint prevents them from doing so.

Beetham (1991) argues that the criteria in Table 6.1 must be met for power or authority to attain legitimacy:[38]

According to Beetham, power gains legitimacy through conformity to its own rules, which gives authority a legal validity. However, such rules must also be given justification by reference to shared beliefs. An example of this is the phrase "In God We Trust" on U.S. currency, a reference to the Christian religion—a belief shared by many Americans at the time of the adoption of the phrase for use on coins in 1864.[39] Finally, legitimacy rests on the consent of the subjects of a power.

Table 6.1 Beetham's Criteria for Legitimate Power

Criteria of legitimacy	Corresponding form of non-legitimate power
1. Conformity to rules (legal validity)	Illegitimacy (breach of rules)
2. Justifiability of rules in terms of shared beliefs	Legitimacy deficit (discrepancy between rules supporting shared beliefs, absence of shared beliefs)
3. Legitimation through expressed consent	Delegitimation (withdrawal of consent)

If any of the above conditions are not met, then the legitimacy of power is threatened. As the table notes, if there is a violation of the rules, the first condition is not met. If the justification for rules is not in accordance with shared beliefs, or if these shared beliefs change while the rules remain the same, the second condition is violated.

If subjects refuse to grant their consent, or if subjects withdraw their consent, the third condition is violated, and legitimacy is threatened.

In the case of prison slavery, we find that the first of these conditions is met. As was shown in Chapter One, prison slavery has legal validity based on the 13th Amendment. Thus, laws regulating prison slavery have a strong Constitutional basis.

However, in terms of the second condition, the justifying of prison slavery, we find that the shared belief is that slavery is morally wrong. No proponents of prison slavery seek to make their case by arguing that inmates deserve to be enslaved, based on some set of common beliefs about crime and punishment. Every proponent of prison labor argues that it is in fact, not slavery, despite the legal validity of slavery in prisons. This itself shows that there is a powerful shared belief that slavery is an unacceptable form of production for inmates or anyone else.

The third condition, that subjects grant their consent, is also not met. Inmates do not grant their consent to prison slavery. Participation in prison slavery is usually mandatory. Where it is not, structures of coercion exist that effectively make individual choice irrelevant. As argued in Chapter One, the labor-power of inmates is owned by the head of the department of corrections. Though not all departments of corrections are able to make full use of all the labor-power which they own, due to limited industrial capacity, this does not equal the consent of inmates.

Prison slavery fails to meet Beetham's criteria for legitimacy. Since prison labor is widespread, existing in nearly every prison in the U.S., we can conclude that the prison system in the U.S. engages in an illegitimate form of treatment to inmates, one that violates our shared understanding of basic human rights.

A prison system that violates human rights loses its authority, which partly stems from its perceived legitimacy as a institution designated to carry out the punishment and rehabilitation of inmates. This lack of legitimacy threatens the normative dimension of the prison system. In other words, inmates no longer follow the rules based on a view of the legitimacy of the rules. Inmates may continue to follow certain rules if the rules are congruent with the individuals' own beliefs—this is the meaning of normative acceptance. However, inmates are less likely follow rules which are not congruent with their own beliefs, because these rules may be seen as illegitimate.

One might think that the issue of legitimacy is rather esoteric, and of limited practical importance in the day to day maintenance of the prison system. Such a view would be incorrect. Legitimacy is a central concern in the prison system.

Bottoms (1999) refers to a major prison riot Manchester Prison, U.K., in 1990. The official inquiry found that the major reason for the disturbance was a widespread sense of injustice on the part of the inmates. This sense of justice or injustice is strongly related to the issue of legitimacy.

In fact, the issue of legitimacy often plays an important role in prison riots and disturbances, indeed in riots outside prison. For example, the Los Angeles riots of 1992 were set off by a widespread sense of illegitimacy of the trial of the officers acquitted of beating Rodney King. Many people felt this acquittal was illegitimate because Rodney King was a black man who was wrongly beaten by white police officers who were motivated in part by racist beliefs. In this case, many observers believed there was a clear violation of the rule that police officers may not brutally beat an unarmed suspect who poses no threat to the safety of the officers, but the finding of the police commission was that no violation had taken place.

In one of the most famous prison riots in U.S. history, the Attica riot of 1971, an underlying factor seems to have been the perceived racial injustice. Black inmates received worse treatment than did white inmates at the hands of a staff of correctional officers who were all white. Inmates saw this as illegitimate treatment, for it contradicted the shared belief in universal human rights.

Since the prison system is one of the main methods of addressing crime in the U.S., an undermining of the legitimacy of the prison system also undermines the criminal justice system as a whole. If individuals feel that the prison system subjects inmates to treatment which is deemed unacceptable, the prison system loses its legitimacy. It can no longer be perceived as an institution that punishes people fairly, with dignity, with the minimum level of respect owed to people. This is partly reflected through the 8th Amendment which reads: "Excessive bail shall not be required, nor excessive fines imposed, nor cruel and unusual punishments inflicted."

There is a long legal tradition of discussion over the issue of how this ought to be interpreted. One ruling argues that the "'basic concept underlying the 8th Amendment' in this area is that the penalty must accord with the 'dignity of man.'" [40]

This reflects the idea that what is considered to be cruel and unusual punishment at one time and place may not be seen differently in another context. It may be that a contradiction exists between the 8th and 13th Amendments, for the 13th Amendment allows 'involuntary servitude' as a punishment for a crime, but this is clearly not consistent with contemporary views that slavery is wrong. To extend the previous argument then, it may be that prison slavery lacks even the first criteria of legitimacy, which is legal validity.

The prison system would lose its legitimacy in the same regard if torture were a widespread practice, if inmates were hung by their arms and beaten, or given electrical shocks, or bound in restraints for long periods for punitive purposes. If torture were legal (which it is not), and yet was widely seen as being wrong, as being against the beliefs that were generally shared in society, then the situation would be similar to the case of prison labor.

Since the prison system represents a visible and important part of the criminal justice system, if the prison system loses its legitimacy, so does the criminal justice system. This may lead people to change their behavior. People may be more likely to engage in criminal activity which does not appear to be detrimental to others, for example, drug related crimes. If the law loses its legitimacy, people are less likely to follow it, which may lead to increased criminal activity.

The preceding discussion has explored the relationship between perceived legitimacy of the prison system, and individuals' propensity to commit crimes. This is not to suggest that legitimacy is the only cause of crime. Economic analyses of crime tend to abstract from social considerations such as legitimacy in favor of a narrow focus on individual decision-making, which stems from individual preferences, themselves exogenously determined. In the interest of concision, this study does not discuss the general causes of crime. We take the perspective that crime is overdetermined by—both the effect of as well as the cause of—many complex, interrelated factors.

NON-EXPLOITATIVE PRISON LABOR

How might prison labor be changed so that it is transformed from the slave class process to some other class process? Marxian theory provides us with some suggestions for a direction of change, though not with the specific details. For example, Marxian theory may not support class transformation which merely moves from one form of exploitation to another. Marx himself praised the abolition of slavery in the U.S. after the Civil War, but argued that the U.S. should go further, abolishing all forms of exploitation. The goal of Marxian theory is communism, the collective production and appropriation of surplus labor by the producers themselves.

It was shown that prison labor is slavery due to its particular class and non-class structure. The class structure has two elements, that the total product of labor is appropriated by the master, and that the reproduction of slave labor-power takes place within the relationship of producer and appropriator. The non-class structure has many different elements, grouped into categories of political, cultural, and economic processes.

In order for the class process to change and be transformed into a non-exploitative one, some or all of the elements of the class and non-class structure must be changed. The class structure must change, so that inmates collectively appropriate their surplus labor. In terms of the non-class structure, inmates must labor on a voluntary basis, free from the coercion of prison authorities, by physical, political, legal, or economic means. Given the unequal power relationship between inmates and correctional officers, it is likely that this area will continue to be a contradiction. The labor-power of inmates must reside in their own ownership and control, not in the hands of the head of the department of corrections. Inmates will always be subject to the power of the correctional guards and other authorities, but this power must be separated from the performance of labor.

The culture surrounding prisons that forms another part of the non-class structure must also be reformed. Inmates cannot continue to be objectified, placed in the dehumanized category of "the criminal"; inmates must be allowed to develop their identities free from the forces currently operating to shape and form that identity into that of a slave.

With regard to the economic aspects of the non-class structure, it may be that the economic incentive to participate in prison slavery could be retained if the other elements were changed; if there is no political authority being brought to bear on an individual, it may be acceptable that the need for a money income motivates an inmate to work. The state welfare might take on a different form, which would transform state welfare from an instrument of slavery in prison household production, to an opportunity for inmates to work together to meet their collective needs, under their own command and control, given a certain amount of resources provided by the state in the form of raw materials and equipment, which the inmates could then decide how best to produce whatever it is they collectively need.

One way that this might be accomplished would be to emulate prisons in the Netherlands, where each group of inmates in a given cell area are given raw materials with which to prepare meals, clean their living areas, and so forth, and must collectively decide who performs labor, and collectively appropriate the products of their labor. Thus the inmates' performance of labor is disconnected from appropriation by the warden of the prison.[41]

A change in one small aspect of this complex class and non-class structure is unlikely to produce a change in the class process. For example, an increase in the master's provision, or in the value of slave labor-power, though it would affect the economic dimension, would leave the others untouched, producing merely slavery with a higher standard of living for the slaves. That may be a positive development in some ways, but it does not transform the class process. What is needed to end prison slavery is a removal of the processes that constitute it. This study aims to begin a discussion of how we might end prison slavery and replace it with a class process that is fair and non-exploitative—however the content of such a class transition must be worked out elsewhere.

CONCLUSION

This study makes several contributions to the literature on the economics of prison. First, the class process of prison labor in the United States at the turn of the millennium is for the first time analyzed and understood from the perspective of the production and appropriation of surplus labor. Indeed, this study offers the first systematic analysis of the industrial organization of prison labor in the contemporary U.S., a fact which underlines the scarcity of studies in the field.

This examination includes both the production of commodities in prison, which has received some attention in the recent literature on prison labor, but also the area of prison household production, which is almost entirely overlooked in the literature. We have shown that the class process occurring in both commodity and prison household producing prison labor is slavery, understood as the slave fundamental class process.

Prison labor is shown to be slavery due to both its class structure, involving the production and appropriation of inmate slave surplus labor, and its non-class structure, including the political, cultural, and economic aspects of both prison life and American culture. The class and non-class structure of prison slavery are mutually related, affecting each other in many complex ways. The analytical focus on class does not imply that class processes are the essential cause of all aspects of prison life; rather the class structure of prisons is seen as one important aspect of prison life among many others. However, the class process of prison labor has never been analyzed, so perhaps it is fair to say that the class process deserves attention and discussion for the light it may shed on other processes taking place in prisons and in society at large.

In the economic realm, prison slavery is supported by a unique form of welfare that inmates receive. This analysis of prison welfare and its interaction with the class processes in prison has never before been systematically examined; this examination may be considered the second contribution of this study. The relationships and interaction of state welfare, slavery, and American society are now visible in terms of their class dynamics, which provides a new understanding of the history of prisons over the last 100 years.

The third contribution is the use of the class analysis to understand in a new way some of the effects of prison slavery on inmates and on society as a whole. We have seen that prison slavery exists in a complex relationship to individuals and social processes. We have considered some of the arguments for possible positive effects of prison slavery, and questioned the assumptions upon which these arguments rest. We have considered some possible negative effects of prison slavery in some detail. A new perspective has been brought to the literature on the legitimacy and desirability of prison slavery.

We have seen that the way criminals are understood in American society—as dehumanized objects, more like beasts or monsters than human beings—serves as a condition of existence for slavery in prisons, and also constructs inmates as heroic rebels who courageously affirm their individuality by breaking the law. Inmates are both lionized and demonized by the same cultural process that fetishizes their status as criminals, focusing on the commission of criminal actions as the essence of an inmate's being. This essentializing of inmates contributes to violence and social disorder by promoting the idea that individual expression and freedom is tied to criminality and violence.

This study has also shown the illegitimacy of prison slavery. Though legal under the U.S. Constitution, prison slavery cannot be justified through shared belief, nor is it the result of collective consent of inmates. This causes the criminal justice system to lose its legitimacy, through its association with, and promotion of, slavery for inmates.

When the criminal justice system that is viewed as illegitimate, people lose respect for the law. If the criminal justice system was seen as legitimate, people may follow laws with which they disagree, even when there is no immediate sanction for disobedience. An example is voting law in Australia, where it is illegal to not vote. Citizens may be fined for failure to vote in an election. As a result, Australia has a very high rate of voter turnout, over 90%. As a point of reference, American elections are often below 50%. Part of the reason Australians follow the law mandating their casting a ballot is because the legitimacy of the law, as it is based on a shared belief in democratic participation. If Australians were asked to vote in an election where there was only one candidate, perhaps because the candidate had managed to seize power over the electoral process, it is likely that fewer would vote, because the law would not be seen as illegitimate—rather than reinforcing democratic values, the law would now be undermining them.

This study has shown that prison labor has many complex effects on other aspects of prison life and society. Thus we should pause at arguments which uphold prison labor as the solution for the problems that plague the criminal justice system, from over-incarceration, to ballooning correctional budgets, to rates of crime and violence. We have shown that prison slavery may well act to increase crime and violence rather than acting to reduce it.

Given that prison labor is a form of slavery, that it is illegitimate and exploitative, the justification for widespread use of this form of slavery in the United States is without basis. It is time to re-evaluate prison labor, to think about how we could transform the slave class process into one that is free of exploitation. It may be that ending the enslavement and exploitation of those we are taught to despise the most may result in a step towards real rehabilitation. If so, such a move would not only potentially save billions of dollars in future criminal justice costs, but also move us one step closer to a truly just society.

Notes

NOTES TO THE INTRODUCTION

1. http://www.ojp.usdoj.gov/bjs/correct.htm
2. Donziger (1996)
3. For a good discussion of the vast differences between U.S. crime policy and that of other countries, see Currie (1998, 12–36)
4. Donziger (1996, 48) See also Gold (1990) From 1976 to 1989, corrections has increased more rapidly then any other spending category, increasing 95%. For comparison, during this same period spending on higher education decreased 6%, while spending on highways declined by 23%. See also Stephan (1999) for an analysis of the period 1990–1996.
5. Miller (1996), Currie (1998), Parenti (2000), Donziger (1996)
6. Correctional Industries Association (CIA) Handbook, 2001
7. We cannot faithfully reproduce this debate here, but for an excellent discussion of the ways in which prisons have been viewed in reference to crime see McLaughlin and Muncie (1996, 157–248).
8. Few reliable statistics exist to measure to incidence of sexual assault within prisons. See Donaldson (1990), (1993), (1995) and Scacco (1975), (1981) for a discussion of rape behind bars. Donaldson (1995) estimates the total number of sexual assaults in prison each year to be a staggering 290,000.
9. See Rosenblatt (1996, 92–99)
10. Donziger (1996, 99–129) Miller (1996, 48–88), Tonry (1995), Marable (2000)
11. The rate of incarceration for African American men in 2001 was 4,848 per 100,000, for Hispanic men, 1,668 while for white men the rate is 705. Men make up the vast majority of the incarcerated population. Bureau of Justice Statistics, http://www.ojp.usdoj.gov/bjs/prisons.htm.
12. This does not include being arrested and spending a night in jail, and thus is limited only to actual sentences, many of which are over 1 year. http://www.ojp.usdoj.gov/bjs/correct.htm. See also Bonczar & Allen (1997). Because of these and other staggering figures describing the incarceration

of minorities in the U.S., Wacquant (2002) argues that mass incarceration serves as a mechanism of both economic domination and social control of African-Americans.

13. See for example, Burton-Rose (1998, 102–133), Parenti (1999, 237), Rosenblatt (1996, 61–72) Individuals from all over the political spectrum have worried about the relationship between prison labor and slavery. Consider the following testimony to Congress by Rep. Charles E. Schumer: "We must be very careful about any new scheme that would say we should farm out prisoners to private enterprises. Farming out prisoners has had a long and sordid history in this country and abroad. In some cases prisoners have been abused as slave labor." See *House of Representatives* (1996, 3) Though Schumer relates his concerns to the past, he suggests that such concerns may also be currently relevant.

14. One exception to this is the work of Mancini (1996), but his argument concerns a historical form of prison labor, not a contemporary one; his argument is explored in Chapter 5. Another exception is Bales (2005, 57–59), but Bales' discussion of prison labor is brief, and his conclusion is ambiguous; he calls prison labor 'a particularly thorny question.'

15. As we will see, there is a strong case to be made that despite the waiting list, prison labor is not voluntary. The above point merely illustrates the complexity of the compulsion of labor in prisons.

16. For an insightful and concise explication of the important differences between a class structure and aspects of markets, such as commodities, the sale of labor-power, etc., see Wolff's contribution to Callari et al. (1995, 394–401)

17. As we'll see, there is an important distinction between owning a person's labor-power—defined as the ability to work in a given amount of time—and owning his person. In prisons, the former is owned, but the latter is not.

18. These forms of appropriation, while important, do not affect the labeling of the class structure as the slave fundamental class process. Appropriation of surplus labor is explored in Chapter 4.

19. Bales (2000) explores several instances of slavery in the modern world, showing that although slavery has been marginalized, it has not disappeared from human society; of course, where one sees slavery is a product of one's definition of slavery.

20. Van der Veen (in Gibson-Graham, Resnick & Wolff, eds. (2000, 121–141)) argues that prostitution may include the *SFCP* or other class processes, depending on the particular setting. While Marxists have explored the connections between aspects of capitalism (especially the reserve army of labor) and crime, none have explored the ways in which surplus labor is produced and appropriated within various types of criminal activity. The classic is Rusche and Kirchheimer (1939), who argue that a society's response to crime is powerfully shaped by the economic structure of the society, including the relations of production, and the relationships between power-wielding elites and the masses. Their most famous point is that criminal activity

and the repression of such activity tends to increase as capitalism enters a period of crisis and decrease during periods of capitalist expansion. Other works in the Marxian literature on crime and class include Garland (1990), Reiman (1984), Lichtenstein (1998), Rosenblatt (1998, 16–46), Sellen (1976), and Wright (1973).

21. Of course, the *SFCP*, being a contradictory totality, may also act to *reduce* crime and violence. Due to the complexity at play in these social processes, there is no way of determining which effect is greater. This study focuses on the role of the *SFCP* in fostering crime and violence because this view is not well-represented in the literature or discourse on prison labor. Most of the studies done on the relationship between prison labor and recidivism, or the conviction of an inmate for a crime committed after his or her release from prison, finds little if any correlation between inmates participation in prison labor (what is conceived here as the *SFCP*) and their criminal behavior after their release. See Maguire et al. (1988). There is one prominent exception to this, the PREP study, Saylor and Gaes (1992), (1995), which is discussed in Chapter 5.

NOTES TO CHAPTER ONE

1. Much of the following discussion is built on the work of two theorists and it seems appropriate to acknowledge that debt here. Feiner (1981), (1988) theorizes the slave class process of the Antebellum south, showing the complex dynamics at play between planters, merchants, banks, and factor houses in the early 19th century. Feiner's work stresses the multiplicity of related social, economic, physical and political processes that mutually constitute both each other and the class processes that form her entry point. Class is consistently defined by surplus labor, and classes are seen as ever-shifting and internally heterogeneous groups that often have conflicted interests. Feiner's nuanced story of the competing class and non-class interests and obligations that shaped the south makes important advances in the theory of slavery.

    Weiner (1999), (2003) uses the work of Feiner and others to take the theory of class in a new direction, showing how a slave class process can exist within a special, privileged site of production in American society—professional baseball—while the rest of the economy is largely capitalist. Weiner delineates class processes from other social processes such as the exercise of power, the accumulation of wealth, racism and social status. Each of these processes is different from the production and appropriation of surplus, and hence none can be used to define the slave class process. Weiner argues that analyses of slavery that are constructed in terms of property—where slavery is seen as the consequence of ownership as opposed to class—slavery appears at certain social sites (which may or may not include the performance and appropriation of surplus labor) and not at others. Weiner argues that the exercise of power is also different from class processes, while the two may shape each other in important ways.

2. At least one prominent economic historian does find Antebellum slavery to be "a form of capitalism"—see Fogel (1992a).Fogel refers to slavery as a form of capitalism only in passing, and offers no real argument for his collapsing of these terms. However, it seems clear that what Fogel considers to be 'capitalism' is the presence of markets, communications and transportation infrastructure, widespreadinformation about prices, and rapid technological growth, all of which says nothing about the question of who appropriates surplus labor. Hence, Fogel's definition of slavery and capitalism is different from those employed here.

3. The phrase 'mode of production' is often associated with an essentialist reading of Marx which argues that a given mode of production contains two elements: the forces of production, or the level of technology and productive capacity, and the relations of production, meaning the relationship between the laborers and the owners of the forces of production. Generally, either the forces or the relations of production are considered the 'essence' of all other aspects of a society, including the cultural institutions, the politics, religion, and so on. See, for example, Sweezy (1968). In contrast, the term 'class structure' indicates a different reading of Marx, in which class is defined through the relationship to the surplus produced at a given site of production, and is seen as one factor continuously shaping, and being shaped by, other social forces in a complex dialectical process of contradiction and continual change. While the debate over essentialism and overdetermination underlies the discussion here, its full scope is outside this study. See Resnick and Wolff (1987, 109–163) Althusser and Balibar (1968)

4. Davis (1984, 8–9). Bloch (1975) , Finley (1980), and Kolchin (1987), (1993) also discuss the difficulties in defining slavery.

5. Fierce (1994, *x*)

6. Anderson (1974) quoted in Finley (1980, 71).

7. Resnick and Wolff (1987), following their reading of Marx, define a five fundamental class processes: capitalist, feudal, slave, ancient (or 'individual') and communist. The first three are exploitative, while the latter two are not.

8. See Fraad, Resnick and Wolff (1989), (1990) and (1994) for a discussion of the class processes occurring within households.

9. See Bloch (1975) for an interesting account of how the form of slavery that existed in the Roman era was gradually transformed into feudalism, and the struggles that accompanied this transformation.

10. For a discussion of some of the theoretical aspects of the communist class process as applied to the Soviet Union, see Resnick and Wolff (2001) in Gibson-Graham et al. (2001, 264–290)). A more detailed discussion can be found in Resnick and Wolff (2002, 3–50)

11. See Cullenberg (1992) for an argument that presents a similarly thin definition of socialism; DeMartino (2000), (2003), offers a brilliant discussion of this definition in terms of class justice; Burczak (2004) also offers an excellent intervention on this topic.

12. Genovese (1967), (1976). Feiner (1981) shows that Genovese is sometimes inconsistent in his use of class, at times defining class by ownership, at

other times defining class by power, as in "the ruling class," while at other times, using geographical notions of class, such as urban and rural or south and north. Feiner argues that this lack of theoretical consistency in defining class weakens Genovese's argument and allows non-Marxian concepts to be inserted into his argument. Feiner's argument reveals the importance of the way that class is defined for both the logic and conclusions of the theory.

13. Patterson (1982). For a detailed and insightful analysis of Jamaican slavery, see Patterson (1969).

14. Bales (2005, 55)

15. Bales (1999, 280)

16. Bales (2005, 57)

17. *Ibid.*, p. 58

18. Is there a country in the world that has a criminal justice system that is completely free of racial, gender, ethnic or class bias? If so, it is not the U.S., Europe, or any of their colonies, as Abu-Jamal (1996), Beresford (1997), Cole (1999), Currie (1998), Donziger (1996), Dyer (2000), Fierce (1994), Free (1996), Marable (2000), Mauer (1999), Miller (1996), Parenti (1999), Reiman (2001), Rosenblatt (1997), Rusche & Kirchheimer (1939), Tonry (1995), Waquant (2002), and Wright (1973) have convincingly shown.

19. Bales (2005, 57)

20. Bales (2005), (1999)

21. Imagine a situation in which a slaveowner could not put all his slaves to work, for reasons outside his immediate control. Say a third of the slaves do labor, and the rest are simply confined to their quarters by violence. Any of the slaves could be put to work at any time, but not all can work at the same time. The slaves are compelled to perform necessary and surplus labor by a variety of social, political, and economic forces, including the master's ownership of the slaves' labor-power. The master appropriates the whole product of labor, and reproduces the labor-power of the productive slaves. Say the slaveowner receives a payment from the government to support the non-working slaves. The slaveowner uses a portion of the proceeds from his slaves' labor to pay the slaves. The rest of the slaves find their confinement monotonous, and they want income, so they sign up for any 'job' that becomes available. This is essentially the situation in American prisons (it holds for British prisons as well, though this study will not offer a detailed argument to support this proposition). It doesn't much matter how individuals got into this situation—whether through a fair trial, a lottery, a corrupt judge, a swindle, or whatever else—these individuals are enslaved.

22. Bales admits that slavery is difficult to define with precision. He writes that "in defining slavery, we must recognize that, in some instances, some or all of the three dimensions of slavery may exist in practices which we do not define as slavery." Bales (2005, 59) Later in the same work, Bales offers this quote from the editors of Scientific American: "We worry that the study of contemporary slavery is more of a protoscience than a science. Its data are uncorroborated, its methodology unsystematic. Few researchers work in the area, so the field lacks the give and take that would filter

out subjectivity. Bales himself acknowledges all this. As we debated his definitions of slavery, he told us, "There is a part of me that looks forward to being attacked by other researchers for my interpretations, because then a viable field of inquiry will have developed."" (*Ibid.*, p. 87)

23. Fogel and Engerman (1974, 233–234); although Fogel and Engerman seem to give a prominent role to the ownership of labor-power, this does not imply that theirs is a class analysis along the lines of this study. Since these scholars do not admit to the existence of surplus labor, they cannot very well analyze its production and distribution.

24. Since the money payment detracts from the gains to productivity, the master must determine whether such an incentive is worth its price; it is often the case though, that relatively small amounts of money serve as an incentive in prisons. For a discussion of money payments as incentives for Antebellum slaves, see Fogel and Engerman (1974, 206, 235–243)

25. Because the bureaucratic structure of corrections is hierarchical, and involves those who are higher in the chain of command delegating tasks to others, it is often the case that those who carry out tasks are different from those who bear the ultimate responsibility. In this case responsibility or culpability may be shared, but the ultimate responsibility for the inmates lies in the hands of the head of the department of corrections, then the warden, and then in the hands of the correctional officers with direct contact with the inmates. Because of this, it makes sense to refer to the hierarchy of command within prisons and the bureaucracy that supports prisons as *prison authorities*.

26. See, for example, Genovese (1967), and Meltzer (1993, 3–6). Kolchin (1993, 5) acknowledges the wide variety of forms slavery as taken, and the problem of using a simple definition to encapsulate them, uses the term 'New World slavery' to deal with some of these issues.

27. *Report to the League of Nations Advisory Committee of Experts on Slavery.* (1938, 16) See Bales (2005, 41–51) for a cogent analysis of the history of international agreements on slavery.

28. Bloch (1975), for example, discusses cases of slavery involving the ownership of a person who tilled a plot of land and was required to deliver a payment in kind to his master as a tribute. Here the slave maintains himself, reproducing his own labor-power by growing crops for his own consumption. He must then continue to labor, providing crops for the tribute to his master. Clearly, this is no longer the slave class process, even though the slave is owned. The slave here meets his own needs, produces surplus, but must distribute a portion of the surplus to his master. Marx (1991, 917–950) discusses the development of 'capitalist ground-rent' from this process of paying tribute to a master, then providing rent in the form of labor to a feudal lord, as slavery transformed into feudalism, then providing rent in the form of money, and so on. Marx ridicules the theorists who argue that rent is somehow a 'natural' or intrinsic part of agricultural production, as if rent was a quality of the earth's crust instead of a social relationship which allows another party to either appropriate the surplus labor or claim a share its distribution.

29. Some Marxian theorists refer to this as 'self-exploitation.' See Gabriel (1990a). In ancient Greek and Roman slavery, it seems that slaves were frequently engaged in the ancient class process. See Bloch (1975, 1–27), Finley (1980, 68–80). While neither discusses surplus labor or the ancient class process directly, (although Finley comes close, with a distinction between 'labor for oneself' and 'labor for others') they show that slaves sometimes had their own small enterprises, in agriculture or manufactures, producing of goods and services for the purpose of exchange, and delivering an ancient subsumed class payment to their owners. Finley describes this as a form of rent paid by slaves to their masters for allowing the slave the freedom to run his or her own enterprise.

30. Feiner (1981, 110) Emphasis appears in original.

31. Feiner (1981, 115)

NOTES TO CHAPTER TWO

1. The term correctional facilities includes federal prisons, state prisons, local or county jails, private prisons, juvenile centers, and INS Detention centers. The term refers to punitive institutions where individuals are punished for committing a crime or held while awaiting trial. In this study, "prison" will serve as a shorthand for all these different institutions unless otherwise noted.

2. These two sites probably make up the majority of labor performed by inmates, but do not by any means describe all of the labor that inmates perform.

3. See Weiner (1999, 85) for a parallel discussion for baseball players, whose labor-power was perpetually owned and controlled by their masters as long as they played professional baseball.

4. Prison authorities may appropriate the surplus, or they may grant the ability to appropriate to others. In either case, they do so due to the combination of non-class processes which give them the cultural, political and legal status as the owners of inmates' labor-power (and the products of their labor) in perpetuity. Note the following passage from California: "Every able-bodied person committed to the custody of the Director of Corrections is subject to an obligation to work as assigned by department staff and by personnel of other agencies to whom the inmate's custody and supervision may be delegated. This may be a full day of work, education, or other program activity, or a combination of work and education or other program activity . . . work assignments, in lieu of enrollment and participation in education, vocational, therapeutic or other institution program assignments, may be made with or without the inmate's consent by a classification committee, a staff member designated as an inmate assignment officer, or by any staff member responsible for the supervision of an unassigned inmate" State of California (2002, 37–38)

5. See for example, Burton-Rose (1998, 102–105), Rosenblatt (1996, 61–72).

6. Wright (1997, 3). Prisons generally do not have long waiting lists for *SFCP* jobs in prison household production, a fact which perhaps is due to the

large relative difference in the master's provision in prison household production versus commodity production. This difference is addressed in detail in Chapter II.

7. See Weiner (1999) for an illuminating discussion of the forms of slavery and the *SFCP*. Patterson (1982) also offers a fascinating study of the different forms of slavery, though not in terms of class as defined here. Both authors clearly show the incredible variety of forms of slavery existing throughout history.

8. Pens (1998, 1)

9. For a description of the astounding number of rules that confront inmates in the State of California, a major state when it comes to corrections, see: "Title 15" at http://www.cdc.state.ca.us/. This 516-page document describes all the rules which inmates in CA must follow.

10. See State of California (2002, 67–123) which stipulates that the following "privileges" may be taken away from inmates who refuse to work: family visits, telephone calls except for emergency calls, access to the yard, educational, or recreational activities, special packages from outside the prison, special purchases, reduction of the inmate's ability to buy items at the prison canteen to a maximum of $45 per month rather than $180 per month, and accrual of excused time off. (If inmates participate in the *SFCP* in California, they can accrue time off at the rate of 8–16 hours per month, but cannot accumulate more than 192 hours. Inmates may use this time off if allowed by the work supervisor.) The document also stipulates on p. 249 that refusing to work is a "Serious Rule Violation" on the same level as violence, theft, use of controlled substances, and compromising the security of the facility.

11. Rosenblatt (1996, 92)

12. Pens (1998, 2)

13. While Patterson provides a brilliant discussion of these cultural and ritualistic practices, he does not connect them to the production and appropriation of surplus labor, as his focus is on the power relationships in slavery rather than the class structure. While Patterson at times mentions various forms of production, he does not make production the central focus of his work. However, Patterson's deft analysis does seem to be, if not complementary, then at least not inherently opposed to an economic analysis.

14. Miller (1996, 178–242) offers a penetrating discussion of the idea that the inferiority of criminals is inherited. The classic in this field is Gould (1981).

15. For an insightful discussion of the ways in which criminals have become the "other" and how this has allowed their punishment to become an acceptable social spectacle, see Foucault (1977).

16. Patterson (1982, 96)

17. Patterson (1982, 55)

18. Patterson (1982, 57)

19. Some numbers have specific meanings, such as the number "69" which has sexual connotations, or the number "23" which, for many people, represents the incomparable skills of basketball star Michael Jordan. Numbers

may, of course, have personal subjective meaning for individuals, but they generally lack wider cultural significance. Perhaps the number 09141996 is important to a person, but you would not be able to tell that number to someone else and expect some reaction.

20. See Wright, ed. (1997, 20)

21. See Stack & Garbus, dirs. (1998), Walsh (1998a), Walsh (1998b)

22. For example, see Abu-Jamal (1996), (1997), (2000) Consider the following poem written by an Unknown author (1969):
    Prison is a place where you learn that nobody needs you, that the outside world goes on without you . . .
    Prison is a place where you write letters and can't think of anything to say. Where you gradually write fewer and fewer letters and finally stop writing altogether . . . Prison is a place where, if you're married, you watch your marriage die. It is a place where you learn that absence does not make the heart grow fonder, and where you stop blaming your wife for wanting a real live man instead of a fading memory of one . . . Prison is a place where you wait for a promised visit. When it doesn't come you worry about a car accident. Then you find out the reason your visitors didn't come; you're glad because it wasn't serious: and disappointed because such a little thing could keep them from coming to see you.

23. Burton-Rose (1998, 103). Wright is editor of *Prison Legal News* and an inmate in Washington state. Wright sharply critical of prison labor, arguing that it should be considered slavery. Wright defines slavery as "unpaid, forced labor." However, it becomes clear in the article that the term 'unpaid' refers to low wages as well. Although we are critical of this position for the reasons expressed earlier, we are highly supportive of many of Wright's conclusions and the general spirit of outrage and advocacy of inmates that fuels Wright's discourse.

24. Except in Texas, Arkansas, and Georgia, which do not provide enslaved inmates with a money income. In these states the actual master's provision has fallen to zero; this is discussed in detail in Chapter 3.

25. Some inmates may be able to rely on outside income from family or other sources, but this is a minority of inmates.

26. Such illegitimate sources of income include selling drugs, sex, protection, tattoos, weapons, or other items considered illegal contraband in the prison setting.

27. Douglass (1994). American slavemasters from the Antebellum period often used their slaves' desire for money income to motivate the slaves to perform more intense labor and meet certain production quotas, a point made in Fogel and Engermann (1974a), Fogel (1992a). Fogel and Engermann also argue that the use of economic incentives may have allowed slavemasters to use less force, including less whipping of slaves.

28. In using this term, I'm following Weiner (1999, 28–29).

29. The so-called 'dirty protests' of incarcerated members of the Irish Republican Army provides one example, in which prisoners refused to wear prison uniforms—the clothing of criminals—for they saw themselves as revolutionaries rather than criminals. Some also engaged in hunger

strikes. In essence, they deprived themselves of as much of the state welfare as possible. See Beresford (1997).

30. Welfare payments could also emanate from another institution, group or individual, but is traditionally associated with the state.

31. It would certainly not surprise an economist if a welfare payment changed an individual's supposed trade-off of labor and leisure.

32. Prison labor programs (which do not generally label themselves as slavery) are likely to be criticized by those who see prison labor as slavery (usually for reasons other than class) and believe it is not a just punishment for a crime. For those who believe that criminals deserve to be enslaved, it may not be a problem that these programs operate at a net loss.

33. Marx (1990, 643–668). Though Marx specifically refers to the capitalist class process in these pages, there is no reason why his remarks cannot be applied to slavery or other class processes.

34. The absolute difference in payments may be quite small. For example, in Louisiana, the payments range from $0.04 per hour to $0.20 per hour. However, the relative difference is quite large, as the inmates receiving the highest payments receive 5 times the inmates receiving the lowest payments.

35. Marx (1992, 233–236, 262–267), Marx (1991, 163–169)

36. Cullenberg (1994, 44–48) discusses this and many other aspects of competition in his discussion of the debate over the falling rate of profit in the Marxian literature.

37. Marx (1990, 528). This point was first made by Richard Wolff.

38. Bowles et al. (1986), Bowles (1985), Elster (1983, 227–252), Reiman (1987)

39. Human choice, as embodied in the utility function, is one of three essences in neoclassical theory. The other two are aspects of physical nature rather than human nature, and are technology, represented by the production function, and resource endowments. For an insightful discussion of the both essentialism and the differences between neoclassical and Marxian economic theory, see Resnick and Wolff (1986, 45–47, 120–122)

40. From personal interviews with correctional officials in Pennsylvania, North Carolina, and Texas, June 1999.

41. Wright argues that many prison industries jobs do not offer valuable job training because they are low-skill menial jobs for which there is little demand outside prisons and the third world. See Burton-Rose (1998, 102). Nonetheless, there are some jobs that offer inmates useful vocational training. The extent and availability of such training, while an important question, is outside the scope of this study.

42. There is a strong tradition and discourse within prisons that prison labor is slavery. See, for example, Burton Rose (1998, 101–110), Bergner (1998), Conover (2000), Cummins (1994), Pens (1998), Wright (1997), and Young (2000) for examples of this view. The idea that inmates are slaves is a strong part of prison culture. Admittedly, the view of slavery

circulating in prisons and in theoretical accounts such as those listed above is different from the slave class process described in these pages. However, given this tradition, it is unlikely that inmates are unfamiliar with the idea that working in prisons is slavery, however slavery is theorized.

43. Marx discusses the differences between his unique notion of class as the appropriation of surplus labor and the various theories of value which focus on an individual's utility. These latter theories are sometimes called "subjective" value theories, since they focus on an individual's own subjective reckoning of the value of a commodity rather than on the "objective" determinants of value such as the amount of social labor embodied in a commodity, which of course exists quite apart from any individual person's desire or distaste for the commodity. Unfortunately, Marx's discussion is only in note form, in his little-known work "Notes on Adolph Wagner," written towards the end of his life. See Marx (1996, 227–257)

44. Correctional Industries Association. (2001) *Annual Directory*. In the federal prison system, a far higher proportion of inmates produce commodities than in the state prisons. 18% of the total number of federal inmates produce commodities, which is about 25% of the inmates medically and institutionally fit for labor, whereas the state average is around 5%. However, the total number of federal inmates is only 145,000—far smaller than the state population of 1.3 million—so the overall average is close to the state average. (Both population numbers are 2000 figures. See the Correctional Industries Association *Annual Directory* for more details) See also U.S. House of Representatives (1997, 14), and Federal Prisons Industries Annual Report (2000).

45. Burton-Rose (1998, 101), Jones (1941), U.S. House of Reps. (1997, 14) These figures are also confirmed by my own observations of prisons in North Carolina, South Carolina, Pennsylvania, Louisiana, Connecticut, Florida, Texas, Arizona and New York.

46. There are several states (Oregon and Texas, for example) as well as the federal system which are exceptions to this in that *all* inmates (except those in high security areas and those medically unfit for labor) are required to perform labor—although the class process (fundamental or subsumed) is not specified. Hence, in the federal prison system, there are few non-laboring inmates. In addition, it is possible that inmates may be involved in other class processes. For example, an inmate who produces a contraband weapon and sells it may well be engaged in an ancient class process involving the individual production and appropriation of surplus. Other inmates may be involved in feudal or other forms of the slave class processes, for example in the production and appropriation of sexual services. These other forms of labor and associated class processes, for the sake of brevity, are not examined here. Other researchers are invited to explore the ways in which these other class processes shape and are shaped by various aspects of prison life.

47. The estimate of 4% of inmates being subsumed slaves comes from the assumption that 10% of all slave workers are needed to provide the conditions of existence for slavery. Based on this figure, about 1% of inmates

are subsumed to commodity production, and 3% are subsumed to prison household production.

NOTES TO CHAPTER THREE

1. See, for example, State of California (2002, 34–133) Other states have similar mandates, but California's Title 15 is notable for the level of detail in which inmate rights (including the right to state welfare) are elaborated.

2. This may have been done to provide a cultural condition of existence for U.S. slavery at the time, to create the appearance that a slave society was caring and humane, more like a family than like the cold, calculated capitalism of the north. Other slave societies, for example in the Caribbean, often did not provide welfare to the aged or the young, as there was an abundance of new slaves of prime working age due to the transatlantic slave trade. See Fogel and Engermann (1974a), Fogel (1992a).

3. See Bergner (1998) for a revealing account of how inmates are provided with NCR_{seg} in LSP Angola, Louisiana's most famous maximum security prison.

4. U.S. Department of Health and Human Services. http://aspe.hhs.gov/poverty/03poverty.htm

5. Oshinsky (1996), Mancini (1998), Lichtenstein (1998)

6. Using the term 'value of labor-power' does not imply that the class process occurring is capitalist. This is the value of *slave* labor-power, not the value of capitalist workers' labor-power. In Chapter I it was shown that slaves are not free to sell their labor-power, but this does not mean that their labor-power has no value. The value of slave labor-power is equal to the amount of socially necessary abstract labor embodied in the goods and services which are necessary to reproduce the labor-power of the slave.

7. Marx argues that the value of labor-power is overdetermined by natural, social, and historical processes in a key section of *Capital*, Volume I: "If the owner of labor-power works today, tomorrow he must again be able to repeat the process in the same conditions as regards health and strength. His means of subsistence must therefore be sufficient to maintain him in his normal state as a working individual. His natural needs, such as food, clothing, fuel, and housing vary according to the climatic and other physical peculiarities of his country. On the other hand, the number and extent of his so-called necessary requirements, as also the manner in which they are satisfied, are themselves products of history, and depend therefore to a great extent on the level of civilization attained by a country; in particular they depend on the conditions in which, and consequently on the habits and expectations with which, the class of free workers has been formed." Marx (1990, 275)

8. Inmates participate in the *SFCP* only in either commodity production or prison household production, but not both, due to time limitations and security issues.

9. Fogel and Engermann (1974a, 38–43)

10. These laws are the Prison Industries Enhancement (PIE) program, which is discussed in detail in Chapter 4.

11. Based on observations of prison labor practices and on interviews with correctional officials in NY, PA, NC, AZ, FL, and TX.

12. State of California (2002, 34)

13. *Ibid*, p. 35

14. *Ibid*, p. 82

15. *Ibid*, p. 78

16. *Ibid*, p. 133

17. *Ibid*, p. 132. Interestingly, the document specifies that inmates may not become small capitalists, as they are prohibited from employing or sub-contracting with other inmates. In addition, inmates may only work together under specific conditions. They must have permission, and each inmate "shall be given recognition if the article is disposed of as a gift by or through the institution. If sold, all inmates involved in its production or creation are to share in any profit as determined by the institution's supervisor of the handicraft program." This is interesting because the document seems to specify a communist class structure for inmates in handicraft production. While more details would be needed to make this argument, it remains an intriguing possibility.

18. *Ibid*, p. 191

19. *Ibid*, p. 319

20. *Ibid*, p. 444–446

21. As discussed in Chapter 2, inmates may lose television, visitation, access to the yard, and other "privileges" for refusing to work, which is considered a disciplinary infraction on the same level as assault or theft.

22. It may be the case that the commodity under consideration here (medical services) is offered at a price below what it would be in the general marketplace. For example, the cost of a medical visit may be $50 rather than $5, in which case the commodity is simply one which has an artificially low price (below the value) due to the Department of Corrections deciding to set the price below the value. What is at issue here is not the "correct" price level, but rather the status of the item, which is no longer part of welfare per se. In a larger sense, inmates are still benefiting from the price subsidy, and hence are still receiving welfare, simply less than before. According to some critics, it is common practice to control medical costs by simply denying inmates medical care.See Burton-Rose (1998, 87), Rosenblatt (1996, 79–91, 115–126)

23. Burton-Rose (1998, 64–69)

24. Pens (1995)

25. Burton-Rose (1998, 101). See also U.S. House of Representatives (1997, 14–22)

26. There are a few laws which relate specifically to segregation, limiting the authority of the warden in certain ways, by stipulating a certain amount of time outside the cell, limiting the amount of time an inmate may be placed in a completely darkened cell, etc. See State of California (2002).

27. Such considerations may or may not be important to the warden. In some prisons, the productivity of prison household production is deliberately kept low, in order to ensure the possibility of enough jobs for all inmates. See U.S. House of Representatives (1997, 14) for a statement from the Director of Federal Prison Industries, Kathleen Hawk: "We basically pad, in essence, some of our other work details. In essence, we probably could function with 20 inmates cooking in food service, but in order not to put all that load on Prison Industries, [commodity production] we may be running food service with 30 inmates when 20 could do the work, and the other 10 could really benefit from being in Prison Industries and developing those kind of job skills and work habits . . . There is some magical number, and I don't know what that is yet because we have never had enough industry jobs to be able to balance that off, and that is that we do require *x* number of inmates to do the work that needs to be done in the institution. If all the inmates worked in a prison industry factory, for example, we would then need staff to do a lot of the things we use inmates for." Note that Ms. Hawk argues that only the production of commodities develops 'job skills' while prison household production does not. One wonders what is the special quality of, say, assembling chairs that is so special in developing job skills but is not present in, say, cooking food.

28. Resnick and Wolff (1987, 117–119)

29. Of course, the history of prisons shows that this has often not been the case, with many wardens using their position of power and a frequent lack of accountability to deliver less to inmates in welfare, so that $(NCR_{PROVE1} - PROV_1)$ is a positive term which is kept by the warden as graft. Wardens have also sought to cut other costs in the prison in order to keep the difference, which would be described as $(NCR_1 - Y_c)$. For a modern example, see Burton-Rose (1998, 64–69).

30. See Bergner (1998) for some descriptions of the unofficial benefits staff receive at Louisiana State Penitentiary at Angola.

31. Marx (1981, 506–513)

32. The name for this type of inmate varies from state to state. Some states have stopped using this term because it has connotations of the brutality and corruption of 19th and early 20th century prisons, conditions which many prison authorities would like to forget.

33. The same holds, to an extent, for the individuals involved in the appropriation of surplus labor. These are not necessarily 'bad' people simply due to their positions as slave masters. The analysis focuses on the exploitation inherent within an exploitative system, and does not place individual responsibility for that system solely on the individuals

involved. To do so would give undue privilege to individual choice. At the same time, we are all collectively responsible for the exploitation in society, since we collectively have the power to change society.

34. See Cummins (1994) for a fascinating account of inmate organizing and agitation for better conditions in California prisons.

35. Parenti (1999, 182–210) very clearly elucidates many of these points. Though Parenti's focus is not on the specific class dynamics taking place within prisons, he is a keen observer of political processes. Much of the above analysis is indebted to his excellent work.

36. Parenti (1999, 170–4, 204)

37. It may well be the case that these inmates are enslaved in yet another instance of the slave fundamental class process, producing sexual services which are appropriated by their inmate masters through force or threat of force. There are numerous instances of these inmate slavemasters selling their slaves' sexual services as commodities. While I believe a strong argument can be made for the *SFCP* in this realm of prison life, it is outside the scope of this study.

38. Parenti (1999, 182–4)

39. *Ibid.*, p. 183

40. See Cummins (1994)

41. Oshinsky (1996, 140–141)

42. Personal interview with correctional officials in North Carolina.

NOTES TO CHAPTER FOUR

1. Public Law 96–157 (codified at 18 U.S.C. 1761(c) and 41 U.S.C. 35)

2. CIA Annual Directory (1997, 98)

3. See http://www.pia.ca.gov/piawebdev/pia_board.html

4. CIA Annual Directory (2001)

5. See for example, State of California (2002, 42). This is discussed in Chapter 2 as part of the development of the forces of production, specifically raising the intensity of labor through competition for higher income. The same tactic was used in the antebellum south. See Fogel and Engermann (1974a, 148–149)

6. The federal prison system refers to prison household production as "performance pay."

7. See Burton-Rose (1998), Pens (1998), Wright (1997), Young (2000) The payment of low wages is used by these authors as evidence for the claim that prison labor is slavery. This is both analytically and rhetorically problematic; analytically, the payment of low wages does not define a production process as slavery or anything else. Rhetorically, it seems unpersuasive to argue that the mark of slavery is low wages, since many see the payment of wages as the very definition of capitalism. Marx shows how capitalists continually seek to take advantage of the conditions of the market to pay lower wages. See Marx (1995). See also Chapter 1. A. of this study.

8. In his testimony before Congress, Michael R. Gale, Director of Government Relations for the American Apparel Manufacturers Association, asserts that Federal Prison Industries prices are higher by an average of 15%. See U.S. House of Representatives (1997, 126) Except to note the effect of such increases in the price on the value theory employed here, such empirical details of the price level of prison commodities are outside the scope of this study.

9. See http://www.pia.ca.gov/piawebdev/pia_board.html

10. Little mention is made in the literature on prison labor of these quasi-private entities that appropriate surplus, a category which also includes Corcraft in New York and PRIDE in Florida. They are generally treated as if it were of no concern whether an organization is public or private. This is a surprising move, given the importance generally placed on the public-private distinction in economics, with ubiquitous arguments for why public enterprises are inferior to private ones.

11. Some prison industries intentionally set their prices below the value of the commodity in order to "pass on" the "benefits" of slave labor to their customers, while some industries sell to the inmates through the canteen system at inflated prices. Evidence that price is equal to value in this case can be found by examining PRIDE's prices and comparing these prices to the market value of the commodities in question. Since this empirical examination of prices would not affect the main argument offered here, it is left to other researchers.

12. The above is based on an average inmate population of 63,528 (obtained by the total spending divided by the annual cost per inmate). However, the Inmate Population Report for the Florida Department of Corrections for 1999 was 68,599. It could be that the difference is due to turnover of inmates, or some other factor. The calculation of the value of state welfare per inmate is based on the latter number.

13. PRIDE Annual Report 2000. Because of turnover, there are more inmates enslaved by PRIDE in the course of a year than there are "inmate positions." However, for our purposes, all that matters is the total number of slave positions. While it affects an individual slave's level of income to lose his job at PRIDE, it does not affect the aggregate non-class revenue to PRIDE, provided that the slave is replaced. Assuming a 50-week work year, the average inmate position entailed 34 hours of labor per week.

14. "PRIDE has advanced funds to related parties for working capital purposes. There are no stated terms for repayment; however, the advances are expected to be repaid within the current operating cycle. The balance of related party receivables is $3,030,656 at December 31, 2000." PRIDE Annual Report (2000, 17)

15. For an interesting discussion of the limits of a number to capture the subjective pain of exploitation, see Fogel and Engermann (1974b, 99)

16. In using the terms 'customer model,' 'employer model' and 'manpower model,' I'm following Sexton (1995).

17. CIA Annual Directory (1998)

18. CIA Annual Directory (2001)

19. Parenti (1999), Dyer (2000)

NOTES TO CHAPTER FIVE

1. See Oshinsky (1996), Mancini (1996), Lichtenstein (1998)
2. Jones (1941), Burton Rose (1998, 101), U.S. House of Reps. (1997, 14) In the early 20th century, the Department of Labor kept records which detailed the proportion of inmates engaged in commodity production as well as those engaged in prison household production. Accounting for the former is still done, but accounting for the latter seems to have fallen out of favor in recent times, making it necessary to make estimates of the number of inmates engaged in prison household production.
3. Goldberg & Breece (1991, 6), Oshinsky (1996, 139, 155, 250). This situation also seems to have occurred in some of the most famous gulags in recent history, such as in the Soviet Union, Nazi Germany, China, and North Korea. See Meltzer (1993, 262–277).
4. Funke et al. (1982, 9)
5. Money to cover means of production (C_1) and commodities for slave sustenance (part of V_1 and $SSCR_1$) in the $SFCP_1$ is already covered by the wardens existing outlays of C_1, V_1 and $SSCP_1$.
6. Oshinsky (1996, 144)
7. *Ibid*, p. 223
8. *Ibid*, pp. 143–145
9. Goldberg & Breece (1991, 15–22)
10. See Jones (1941, 10): "Various authorities estimate that in the average penal institution, not more than 25 percent of inmates are actually needed for this type of work [the $SFCP_2$]"
11. U.S. Department of Labor (1940, 4) notes that "the systems of work which permitted the exploitation of the prison population for private gain have practically disappeared . . . The lease system, the most condemned of all, had disappeared by 1923."
12. Burns (1997) later admitted to some embellishments in his account, but his account is generally consistent with other first-hand accounts, even by guards. See also Powell (1891).
13. McShane & Williams (1996, 71–73, 253–254)
14. Free (1996), Oshinsky (1996), Marable (2000), Lichtenstein (1998), Mancini (1996)
15. Marable (2000, 109)
16. Cummins (1994, 1–21), Gill (1931, pp. 83, 100–101)
17. Williams (1979, 212), and Cummins (1994, 33–62) discuss the rise of inmate celebrities such as best-selling authors Caryl Chessman, Eldridge Cleaver and George Jackson. Cleaver and Jackson were famous for their outspoken political radicalism.
18. Reynolds (1985)
19. Parenti (1999), Burton-Rose (1998, 171–181), Rosenblatt (1996, 13–78, 195–240, 251–278)
20. Miller (1996, 48–89), Donziger (1996), Reiman (2001), Marable (2000, 124–126), Currie (1998, 110–161), Dyer (2000), Free (1996), Wacquant (2002), Gabriel (1990b)

21. See **http://www.ojp.usdoj.gov/bjs/correct.htm.**
22. Cummins (1994, 63–93)
23. McShane & Williams (1996, 43)
24. Cummins (1994, 128–150)
25. Marable (2000, 128)
26. Lusane (1991, 25–53)
27. Marable (2000, xvii–xxxix)
28. Chicano is an ethnic / linguistic category rather than a racial category per se, which hints at the vague, unscientific quality of modern racial constructions; however it makes sense to include Chicanos with African Americans, for many aspects of discrimination faced by the two groups are similar.
29. Hernnstein and Murray (1994), Wilson and Hernnstein (1985)

NOTES TO CHAPTER SIX

1. Marx (1973), (1995), (1996) Engels (1962)
2. Marx argues that in a world without exploitation, the difference between necessary and surplus labor may become insignificant, and that when this takes place, then all work may be considered to be, in some sense 'necessary.' See Marx (1977, 369 note I)
3. Johnson (1996), Johnson & Toch (2000). Prison may be seen as simply a harsher extension of a society which also systematically denies many individuals the ability to pursue meaningful work, for the simple reason that there are not enough jobs to go around.
4. Smith (1994, 33)
5. Marx (1977, 368–370). Emphasis added. Marx refers to Adam Smith in this passage as 'A. Smith' which I have altered for purposes of clarity.
6. Robert Leon, North Carolina Correctional Industries, personal communication, May 1999. All the civilians I spoke to who work in correctional industries do not describe the inmates as enslaved, but rather as 'employed.'
7. See Wright (1997), Young (2000), Burton-Rose et al. (1998) There is not one mention in any of these works that prison labor may have a positive dimension.
8. See for example, U.S. House of Representatives (1996).
9. For one example, see Louisiana Prison Enterprises brochure.
10. Maguire et al. (1988) provide an excellent survey of the relevant literature, as well as finding no concrete relationship between an inmate' participation in prison labor and his or her likelihood of returning to prison.
11. The authors would not release their original data, so a reconstruction of their statistical results was not possible.
12. The class processes occurring in occupational training are not investigated in this study; to my knowledge, no other researchers have examined the question.

13. The contribution to a victim fund is part of the sum of deductions made from the master's provision which is granted to inmate-slaves. Depending on whether a private firm is involved in the production process, the mandatory contribution to the victim fund would be some portion (usually 10–15%) of either or . See Chapter III, Table 3.1.

14. Rosenblatt (1996, 47–61), Reiman (2001, 31–35).

15. Marx (1977, 77–87)

16. Silberman (1995, 83), Durkheim (1933, 233–256)

17. Silberman (1995, 84)

18. *Ibid.*, 83

19. *Ibid.*, 85–86

20. *Ibid.*, 53

21. See Rosenblatt (1996, 70–71)

22. For an excellent description of this process of escalating threat and pre-emptive strikes, see Johnson (1996).

23. Rosenblatt (1996, 320). Johnson (1996) argues that such encouragement of violence is the exception, and that most correctional officers work toward a correctional agenda, meaning one which focuses on the rehabilitative or correctional aspects of prison life, rather than what Johnson calls the 'custodial agenda,' or a focus on security, merely warehousing the inmates until their death or release.

24. Although Aptheker (1968) has shown that a constant theme of American slavery was resistance and revolt, it is still the case that the number of slave revolts was low, especially when compared to the number of slaves and the size of the region in which slavery was the rule.

25. Some of these efforts have been successful while others have not. The first union of prisoners in the U.S. was started at California's Folsom Prison in 1970, but it would crumble before the might of the California Correctional Officers Association. Although a 1979 court decision gave inmates the right to wear Union buttons, the union had effectively ended as a political or economic force inside prisons, though it did serve as a political lobbying organization outside prisons. See Williams (1979, 211–213), Cummins (1994, 255–257)

26. Butler & Henderson (1990, 18–33)

27. Silberman (1995)

28. Donziger (1996, 65–73)

29. Silberman (1995)

30. Williams (2001, 7) See also Shakur (1996).

31. See for example, Wood (1993, 395–401) for an interesting argument about the controversy surrounding Thomas Jefferson's supposed sexual relationship with Sally Hemings for insight into America's shame about its slave past.

32. Human Rights Watch (2001, 57–60) For the full text of the 1926 Slavery Convention signed in Geneva, see http://www.anti-slaverysociety.addr.com/cxslavery.ht. See also the text of the 1930 Abolition of Forced Labor Convention, which abolishes all forms of coerced labor. http://193.194.138.190/html/menu3/b/32.htm See also Bales (2005).

33. A rare exception to this is Mancini (1996). In discussing convict leasing, Mancini argues that convict leasing was not slavery, but rather a "form of unfree labor"—without any discussion of why this would be a relevant or important distinction. Mancini does not employ a class-based theory, but rather uses a cultural-political theory inspired by Patterson (1982). Bales (2005) offers a systematic theory of slavery, but his conclusions on prison labor are undeveloped and ambiguous; he does not address the question of whether or not prison labor in the U.S. matches his criteria, though it seems likely he would argue it does not.

34. See for example, Ressler and Schachtman (1994). In their account of profiling violent criminals, the authors' title is instructive: *Whoever Fights Monsters*.

35. Donziger (1996), Currie (1998)

36. Recent trends indicate a possible regression toward older forms of punishment. The widespread use of capital punishment in the U.S., polls indicating many Americans are in favor of allowing torture for suspected terrorists, the call for a return to the 'stigma' of incarceration, and a general mood of anger and retribution toward criminal offenders may all signal the beginning of a move back to corporal punishment.

37. In Tonry and Petersilia (1999, 255)

38. The table is taken from Bottoms, in Tonry & Petersilia (1999), while the content is from Beetham (1991, 19), who argues that for power to gain legitimacy "three conditions are required: its conformity to established rules; the justifiability of the rules by reference to shared beliefs; the express consent of the subordinate, or of the most significant among them, to the particular relations of power."

39. For a description of the history of this phrase and its use on U.S. currency, see http://www.ustreas.gov/education/fact-sheets/currency/in-god-we-trust.html

40. Trop v. Dulles (1958) 356 U.S. 86, 99, 100.

41. Donziger (1996)

Glossary

Φ_C = the price of means of production used in the SFCP[2];

Φ_{retail} = the retail price of a prison commodity, assumed to be equal to its value;

Φ_s = the price of a prison commodity that may result from a non-competitive market where the master seeks to obtain greater market share by lowering the price of the prison commodity below the market unit value;

Φ_s^M = the price of a prison commodity that may result from a non-competitive market where the master seeks to use his substantial market share to raise the price of the prison commodity above the market unit value;

$\Phi_{slave-rental}$ = the rental price of slave labor-power that a private firm must pay in the manpower model = PPIE;

$\Phi_{wholesale}$ = the wholesale price of a prison commodity, or the price paid by a private enterprise acting as merchant in the customer model;

C = constant capital, or embodied labor, defined as the amount of SNALT in the raw materials and depreciation on equipment used in production, which is transferred to the commodity;

C_1 =   the constant capital used to produce prison slave commodities, equal to the value of the raw materials and depreciation on equipment used in production;

C_{ncp} =   the constant capital used to produce prison household use-values, equal to the value of the raw materials and depreciation on equipment used in production;

$CFCP$ =   the communist fundamental class process, a form of production, appropriation, and distribution of surplus labor where those who produce also collectively appropriate the surplus labor, and may also distribute the surplus on the basis of need. This class process which has long been seen as the goal of Marxian economic theory;

CL_1 =   the value of the cleaning services done by slaves in prison household production which is consumed by inmates;

CL_2 =   the value of the cleaning services done by slaves in prison household production which is consumed by non-inmates;

F_1 =   the value of the meals prepared by slaves in prison household production which is consumed by inmates;

F_2 =   he value of the meals prepared by slaves in prison household production which is consumed by non-inmates;

FPI =   an acronym which stands for "Federal Prison Industries, Inc.," the state agency charged with production and appropriation of commodities in federal prisons. FPI represents the largest single producer of prison commodities in the U.S. (See UNICOR);

G_1 =   the value of the groundskeeping services done by slaves in prison household production which is consumed by inmates;

G_2 =   the value of the groundskeeping services done by slaves in prison household production which is consumed by non-inmates;

L	=	funds loaned by PRIDE;
L_1	=	the value of the laundry services done by slaves in prison household production which is consumed by inmates;
L_2	=	the value of the laundry services done by slaves in prison household production which is consumed by non-inmates;
M_1	=	the value of the maintenance services done by slaves in prison household production which is consumed by inmates;
M_2	=	the value of the maintenance services done by slaves in prison household production which is consumed by non-inmates;
N	=	the total inmate population;
N_{seg}	=	the total inmate population in segregation (it is assumed that all these inmates receive a lower amount of state welfare);
$NCP_{welfare}$	=	a non-class payment paid by the warden qua master in prison household production due to his state-mandated responsibility to provide welfare to all inmates;
NCR_C	=	a non-class revenue received by the warden qua master in prison household production due to the provision by the state of the raw materials, tools, equipment, and so forth needed to produce prison household use-values;
$NCRM$	=	the non-class revenue flowing the master in commodity production who has managed to raise the price of the prison commodity above the market unit value. This non-class revenue may be common in jurisdictions where a state entity is given a monopoly on sales to state agencies;
NCR_{laws}	=	a non-class revenue existing due to less restrictive laws in prison which allow private firms to escape costs which they

would otherwise have to bear, for example, occupational health and safety laws;

NCR_{PRIDE} = a non-class revenue which flows to PRIDE, the semi-government, semi-private entity charged with production, appropriation, and sale of commodities in Florida prisons, due to PRIDE's lowering of the actual master's provision below the value of slave labor-power;

NCR_{rent} = a non-class revenue in the form of free rent on space and possible on equipment, which flows to private enterprises in the manpower and employer models, who not charged for the use of prison space, and the use of machinery and equipment that may be owned by the state agency;

NCR_{seg} = the total welfare received by an inmate in segregation;

$\dot{N}CR_{seg}$ = the total welfare received by all inmates in segregation, equal to $\left(NCR_{seg} \cdot N_{seg} \right)$;

NCR_{state} = the total welfare received by an inmate in the general population;

$\dot{N}CR_{seg}$ = the total welfare received by inmates in the general population, equal to ;

NCR_V = a non-class revenue flowing to the warden qua master in prison household production due to the state welfare, which allows the P2 to fall below V2;

NCR_w = a non-class revenue flowing to the master in commodity production due to the state welfare, which allows the P1 to fall below V1;

P_{slave} = the actual master's provision granted to slaves in prison, encompassing both V1 and V2;

P_1 = the actual master's provision granted to a slave in commodity production. Due to certain laws, the actual master's provision varies depending on whether or not private enterprises are involved in the production process, therefore P1 includes both PPIE , where private enterprises are involved, and Ps, where only state-run entities rather than private enterprises are involved;

$\dot{P}_1$ = the total actual master's provision granted to all slaves in commodity production;

P_2 = the actual master's provision granted to a slave in prison household production;

$\dot{P}_2$ = the actual master's provision granted to all slaves in prison household production;

Ps = the actual master's provision in state-run commodity production;

P_{PIE} = the actual master's provision in commodity production involving private enterprises;

PIA = an acronym which stands for "Prison Industry Authority," the state agency charged with producing and appropriating prison commodities in the state of California;

PIE = an acronym which stands for "Private Industries Enhancement" a 1979 federal law which loosened certain restrictions on the market for prison produced commodities;

PRIDE = an acronym which stands for "Prison Rehabilitative Industries and Diversified Enterprises," the semi-government, semi-private entity charged with production, appropriation, and sale of commodities in Florida prisons;

$PROV_1$ = the direct provision of commodities which are produced outside the prison to inmates;

$PROV_2$ = the hypothetical cost of substituting commodities (meals, cleaning services, laundry service, etc.) for prison-produced prison household use-values;

S = surplus value. The amount of value produced by labor which is above and beyond the needs of the worker;

S_1 =   surplus value produced by slaves in prison commodity production. The amount of value produced by slave labor which is above and beyond the needs of the slave;

S_c =   surplus value produced by workers outside prisons. The amount of value produced by labor which is above and beyond the needs of the worker;

S_e =   the surplus value appropriated by private firms who are masters in the employer model;

S_m =   the surplus value appropriated by private firms who are masters in the manpower model;

S_p =   the surplus value in commodity production appropriated by private prison masters;

S_{slave} =   the general term for slave surplus value in prisons. The amount of value produced by a given slave's labor which is above and beyond the needs of the slave;

$\left(\dfrac{S_1}{C+V_1}\right)$ =   the value rate of profit within PRIDE, equal to the slave surplus value divided by the cost of production;

$\left(\dfrac{S_1}{V_1}\right)$ =   the rate of slave exploitation in prison commodity production;

$\left(\dfrac{S_c}{V_c}\right)$ =   the rate of capitalist exploitation in commodity production outside prisons;

SFCP   =   the slave fundamental class process, a form of production, appropriation, and distribution of surplus labor with two key characteristics: 1. the appropriator, or master, takes the whole product of the slave producer's labor, and 2. the reproduction of the slaves' labor-power takes place within the relationship of master and slave. The *SFCP* also has a unique non-class structure, consisting of physical, social, religious, economic, and a myriad of other processes which participate in overdetermining the class structure of the *SFCP*.

$SFCP_1$	=	the slave fundamental class process in prison industries, or commodity production;
$SFCP_2$	=	the slave fundamental class process in prison household production;
SL_{ncp}	=	the slave surplus labor performed in prison household production;
$SNALT$	=	socially necessary abstract labor time, the source of value in Marxian theory;
$SSCP_1$	=	the sum of subsumed class payments the master in the $SFCP_1$ must make to secure his or her conditions of existence;
$SSCP_m$	=	the sum of subsumed class payments made by private firms who are masters in the manpower model;
$SSCP_e$	=	the sum of subsumed class payments made by private firms who are masters in the employer model;
$SSCP_p$	=	the sum of subsumed class payments made by private prison masters;
$SSCP_{adm}$	=	a subsumed class payment the warden makes to inmate administrators within the $SFCP_2$;
$SSCP_{cu}$	=	a subsumed class payment the warden makes to the inmates outside the production process who provide cultural conditions of existence for the $SFCP_2$ by encouraging inmates to get involved in existing prison programs such as the $SFCP$ or other activities and not to challenge the rules of the prison;
$SSCP_{gang}$	=	a subsumed class payment the warden makes to certain inmates outside the production process who provide political conditions of existence for the $SFCP_2$ by their cooperation with the prison system, by enforcing order among their members and other inmates, by disciplining inmate

troublemakers who refuse to follow orders, threaten or harm guards, etc.;

$SSCP_{manager}$ = a subsumed class payment the warden makes to inmate managers within the $SFCP_2$;

$SSCP_{ncp}$ = the sum of subsumed class payments the warden must make to secure the conditions of existence for the $SFCP_2$, and hence remain the master within prison household production;

$SSCP_{payroll}$ = a subsumed class payment made by PRIDE to pay for the administrative and managerial citizens who work for PRIDE, many of whom are involved in sales activities (see PRIDE);

$SSCP_{rape}$ = a subsumed class payment the warden makes to certain inmates outside the production process who provide political conditions of existence for the $SFCP_2$ by sexually assaulting other inmates, thus terrorizing the inmate population as a whole, and to a certain extent deterring inmates from certain activities which threaten the prison authorities;

$SSCP_{snitch}$ = a subsumed class payment the warden makes to certain inmates outside the production process who provide political conditions of existence for the $SFCP_2$ by their willingness to provide inside information about inmate activities which are unknown to the prison authorities;

$SSCP_{staff}$ = a subsumed class payment the warden makes to the prison staff to secure the participation of the staff as a subsumed class and hence meet a condition of existence for the $SFCP_2$;

$SSCR_1$ = a subsumed class revenue received by slaves who are subsumed to the $SFCP_1$;

$SSCR_2$ = a subsumed class revenue received by slaves who are subsumed to the $SFCP_2$;

$SSCR_{\text{merchant}}$ = a subsumed class revenue received by a private enterprise which acts as a merchant in the customer model of prison commodity production. Here the state appropriates the surplus and distributes a portion of it to the private enterprise for selling the commodity;

$SSCRPIE$ = a subsumed class revenue received by slaves who are subsumed to the $SFCP_1$ in a production process involving private enterprise;

$SSCRs$ = a subsumed class revenue received by slaves who are subsumed to the $SFCP^1$ in a production process involving a state entity rather than private enterprise;

State agency: the general term used for an institution which may be a quasi-private organization, a private organization, or a part of the state department of corrections, which is given the responsibility for the production of commodities within prisons;

$\sum c$ = the sum of charges to inmates for basic services, which act as a reduction of the state welfare;

$\sum d_s$ = the sum of deductions from the actual master's provision in state-run commodity production (Ps);

$\sum d_{PIE}$ = the sum of deductions from the actual master's provision in commodity production involving private enterprises in the manpower model (PPIE). This term is also considered the revenue to the state from renting slave labor-power to a private firm;

uv = the number of use-values produced in a production process, where a use-value is defined as a useful thing, either a good or service;

uvC = the number of use-values used in the $SFCP_2$;

UNICOR = another name for Federal Prison Industries, Inc., the master of the $SFCP_1$ in federal prisons (See FPI);

V	$=$	the value of labor-power. The social labor needed to reproduce a workers' labor-power at the level deemed appropriate in society;
V_1	$=$	the value of slave labor-power in commodity production ($SFCP_1$), termed the master's provision;
$\dot{V}_1$	$=$	the total value of slave labor-power in commodity production ($SFCP_1$), termed the master's provision;
V_2	$=$	the value of slave labor-power in prison household production ($SFCP_2$), termed the master's provision;
$\dot{V}_2$	$=$	the total value of slave labor-power in prison household production ($SFCP_2$), termed the master's provision;
V_c	$=$	the value of labor-power outside prison, representing the social labor needed to reproduce a worker's labor-power at the level deemed appropriate in society;
V_{slave}	$=$	the value of slave labor-power in prison, representing the social labor needed to reproduce a slave's labor-power at the level deemed appropriate in society. This general term encompasses both V_1 and V_2;
W	$=$	the value of a commodity, defined as the socially necessary abstract labor time embodied in it;
W_1	$=$	the value of a commodity produced by a slave in prison, defined as the socially necessary abstract labor time embodied in the prison slave commodity;
W_{ncp}^{i}	$=$	the value of the prison household use-values produced by slaves which goes to inmates;
W_{ncp}^{o}	$=$	the value of the prison household use-values produced by slaves which goes to non-inmates, mostly prison staff;
W_{ncp}^{T}	$=$	the total value of the prison household use-values produced by slaves;

W_{PROV_2} = the value of the commodities produced outside prisons that are granted to inmates as part of the state welfare;

W_{slave} = the value of a commodity produced by a slave, defined as the socially necessary abstract labor time embodied in it;

$\left(\dfrac{W}{uv}\right)$ = the market unit value of a commodity, or the total value produced divided by the total number of use-values produced;

$X_{merchant}$ = the sum of expenditures a private enterprise involved in the selling of prison slave commodities must make in order to procure the subsumed class revenue ($SSCR_{merchant}$);

Y_m = the sum of non-class payments made by private firms who are masters in the manpower model in order to obtain non-class revenues;

Y_e = the sum of non-class payments made by private firms who are masters in the employer model in order to obtain non-class revenues;

Y_{inmate} = the income of an inmate in the general population who is not enslaved;

Y_{seg} = the income of an inmate who is in segregation and is therefore not enslaved;

Y_{slave} = the potential income of an inmate who is enslaved;

YSS_1 = the income of an inmate who is enslaved as an unproductive slave, subsumed to the slave class process of commodity production;

YSS_2 = the income of an inmate who is enslaved as an unproductive slave, subsumed to the slave class process of prison household production;

Y^A_{slave} = the actual income of an inmate who is enslaved;

Y_1^A =   the actual income of an inmate who is enslaved in commodity production;

Y_2^A =   the actual income of an inmate who is enslaved in prison household production

Bibliography

Abbott, Jack H. (1981) *In the Belly of the Beast*. New York: Vintage.

Abu-Jamal, Mumia. (1996) *Live From Death Row*. New York: Avon Books.

———. (1997) *Death Blossoms*. London: Plough Publishing House.

———. (2000) *All Things Censored*. New York: Seven Stories Press.

Althusser, Louis. (1970) *For Marx*. New York: Vintage Books.

Althusser, Louis and Ettiene Balibar. (1970) *Reading Capital*. London: New Left Books.

Anderson, Perry. (1974) *Passages from Antiquity to Feudalism*. London: New Left Books.

Aptheker, Herbert (1968) *American Negro Slave Revolts*.

Arrow, Kenneth J. and Frank H. Hahn. (1971) *General Competitive Analysis*.

Bales, Kevin. (1999) *Disposable People: New Slavery in the Global Economy*. Berkeley, CA: University of California Press.

———. (2005) *Understanding Global Slavery*. Berkeley, CA: University of California Press.

Becker, Gary S. (1971) *The Economics of Discrimination*. 2nd ed. Chicago: University of Chicago Press.

———. (1968) "Crime and Punishment: An Economic Approach." *Journal of Political Economy* 76. pp. 169–217.

Becker, Gary S. and George J. Stigler. (1974) "Law Enforcement, Malfeasance, and Compensation of Enforcers." *Journal of Legal Studies* 1.

Beetham, David. (1991) *The Legitimation of Power*. Atlantic Highlands: Humanities Press International.

Beresford, David. (1997) *Ten Men Dead: The Story of the 1981 Irish hunger Strike*. New York: Atlantic Monthly Press.

Bergner, Daniel. (1998) *God of the Rodeo*. New York: Crown Publishers, Inc.

Bloch, Marc. (1975) *Slavery and Serfdom in the Middle Ages*. Trans. William R. Beer. Berkeley, CA: University of California Press.

Bonczar, Thomas & Allen Beck. (1997) "Lifetime Likelihood of Going to State or Federal Prison." *Bureau of Statistics Special Report*. Washington, D.C.: Bureau of Justice Statistics.

Bowles, Samuel, David Gordon, & Thomas Weisskopf. (1986) "Power and Profits: The Social Structure of Accumulation and the Profitability of the U.S. Economy." *Review of Radical Political Economics.* 18 (1/2): 132–167.

Bowles, Samuel and Herbet Gintis. (1999) "The Evolution of Strong Reciprocity." Mimeo, University of Massachusetts at Amherst.

Bugliosi, Vincent (2001) "None Dare Call It Treason." *The Nation.* Jan 18, 2001. http://www.thenation.com/doc.mhtml?i=20010205&s=bugliosi&c=1.

Burczak, Theodore. (2004) "Focusing on Appropriative Class Justice: A Comment on DeMartino's "Realizing Class Justice." *Rethinking Marxism.* 16:2, 207–209.

Burns, Robert E. (1997) *I Am a Fugitive from a Georgia Chain Gang.* University of Georgia Press. First published 1932.

Burns, Robert. (1998) *Rethinking the Law of the Tendency for the Rate of Profit to Fall.* IWGVT Paper. http://www.iwgvt.org/files/98fri3b-bur

Braswell, Michael, Steven Dillingham and Reid Montgomery, Jr., eds. (1985) *Prison Violence in America.* 1st Edition.

Burton-Rose, Daniel, Dan Pens and Paul Wright, eds. (1998) *The Celling of America: An Inside Look at the U.S. Prison Industry.* Monroe, ME: Common Courage Press.

Butler, Anne and C. Murray Henderson (1990) *Angola: Louisiana State Penitentiary: A Half-Centruy of Rage and Reform.* Lafayette, LA: Center for Louisiana Studies.

Callari, Antonio, Stephen Cullenberg, & C. Biewener. (1995) *Marxism in the Postmodern Age.* New York: Guilford Press.

Colander, David. (2002) "The Death of Neoclassical Economics." *Middlebury College Economics Discussion Paper,* No. 02–37. http://www.middlebury.edu/~econ.

Cialdini, Robert. (1996) "Activating and Aligning Two Kinds of Norms in Persuasive Communications." *Journal of Interpretation Research.* Vol 1: 1. http://www.journalofinterpretationresearch.org/issues/v1n1/article1.html

Cole, David. (1999) *No Equal Justice: Race and Class in the American Criminal Justice System.* New York: The New Press.

Conover, Ted. (2000) *New Jack: Guarding Sing Sing.* New York: Random House.

Correctional Industries Association. (1998) *Annual Directory.* Published by the Correctional Industries Association, Inc.

Correctional Industries Association. (2001) *Annual Directory.* Published by the Correctional Industries Association, Inc.

Corry, T.M. (1977) *Prison Labour in South Africa.* Cape Town, South Africa: National Institute for Crime Prevention and the Rehabilitation of Offenders.

Cullenberg, Stephen. (1992) "The Burden of Socialism: Towards a Thin Definition of Socialism," *Rethinking Marxism,* 5:2 (Summer 1992): 64–83.

———. (1994) *The Falling Rate of Profit: Recasting the Marxian Debate.* London / Boulder, CO: Pluto Press.

Cullenberg, Stephen, Jack Amariglio, & David Ruccio. (2001) *Postmodernism, Economics and Knowledge.* London / New York: Routledge.

Cummins, Eric. (1994) *The Rise and Fall of California's Radical Prison Movement.* Stanford, CA: Stanford University Press.

Currie, Elliot. (1998) *Crime and Punishment in America*. New York: Henry Holt & Co.

Davis, David Brion. (1966) *The Problem of Slavery in Western Culture*. Ithaca, NY: Cornell University Press.

———. (1975) *The Problem of Slavery in the Age of Revolution, 1770–1823*. Ithaca, NY: Cornell University Press.

———. (1984) *Slavery and Human Progress*. Oxford, UK: Oxford University Press.

DeMartino, George. (2000) *Global Economy, Global Justice: Theoretical objections and policy alternatives to neoliberalism*. London: Routledge.

———. (2003) "Realizing Class Justice." *Rethinking Marxism*. 15:1, 1–31.

Donaldson, Stephen. (1990) "Rape of Males" in the *Encyclopedia of Homosexuality*. Wayne R. Dynes, ed. NY: Garland Publications.

———. (1993) "The Rape Crisis Behind Bars" *The New York Times*. 29 Dec 1993. P.

———. (1995) *The Rape of Males: A Preliminary Statistical Look at the Scope of the Problem*. 7th ed. Stop Prisoner Rape.

Donziger, Stephen, ed. (1996) *The Real War on Crime*. New York: Harper Perennial.

Douglass, Frederick. (1994) *Autobiographies*. New York: The Library of America.

Durkheim, Emile. (1933) *The Division of Labor in Society*. New York: The Free Press.

Dyer, Joel. (2000) *The Perpetual Prisoner Machine : How America Profits from Crime*. Boulder, Colo. : Westview Press

Econ Incorporated. (1978, I) *Study of the Economic and Rehabilitative Aspects of Prison Industry: Analysis of Prison Industries and Recommendations for Change*. U.S. Dept. of Justice. National Institute of Law Enforcement and Criminal Justice.

———. (1978, II) *Study of the Economic and Rehabilitative Aspects of Prison Industry: Technical Tasks and Results*. U.S. Dept. of Justice. National Institute of Law Enforcement and Criminal Justice.

Elster, Jon (1983). "Exploitation, Freedom and Justice," in J. Roland Pennock and John Chapman, eds. *Nomos XXVI: Marxism*. New York: New York University Press.

———. (2000) *Ulysses Unbound*. Cambridge: Cambridge University Press.

Engels, Frederick. (1962) *Anti-Dühring: Herr Eugen Dühring s Revolution in Science*. Moscow: Foreign Languages Publishing House.

Fehr, Ernst and Simon Gächter. (2000) Fairness and Retaliation: The Economics of Reciprocity. *Journal of Economic Perspectives. 14:3.* pp 159–181.

Fehr, Ernst and Klaus Schmidt. (2001) "Theories of Fairness and Reciprocity— Evidence and Economic Applications." *Institute for Empirical Research in Economics*, University of Zurich, Working Paper 75.

Feiner, Susan. (1988) "Slavery Classes, and Accumulation in the Antebellum South." *Rethinking Marxism*. Vol 1, No. 2

———. (1981) *The Financial Structures and Banking Institutions of the Antebellum South: 1811–1832*. Ph.D. Dissertation, University of Massachusetts Amherst.

Fellner, Jamie and Marc Mauer. (1998) *Losing the Vote:The Impact of Felony Disenfranchisement Laws in the United States.* Human Rights Watch and the Sentencing Project. http://www.hrw.org/reports98/vote/

Finley, M.I. (1980) *Ancient Slavery and Modern Ideology.* New York: Penguin.

Florida Department of Corrections Annual Budget, Fiscal Year 1999–2000. http://www.dc.state.fl.us/pub/annual/9900/index.html

Fogel, Robert William and Stanley L. Engermann. (1974a) *Time on the Cross: the Economics of American Negro Slavery.* Boston, Toronto: Little, Brown & Co.

———. (1974b) *Time on the Cross:Evidence and Methods—a Supplement.* Boston, Toronto: Little, Brown & Co.

Fogel, Robert William. (1992a) *Without Consent or Contract: the Rise and Fall of American Slavery.* New York, London: W.W. Norton & Co.

———. (1992b) *Without Consent or Contract: the Rise and Fall of American Slavery—Evidence and Methods.* New York, London: W.W. Norton & Co.

Forché, Carolyn. (1993) *Against Forgetting: 20th Century Poetry of Witness.* New York: Norton.

Foucault, Michel. (1979) *Discipline & Punish: The Birth of Prison.* New York: Vintage.

Funke, Gail S., Billy L. Wayson, and Neal Miller. (1982) *Assets and Liabilities of Correctional Industries.* Lexington, MA: Lexington Books.

Fierce, Milfred C. (1994) *Slavery Revisited: Blacks and the Southern Convict Lease System, 1865–1933.* New York: Africana Studies Research Center.

Fraad, Harriet, Stephen A. Resnick, and Richard D. Wolff. (1989) "For Every Knight in Shining Armor, There's a Castle Waiting to be Cleaned: A Marxist-Feminist Analysis of the Household." *Rethinking Marxism* 2, no. 4: 10–69.

———. (1990) "Class, Patriarchy and Power." *Rethinking Marxism* 3, no. 2: 124–44.

———. (1994) *Bringing It All Back Home: Class, Gender & Power In The Modern Household.* London: Pluto Press.

Free, Marvin D. Jr. (1996) *African Americans and the Criminal Justice System.* New York and London: Garland Publishing, Inc.

Frey, Bruno S., Felix Oberholzer-Gee, and Reiner Eichenberger. (1996) "The Old Lady Visits Your Backyard: A Tale of Morals and Markets." *Journal of Political Economy.* Vol. 104, No. 6, pp. 1297–1313.

Friedman, Milton. *Capitalism and Freedom.*

Gabriel, S. (1990a). "Ancients: A Marxian Theory of Self-Exploitation." *Rethinking Marxism.* 3(1): 85–106.

———. (1990b). "The Continuing Significance of Race: An Overdeterminist Approach to Racism." *Rethinking Marxism.* 3(3–4): 65–78.

Garland, David. (1990) *Punishment and Modern Society: A Study in Social Theory.* Chicago: University of Chicago Press.

Genovese, Eugene D. (1967) *The Political Economy of Slavery.* New York: Vintage Books.

———. (1976) *Roll, Jordan, Roll: The World the Slaves Made.* New York: Vintage Books.

Gibson-Graham, J.K., Stephen Resnick, and Richard Wolff. (2000) *Class and Its Others*. Minneapolis & London: University of Minnesota Press.

————. (2001) *Re/Presenting Class: Essays in Postmodern Marxism*. Durham & London: Duke University Press.

Gill, Howard B. (1931) "The Prison Labor Problem." *Annals of the American Academy of Political and Social Science*. Volume 157, Sept 1931.

Gold, Steve. (1990) *The State Fiscal Agenda for the 1990's*. Albany, NY: Center for the Study of the States, Nelson A. Rockefeller Institute for the Study of Governement.

Goldberg, Kenneth D., and Yvonne S. Breece. (1990) *An Overview of the History of Prison Industries*. Mimeographed Paper, obtained from PRIDE Enterprises of FL, or from Taylor, Brion, Buker & Greene P.O. Box 11189 Tallahassee, FL 32302.

Gordon, Robert Ellis. (2000) *The Funhouse Mirror: Reflections on Prison*. Pullman, WA: Washington University Press.

Gould, Stephen Jay. (1981) *The Mismeasure of Man*. New York, London: W.W. Norton & Company.

Gutman, Herbert G. (1975) *Slavery and the Numbers Game: A Critique of "Time on the Cross."* Chicago: University of Chicago Press.

Hernnstein, Richard and Charles Murray. (1994) *The Bell Curve: Intelligence and Class Structure in American Life*. New York: Free Press.

Hindess, Barry and Paul Hirst. (1975) *Pre-capitalist Modes of Production*.

Hirst, J.B. (1983) *Convict Society and its Enemies*. Sydney: George Allen & Unwin.

Hornblum, Allen M. (1998) *Acres of Skin: Human Experiments at Holmesburg Prison*. London: Routledge.

Human Rights Watch (2001) *No Escape: Male Rape in U.S. Prisons*. New York: Human Rights Watch.

James, C.L.R. (1980) *Spheres of Existence*. London: Allison & Busby

Johnson, Robert (1996). *Hard Time: Understanding and Reforming the Prison*. London: Wadsworth Publishing Company. 2nd edition.

Johnson, Robert and Hans Toch, eds. (2000). *Crime and Punishment: Inside Views*. Los Angeles, CA: Roxbury Publishing Company.

Jones, Richard Francis. (1941) *Prison labor in the United States, 1940*. Washington, D.C.: U. S. Govt. Printing Office. Bulletin of the U.S. Bureau of Labor Statistics; 698.

Kolchin, Peter. (1987). *Unfree Labor: American Slavery and Russian Serfdom*. Cambridge, MA and London, England: Belknap Press, Harvard University Press.

————. (1994) *American Slavery, 1619—1877*. New York: Hill and Wang.

Lee, Frederic. (2003) "Neoclassical Economics: Should Heterodox Economists Afford it Any Respect?" Presentation at the *American Economics Association Annual Conference*, January 3–5, 2003.

Levin, Kenneth. (1999) *Hybrid Class Processes in High-Tech Industry*. University of Massachusetts at Amherst. Unpublished dissertation outline.

Louisiana Prison Enterprises: Sensible Savings Through Work and Training. Brochure.

Lichtenstein, Alex. (1998) *Twice the Work of Free Labor*. London: Verso.

Maguire, Kathleen E., Timothy J. Flanagan and Terence P. Thornberry. (1988) "Prison Labor and Recidivism." *Journal of Quantitative Criminology*. Vol. 4., No. 1, pp. 3–18

Mancini, Matthew J. (1996) *One Dies, Get Another: Convict Leasing in the American South, 1866–1928*. University of South Carolina Press.

Marable, Manning. (2000) *How Capitalism Underdeveloped Black America*. Updated Edition. Boston, MA: South End Press. First edition, 1983.

Mauer, Marc. (1999) *Race to Incarcerate*. New York : New Press.

Marx, Karl. (1973) *Grundrisse: Introduction to a Critique of Political Economy*. New York: Vintage Books.

———. (1977) *Selected Writings*. David McLellan, ed. Oxford: Oxford university Press.

———. (1990) *Capital: A Critique of Political Economy. Volume I*. London: Penguin Classics. First published 1867.

———. (1992) *Capital: A Critique of Political Economy. Volume II*. London: Penguin Classics. First published 1884.

———. (1991) *Capital: A Critique of Political Economy. Volume III*. London: Penguin Classics. First published 1894.

———. (1995) *Value, Price, and Profit*. Eleanor Marx Aveling, ed. Transcriber: Mike Ballard. http://csf.colorado.edu/psn/marx/Archive/1864-IWMA/1865-VPP/

———. (1996) *Marx: Later Political Writings*. Terrell Carver, ed. London: Cambridge University Press.

McCloskey, Donald N. (1985) *The Applied Theory of Price*. New York: Macmillan Publishing Co. 2nd edition.

McLaughlin, Eugene and John Muncie, eds. (1996) *Controlling Crime*. London: SAGE

McShane, Marilyn D. and Frank P. Williams III (1996) *The Encyclopedia of American Prisons*. New York and London: Garland Publishers.

Melossi, Dario and Massimo Pavarini. (1981) *The Prison and the Factory: Origins of the Penitentiary System*. Trans. Glynis Cousin. Totowa, N.J.: Barnes and Noble.

Meillassoux, Claude. (1991) **The Anthropology of Slavery : The Womb of Iron and Gold**. translated by Alide Dasnois Chicago : University of Chicago Press,

Meltzer, Milton. (1993) *Slavery: A World History*. Updated edition. New York: Da Capo Press.

Meyer, Peter B. (1976) **Drug Experiments on Prisoners**. Lexington, MA: Lexington Books.

Miller, Jerome G. (1996) *Search & Destroy: African-Americans in the Criminal Justice System*. Cambridge: Cambridge University Press.

More, Thomas. (1994) *Utopia*. New York: Everyman's Library. Paperback Revised edition (First published 1919).

Moseley, Fred. (1991) *The Falling Rate of Profit in the Postwar United States Economy*. New York: St. Martin's Press.

———. (1982) *The Rate of Surplus Value in the U.S., 1947–1977*. University of Massachusetts, Amherst Ph.D. Dissertation.

Oshinsky, David. (1996) *Worse Than Slavery: Parchman Farm and the Ordeal of Jim Crow Justice*. New York: Free Press.

Parenti, Christian. (1999) *Lockdown America*. London: Verso.

Patterson, Orlando. (1969) *The Sociology of Slavery: An Analysis of the Origins, Development and Structure of Negro Slave Society in Jamaica*. Rutherford: Fairleigh Dickinson Press.

———. (1982) *Slavery and Social Death*. Cambridge, MA: Harvard University Press.

Pens, Dan. (1995) "VitaPro Fraud in Texas". *Prison Legal News*. May, 1995.

———. (1998) "Oregon's Prison Slaveocracy". *Prison Legal News*. Vol. 9, No. 5.

Powell, J.C. (1891) *The American Siberia, or 14 Years Experience in a Southern Convict Camp*. Chicago: H.J. Smith & Co.

PRIDE Enterprises Annual Report. Fiscal Year 2000. http://www.peol.com/about. htm

Reiman, Jeffrey H. (1984) *The Rich Get Richer and the Poor Get Prison*. New York: Macmillan. 2nd edition.

———. (2001) *The Rich Get Richer and the Poor Get Prison*. Boston: Allyn and Bacon. 6th edition.

———. (1987) "Exploitation, Force, and the Moral Assessment of Capitalism: Thoughts on Roemer and Cohen." *Philosophy and Public Affairs*, 16, pp. 3–41.

Resnick, Stephen A. & Richard D. Wolff, eds. (1985) *Rethinking Marxism*. New York: Autonomedia.

———. (1987a) *Economics: Marxian versus Neoclassical*. Baltimore / London: Johns Hopkins Press.

———. (1987b) *Knowledge & Class*. Chicago: Univ. of Chicago Press.

———. (2002) *Class Theory and History: Capitalism and Commuism in the U.S.S.R*. New York and London: Routledge.

Ressler, Robert K. & Thomas Schachtman. (1994) *Whoever Fights Monsters*. St. Martins Press.

Report to the League of Nations Advisory Committee of Experts on Slavery. (1938) Geneva, April 5, 1938, vol. 6.

Reynolds, Morgan O. (1985) *Crime By Choice*. Fischer Publishing.

———. (1996) "Factories Behind Bars." *National Center for Policy Analysis Policy Report*. 206: Sept 1996. http://www.ncpa.org/

Rosenblatt, Elihu. (1997) *Criminal Injustice*. Boston: South End Press.

Rossi, Peter H., Richard Berk and Kenneth Lenihan. (1980) *Money, Work, and Crime*. New York: Academic Press.

Rusche, Georg, and Otto Kirchheimer. (1939) *Punishment and Social Structure*. New York: Columbia University Press.

Ryan, William. (1976) *Blaming the Victim*. New York: Vintage Books. p. 3–30

Sawyer, Roger. (1986) *Slavery in the Twentieth Century*. London: Routledge & Kegan Paul.

Saylor, William G. and Gerald G. Gaes. (1992) "Prison work has meaurable effects on post-release success." *Federal Prisons Journal*. Vol 2, no. 4. 32–36

————. (1995) *Interim Report*: "The Effect of Prison Work Experience, Vocational and Apprenticeship Training on the Long-Term Recidivism of U.S. Federal Prisoners." U.S. Federal Bureau of Prisons. October 26.

Scacco, Anthony M., Jr. (1975) *Rape in Prison*. Springfield, IL: Charles C. Thomas.

Schulze, Guenther G. and Bjorn Frank. (2000) "Deterrence versus Intrinsic Motivation: Experimental Evidence on the Determinants of Corruptibility." *Econometric Society World Congress 2000 Contributed Papers*. Econometric Society, 0950.

Sellen, J. Thorsten. (1976) *Slavery and the Penal System*. Amsterdam: Elsevier

Sexton, George E. (1995) *Work in American Prisons: Joint Ventures with the Private Sector*. National Institute of Justice Program Focus. (www.ncjrs.org)

Shakur, Sanyika. (1998) *Monster: The Autobiography of an LA Gang member*. New york: Addison-Wesley.

Silberman, Matthew. (1995) *World of Violence*. Belmont, CA: Wadsworth Publishing Co.

Smith, Adam. (1994) *An Inquiry into the Nature and Causes of the Wealth of Nations*. New York: Modern Library.

Stack, Jonathan and Elizabeth Garbus, directors. (1998) Film: *The Farm: Angola USA*. Independent. 88 Minutes. PG-13.

State of California. (2002) *Title 15*. California Code of Regulations. 31 January, 2002. Register 91, No. 6. http://www.cdc.state.ca.us/Regulations/Regulations.htm.

State of New York. (2001) *Subtitle AA: State Commission of Correction*. 11 April 2001. http://www.scoc.state.ny.us/nysscoc/manuals.htm

Steiner, Jesse F. and Roy M. Brown. (1969) *The North Carolina Chain Gang*. Montclair, New Jersey: Patterson Smith.

Stephan, James J. (1999) "State Prison Expenditures, 1996." US Department of Justice, Office of Justice Programs, Bureau of Justice Statistics. http://www. ojp.usdoj.gov/bjs

Sweezy, Paul M. (1968) *The Theory of Capitalist Development*. New York and London: Modern Reader Paperbacks. First published 1942.

Tatum, Beverly Daniel. (1999) *Why are all the black kids sitting together in the cafeteria?* New York: Basic Books

Titmus, Richard. (1971) *The Gift Relationship: From Human Blood to Social Policy*. New York: Pantheon Books.

Tonry, Michael. (1995) *Malign Neglect: Race, Crime & Punishment in America*. New York: Oxford University Press. p. 181–209

Tonry, Michael and Joan Petersilia, eds. (1999) *Prisons. Crime and Justice: A Review of Research*. Chicago and London: University of Chicago Press.

U.S. General Accounting Office. (1996) *Private and Public Prisons: Studies Comparing Operational Cost and/or Quality of Service*. GAO/GGD-96–158, August 1996.

U.S. House of Representatives (1996) *Federal Prisons Industries, Inc. Hearing Before the Subcommittee on Crime of the Committee on the Judiciary*. 104th Congress. 18 Sept 1996. Serial no. 121.

U.S. House of Representatives (1997) *Options to Improve and Expand Federal Prisons Industries. Hearing Before the Subcommittee on Crime of the Committee on the Judiciary*. 105th Congress. 30 Oct 1997. Serial no. 107.

Unknown author(s). (1969) "Prison is a Place." *The Fortune News*. September, 1969.

Van Zyl Smit, Dirk and Frieder Dünkel, eds. (1999) *Prison Labour: Salvation or Slavery?* Aldershot, UK: Dartmouth.

Wacquant, Loïc. (2002) From Slavery to Mass Incarceration. *New Left Review*. 13: 41–60.

Walker, Donald R. (1988) *Penology for Profit: A History of the Texas Prison System, 1867–1912*. Texas A&M University Press.

Walsh, David (1998a) "Life in Prison." *World Socialist Web Site*. 23 May 1998. Film Reviews. http://www.wsws.org/arts/1998/may1998/farm-m23.shtml

———. (1998b) "What is society going to do with the surplus humanity?": An interview with Jonathan Stack, co-director of the Farm: Angola USA. *World Socialist Web Site*. 23 May 1998. Film Reviews. http://www.wsws.org/arts/1998/may1998/farm-m23.shtml

Walvin, James. (1983) *Slavery and the Slave Trade*. Jackson, MS: University of Mississippi Press.

Ward, Robert D. and William W. Rogers. (1987) *Convicts, Coal, and the Banner Mine Tragedy*. Tuscaloosa: University of Alabama Press.

Weiner, Ross. (1999) *The Political Economy of Organized Baseball*. Ph.D. Dissertation, University of Massachusetts.

———. (2003) "Power Hitters Strike Out: New Perspectives on Baseball and Slavery." *Rethinking Marxism*. 15: 1. pp. 33–48.

West, Jude P. and John R. Stratton, eds. (1971) *The Role of Correctional Industries*. Center for Labor and Management. Iowa City: University of Iowa.

Williams, Eric. (1994) *Capitalism and Slavery*. Chapel Hill, NC: University of North Carolina Press.

Williams, Patricia J. (1991) *The Alchemy of Race and Rights*. Cambridge, MA: Harvard University Press.

Williams, Stanley "Tookie." (2001) *Life in Prison*. SeaStar Books.

Williams, Vergil L. (1979) *Dictionary of American Penology*. London: Greenwood Press.

Wilson, Walter. (1933) *Forced Labor in the United States*. New York: International Publishers.

Wilson, James Q. and Richard Hernnstein (1985) *Crime and Human Nature*. New York: Simon & Schuster.

Winks, Robin W., ed. (1972) *Slavery: A Comparative Perspective*. New York: New York University Press.

Wolff, Richard D. (1995) "Markets do not a class structure make". In *Marxism and the postmodern age*. Antonio Callari, Stephen Cullenberg, Carole Biewener, eds. New York and London: Guilford Press.

Wood, Gordon S., in Onuf, P.S., ed. (1993) *Jeffersonian Legacies*. Charlottesville: University Press of Virginia.

Wright, Erik Olin. (1973) *The Politics of Punishment*. New York: Harper Torchbooks.

Wright, Paul. (1997) "Making Slave Labor Fly: Boeing Goes to Washington." *Prison Legal News*. Vol. 8, No. 3. (March)

Young, Ronald. (2000) "Slave Labor Supplanting Welfare State". *Prison Legal News*. Vol. 11, No. 11. (November)

Zimring, Franklin E. & Gordon J. Hawkins. (1973) *Deterrence*. Chicago: University of Chicago Press.

Index

A

Absolute surplus value, 38
Abstract labor, 49, 64 *See also* Socially necessary abstract labor; Value
Accomplishment of goals, 130
Achilles tendon, 141
Administrative segregation, 26, 68
    and Welfare, 50–51, 69, 92, 138, 139
Advertisers, 103
Affirmative action, 124
African Americans, 2, 119, 122–124
    proportion incarcerated, 122
Alienation, 129–130,
    causes of, 138
    contradictions of, 136
    forms of, 136–138
    influence of Marx's theory of, 136
    and powerlessness, 136
American eugenics movement, 124
American ideals, 127
Anger, inmates' response to, 140–141
Angola prison, 32, 78, 141
Animal-grade soybeans, 63
Antebellum South, 10, 18–19, 35, 50, 57, 69, 107, 109, 114, 141, 157–169
Anthropology, 136
Arizona, 31, 62
Arkansas, 56, 88
Ashurst-Summers Act, 115
Assassination, 124
Attica prison, 123, 142, 148
Auburn prison, 112
Auschwitz concentration camp, 130
Australia, 153
Autonomy, 128

B

Bales, Kevin, 13–15
Beetham's criteria for legitimate power, 146–149
The Bell Curve, 124
Black market, 63
Black Muslims, 123, 124
Black Panthers, 123
Bottoms, A., 146
Burden rate, 103–104
Burns, Robert, 118

C

California, 34, 42, 59–62, 89, 95–7
Capital,
    circulation of, 39
    turnover time of, 39
Caribbean, 82, 109
Charges for medical care, 62
Chattel, 119
Chicanos, 124
China, 82
Christian religion, 146
Civil rights struggle, 123
Civil War, U.S., 82, 118, 119
Class,
    analysis, 5, 8, 66, 82, 110, 123, 152
    conflict, 29, 131, 136
    dynamics, 110
    grouping, 43–46
    process, 11, 71, 151–152
    process and criminal behavior, 6–8
    structure, concept of, 11
Coercion in prison, 26, 150
COINTELPRO, 123

Collective appropriation of surplus labor, 12, 68, 150–152
Commodities,
　circuit of, 39
　illicit, *See* Black market
　price of, 39
　production of, 21, 37
　sale of, 37, 94–96
　value of, *see* Value
Communism, 150
Communist class process, 68
Competition,
　for income, 39
　market, 40
Complexity of social processes, 9
Compliance, practices which lead to, 146
Concentration on a task, 130
Conditions of existence, 44
Conflicts between inmates and staff, 29
Conservative attack on liberalism, 122
Constant capital, 101
Constitution, U.S.,
　8th Amendment, 149
　13th Amendment, 24, 145–149
Constraints, 146
Consumption, level of, 42, 51, 63–65, 108, 111, 118, 121
Contraband, 36
Control group, 133
Convict leasing, 10
　abolition of, 117
　historians view of, 131
Cool Hand Luke, 129
Corporation,
　private, 103–107
　semi-private, 96–101
Correctional authorities, obedience to, 2 *See also* Prison authorities
Correctional Industries Association, 45
Corruption in prison administration, 118
Cost of living, 52
Cost of production, 95, 104
Cotton, 110
Criminality,
　meaning of, 28
　and race, 124
Criminologists, 121
Crime,
　and class, 5–8
　non-violent, 124
　and punishment, 61, 144–145
　romanticization of, 143
　as a social failure, 122
　victimless, 135
　violent, 144
Crime and Human Nature, 124
Crips gang, 143
Critics of prison labor, 37, 91, 95–96, 107, 115, 131–135
Currency, U.S., 146
Customer model, 96, 102–103

D
Decline of prison slavery, 122
Deductions from the actual master's provision, 89–91
Defense attorneys, 122
Dehumanization, 27–34, 83, 144
Delegitimation, 147
Democratic National Convention, 123
Democratic values, 153
Demographic shifts, 120
Department of Corrections, 21, 96–97
Depression, 29
Deprivation in prison, 128
Desperation, 124
Development of prison industries, 23–24
Dialectic, 12
Dignity of man, 149
Dillard, Eddie, 81
Disciplinary record, 84, 133
Discrimination, 119
Disincentives, 146
Distribution,
　of profits, 103
　of slave surplus labor, 74
　of slave surplus value, 99–101
　sphere of, 41, 92
Dividends, 105
Dobb, Maurice, 9
Drug and alcohol abuse, 140
Drugs, 79

E
Economic deprivation, 119
Emasculation of inmates, 138–139
Embodied labor, 65, 92
Employer model, 105
Engerman, Stanley, 15
Entrapment, 124
Essentialism, 25, 41, 86, 134, 144, 152
Executive Order 325A, 115
Expenditure, 71–75
Experimental group. 133

Exploitation,
    feeling of, 102
    and happiness, 127
    Marxian definition of, 41
    Neoclassical definition of, 41
    rate of, 56, 94, 101–102
    slave, 47
Eyeglasses, 60

F

False consciousness, 42
Fear of criminals, 142
Federal Bureau of Investigation, 123
Federal Prison Industries, 91, 97
Federal prison system, 45, 57
Feiner, Susan, 19
Feudalism, 9–10, 17
Florida, 5, 56, 88, 97–102
Fogel, Robert, 15
Food preparation, 64, 68, 76
Forces of production, 38
Fruits of human labor, 47

G

Gaes, G., 132–134
Gangs, 79–80
    conflicts between rival, 141
Geneva Convention on the Treatment of
        Prisoners, 145
Genovese, Eugene, 13
Georgia, 56, 88
Gold, 110
Great Migration, 119

H

Hawes-Cooper Act, 115
Hearst, Patty, 123
Hierarchy in prison, 140
High-skill tasks, 70
Hip-hop clothing, prison influence, 142
Holland, *See* Netherlands prisons
Hollywood, 118
Holy Grail of penology, 5
Homosexuals, 140
Human development, 127
Human rights, 145

I

Illegitimacy of prison slavery, 152
Immigration, 120
Incapacitation of criminals, 122
Incarceration rate, United States, 1

Incarceration,
    cost of, 1, 5, 107, 110–122, 131, 134,
        153
    effects of, 2
    increases in, 119–122
    purposes of, 1
    rate of, 120
    of slaves prior to the Civil War, 119
    stigma of, 135
    total number, United States, 1, 119
Incentives, 146
    for good behavior, 66
Income, need for, 34–35, 42
Indigo, 110
Informant, 80
Inmate education, 122
Instrumental behavior, 146
Interest,
    payments, 60, 100–101, 105
    rate, 60
Internal/External scale, 137
International Slavery Convention, 145
Interstate commerce, 89, 115
Intolerance, 124
Investment in technology, 96
J
Jamaica, 13
Job opportunities for former inmates, legiti-
        mate, 135
Job training, 42
Johnson, Luke, 129

K

Kent State University, 123
Kerouac, J., 142
Keynesian economic policies, 122
King, Rodney, 148

L

Labor,
    contradiction of, 130
    as development and fulfillment, 128
    division of, 65–68
    factory, 125
    hard, 125, 129
    intensity of, 38, 94, 114, 130
    living, 93
    pointless, 129
    pleasure and, 130
    process, 38–39
    unions, 89, 115
Labor-power,

market for, 12
ownership of, 13–16, 44, 111
reproduction of, 11
sale of another's, 15, 23, 104, 111
value of, 51–54, 92–94, 98–99, 111
Laundry, 64
Lawmakers, 100
Legitimacy,
   of the legal system, 8, 149
   of the prison system, 146–149
Lewis, Sam, (Dept of Corrections AZ) 62
Liberalism, 122
Liberty, 128
Lockdown, 68, 69
Louisiana, 78, 141
Low-skill tasks, 70
Lusane, Clarence, 124

M

Maguire, K., 133
Maintenance, 64
Management salaries, 105
Manchester prison, UK, 148
Mandatory source requirement, 95
Manpower model, 96, 103–104
Marable, Manning, 123–124
Markers of slave status, 31–32
Market for prison commodities, 115
Market, non-competitive, 95
Marketing costs, 103, 105
Marx, Karl, 5, 22, 38–40, 45, 53–54, 75, 93,
      102, 128–130, 136–137, 150
Master's provision, 35, 69–71
Means of production, 72
Media, 101
Media coverage of violent crime, 142
Methodological flaws in the PREP study,
      132–134
Minimum wage, 52, 88, 103
Mississippi, 85, 112, 131
Mode of production, 9–10, 92
Monopoly power, 95
Moral depreciation, 40

N

National Guard, 123
Necessary labor,
   definition of, 4
   of inmates, 49, 54
Netherlands prisons, 151
New York, 112
Newman, Paul, 129

Non-class payment, 71–73
Non-class position, 50
Non-class revenue, 50, 71–73, 94–95, 98–99
Non-class structure, concept of, 12
Non-exploitative class structure, 150
Non-laboring inmates, 23, 43–46
Norms of compliance, 146

O

Objectification, 27–34, 83, 142
Occupation Safety and Health rules, 104
Occupational training, 133
The Open Road, 142
Oppression, forms of, 121
Oshinsky, David, 85, 131
Outlaws and American culture, 142
Overdetermination, 12, 21–25, 51–53, 72,
      86–88, 109–110, 123, 136, 149
Ownership of human chattel, 3, 17–19, 46

P

Parchman prison farm, 85, 112, 114
Parenti, Christian, 80–81
Patterson, Orlando, 27–32
Penological literature, 131
Perfection of prisons through science, 121
Personal development, 78
Philosophy, 136
Pick, 130
Plumber, 75
Political activity of inmates, 121
Political prisoners, 121
Political science, 136
Post-Release Employment Program, 132
Poverty, 119, 124
Poverty line, 52
Preference for enslavement over idleness, 66
Price,
   retail, 102
   of slave rental, 104
   and value, 95, 102, 117
   wholesale, 102
Prison,
   authorities, definition, 21
   classes, *See* Class
   and culture, 142–143
   as a gladiator school, 143
   household production, 5, 43–46, 64–86,
      150–151
   Industries Enhancement (PIE), 88–90,
      117–118
   Industry Authority (PIA), 34, 89, 95–97

managers, 130
programs, spending on, 3
rodeo, 78
Prison labor,
  contradictions, 127–131
  effect on society, 141–149
  and security problems, 131
Prison slavery, justifications for, 147
Prisonization, 142
Private enterprise in prison, rules, 88–89
Production,
  facilities, 101
  quota, 57
Productivity, 39
Profits, 37
Profit maximization, 107
Property ownership,
  laws of, 25
  personal, 128
Protests by inmates, 36
PRIDE, 97–102
Privacy, 128
Privatized prison labor, 106–107
Prohibitory Act, 115
Prostitution, 79
Punishment,
  corporal, 145
  cruel and unusual, 149
  of inmates, 26, 144
  seen as counterproductive, 122

R
Race and incarceration rates, 2
Racial injustice, effects of, 148
Racism, 2–3, 121–124
Rape, *See* Sexual assault
Rate of inmate enslavement, 46, 111, 115–118
Rate of incarceration versus rate of exploitation, 131
Reagan, Ronald, 124
Rebel Without a Cause, 142
Recidivism,
  and class processes, 132–134
  definition of, 132–133
Regression analysis, 134
Regulatory setting, lax, 104
Rehabilitation of inmates, 122, 127
  and internal decision, 133
Relationships, effect of prison on, 32, 128
Relative surplus value, 38
Rent, free, 104

Restitution, 131 *See also* Victim compensation
  and inequality, 135
  paradox of, 135
Restrictions on prison labor, 115
Revenue, 71–72
Reynolds, M., 131, 134
Rideau, Wilbur, 80
Riots in prison, 25, 68, 86, 139, 148
Riots, political, 123
Robertson, Wayne, 81
Room and board payments, 135
Roosevelt, Theodore, 115
Rome, 82
Rules of prison life, unwritten, 2

S
Salt, 110
Sambo, stereotype of, 28
San Quentin prison, 123, 142
Saylor, W., 132–134
Scacco, Anthony, 80
Security costs, 98–99, 107
Selection bias, 133
Self-destructive behavior, 29, 140
Self-mutilation, organized, 141
Self-sufficient prison, 5, 112–114
Self-sufficient prison labor program, 96, 99
Sellout, 84
Sentencing of minorities, 122
Serf, 11–12
Sex offender, 140
Sexual assault, 2, 80–81
Shareholders, 103
Shovel, 130
Silberman, M., 137
Sing-Sing prison, 112
Slave,
  administrator, 75
  Fundamental Class Process (*SFCP*), 10–11
  manager, 75–76
  master, 4, 11
  identity, 27–34
  rental market, 104, 111 *See also* Labor-power, sale of another's
  surplus labor, 11–12
Slavery,
  abolition of, 145, 150
  class structure of, 11
  cultural conditions of existence of, 27–34
  definition of, 12
  economic conditions of existence of, 34–40

forms of, 10–11
and legitimacy, 143–149
and moral acceptability, 143
political conditions of existence of, 22–27
punitive, 144–145
Smith, Adam, 128
Smoking ban, 74
Snitch, 80, 84, 140
Social experiment in incarceration, 1
Socially necessary abstract labor time, 39–40, 92–93
Society,
just, 153
and prison, relationship between, 134
Solitary confinement, 26 *See also* Administrative segregation
South Carolina, 105
Standard of living, 139
State enterprise model, 96–102
State law, 100
Strikes in prison, 124, 139
Subsidy, indirect, 99–101, 108, 117
Substitution of labor for capital, 40
Subsumed class process, 43–46, 77–82
Subsumed class payment, 72–82, 101, 105
Sugar, 110
Supporters of prison labor, 101, 131–134, 144
Surplus labor, *See also* Slave surplus labor
appropriation of, 16
definition, 4, 49
performance of, 127
Surplus-value, 92–94, 101
Survival time, definition, 133
Sweezy, Paul, 9
Symington, Fife, (Governor of AZ) 62

T

Tattoos, prison, 142
Tennessee, 105
Texas, 56, 63, 74
Texas Department of Criminal Justice, 63
Theft, petty, 144
Tobacco, 110
Transformation of the labor process, 128
Transformation of the prison system, 119
Treatment Era, 121–122
Trusty, 76, 84–85, 88, 114

U

Unemployment, 119
UNICOR, *See* Federal Prison Industries
Unionization in prison, 124

Unions, 125
Use-values, 38, 58, 64–68, 71–73, 78, 94

V

Validity, legal, 146
Value, *See also* Socially necessary abstract labor time
commodity, 39, 93
equivalent, 49
of fixed capital, 93
of machinery, 40
unit, 95
Value of machinery, 40
Variable capital, 93
Victim compensation, 89–90, 134–135
Violence,
atmosphere of, 141
and class conflict, 5–7, 131
domestic, 141
inmate-on-inmate, 141
Visibility of inmates in the culture, 121
Voter turnout rate, Australia, 153

W

Wage,
fair, 41
and marginal product of labor, 41
and master's provision, 53
slave, 91

W

Walsh-Healey Public Contracts Act, 115
War on Drugs, 124
Warden, 21
Warden as slavemaster, 66–69
Washington, 62
Weiner, Ross, 19, 61
Welfare,
in California prisons, 59–61
cost of, 98–99
decrease of, 113
increase in, 118–119
in prisons, 4–5, 36–37, 49–73
state, 122
West Africa, 13
The Wild Ones, 142
Witherspoon, Ashanti, 78
Work and meaningful existence, 128
Work ethic and prison labor, 134
Worker, non-union, 107
Workman's compensation, 104
Wright, Paul, 34

For Product Safety Concerns and Information please contact our EU
representative GPSR@taylorandfrancis.com Taylor & Francis Verlag GmbH,
Kaufingerstraße 24, 80331 München, Germany

Printed and bound by CPI Group (UK) Ltd, Croydon, CR0 4YY
08/05/2025
01864415-0001